CAIRO

INSIGHT *City* GUIDES

Edited by John Rodenbeck
Principal Photographers: Richard Nowitz, Marcus Wilson-Smith
Managing Editor: Andrew Eames

A P A
PUBLICATIONS

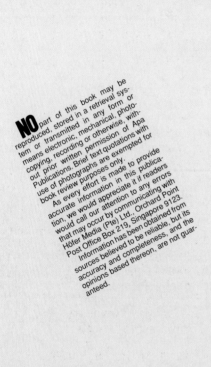
CAIRO

First Edition
© **1992 APA PUBLICATIONS (HK) LTD**
All Rights Reserved
Printed in Singapore by Höfer Press Pte. Ltd

ABOUT THIS BOOK

Cityguide Cairo is the middle brother in a triumvirate of books on Egypt in the award-winning Insight Guide series from Apa Publications. Following the success of *Insight Guide: Egypt*, which since its initial publication in English has been translated into German, French, Spanish and Chinese, Apa Publications set about commissioning two new books: one on the River Nile and the other on Cairo, the Mother of the World herself.

Many of the contributors to this new volume, therefore, will be well-known to fans of *Insight Guide: Egypt*, particularly editor **John Rodenbeck** who has lived in Cairo off and on since 1964, where he has worked as scholar, writer, actor, and publisher. For nine years he headed the American University in Cairo Press and was the publisher of Nobel prizewinner Naguib Mahfouz. In 1979 he founded SPARE (The Society for the Preservation of the Architectural Resources of Egypt) and he continues to be a leading figure in campaigns to preserve historic Cairo. He is currently a professor of English and comparative literature at the American University.

Angela Milward Jones, who wrote the sections on ancient history, Pharaonic sites, and "Old Cairo" (Misr al-Qadimah) is an Egyptologist well known in the field. She first lived in Egypt as a student assistant on digs at Luxor, Abydos and Gizah. In 1985, fed up with the inconvenience of commuting 3,000 miles, she left London to settle for an indefinite period in Cairo. Since then she has travelled the length and breadth of Egypt and lectured on ancient history and archaeology for the American Research Center.

William Lyster, who was rather improbably born in Texas, also contributed to *In-sight Guide: Egypt*. He has spent more than two decades travelling throughout the Middle East, and made his first visit to Egypt in 1968. In the late 1970s he moved to Cairo, settled down to the serious study of Islamic art, architecture and history, and is now a recognised authority on all three. The author of a book on the Citadel, he lectures on the Islamic art of Egypt and lives in Heliopolis.

Max Rodenbeck, John's son, who wrote the sections on recent history, the economy and religion, likewise contributed to the original Egypt book. He is the Cairo correspondent of *The Economist,* but his name is also familiar to readers of *Middle East International* and the *Financial Times*. Brought to Cairo when he was two years old, he has lived most of his life in the city and is virtually an *ibn al-balad* (Cairene) although he is happily married to an Alexandrian. He reads, speaks and writes Arabic fluently.

The right team

Another internationally known professional is **Stephen Hubbell**. "To the horror of close relatives," he notes, "I forsook a cushy job as managing editor of *Interview* magazine in New York for the unpredictability of life along the banks of the Nile – and have never looked back." Now working as a freelance journalist, he is correspondent for the *Nation* and the *Atlanta Constitution* and travels widely throughout the region. He is an accomplished Arabist.

An Egyptian citizen, **Heba Saleh** has degrees in English literature from the American University in Cairo and in film studies from the University of East Anglia in England. Editor of an English-language magazine since

John Rodenbeck *Jones* *Max Rodenbeck* *Lyster*

1986, she has written features and helped to make television and radio programmes on a wide variety of Egyptian topics, particularly about Egyptian women – chiefly, she says, to correct the simple-minded misrepresentations of Egyptian women in the Western media.

Elizabeth Maynard has lived in Egypt for over 20 years, for 12 of which she has been general factotum for SPARE. Another contributor to *Insight Guide: Egypt*, she has also been an editor of *Cairo Today* and is currently the Egyptian representative of the London-based journal *Arts and the Islamic World*. She has worked as an archaeological draughtsman and is a skilled cartographer.

When **Jasper Pleydell Bouverie** came to Cairo from the UK in 1987, he intended to spend a year teaching at one of the more respectable language institutes. When the year was up, however, he stayed on to edit the leading English-language monthly, then became a freelance journalist. He has also sold photographs and acted in television commercials. "I like to live a varied existence," he says. "For a Westerner living in Cairo, life is seldom dull." In the line of journalistic duty he has been detained by Egyptian police for 48 hours on suspicion of spying for Sussex.

Fresh from his British university **David Tresilian** came to Cairo in the summer of 1989 to teach at the American University. He now writes for Cairo's English-language *Al-Ahram Weekly*.

Andrew Humphreys grew up in the UK, studying architecture for four years in London. Working for London Regional Transport, he met an author preparing a book on the London Underground and joined him researching tunnels, ticket halls and other dark, damp places. In 1988 he came to Cairo for a brief holiday and stayed, collaborating with William Lyster on his book on the Citadel.

Ian Portman has lived in Egypt for 14 years. Despairing, he says, of a career as a teacher, he drifted into publishing and literary pursuits, founding the Palm Press in Cairo, which he now manages. He has written guidebooks to Luxor and to several individual ancient Egyptian temples, while never ceasing to be amazed at the gulf in understanding between Egyptians and their foreign guests.

Chris Flammer, who compiled much of the *Travel Tips* section, is a graduate in psychology, and professes fascination with the Muslim world. Before coming to Cairo for a two-year stay in 1988, she lived in Ankara, where she contributed the *Travel Tips* section to the *Insight Guide: Turkey*. Currently resident in Qatar, she is polyglot and speaks both Turkish and Arabic.

The Photographers

Photographs in this book are primarily the work of US-based **Richard Nowitz**, an Insight Guide regular who contributed extensively to the books on Jerusalem, London and Wales, and **Marcus Wilson-Smith**, a London-based freelance who has spent many months in Egypt researching his own book on the desert areas of the country. Other images came from regular Insight contributors **Tor Eigeland**, **Lyle Lawson**, **Christine Osborne** and **Eddy Posthuma de Boer**.

The book was produced by Apa London under the eye of Managing Editor **Andrew Eames**. Proof-reading and indexing were completed by **Dorothy Stannard**, while **Jill Anderson** and **Loh Ai Leen** bullied the text through various Macintosh computers.

Saleh

Maynard

Hubbell

Portman

History

Features

Maps

TRAVEL TIPS

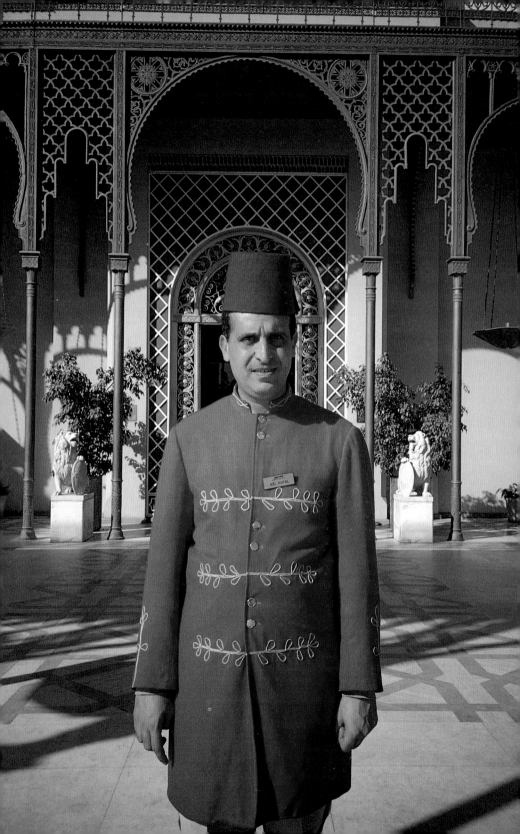

THE MOTHER OF THE WORLD

Ibn Khaldun, the great Arab historian, called Cairo "The Mother of the World." So did the anonymous author of the *Arabian Nights*. Since then, continuous attempts to transform it into a sort of Nile-side Los Angeles have adorned the Mother of the World with flyovers, shopping malls, and lethal smog, but they have not yet obliterated its fundamental charm.

To Cairenes, the city has exactly the same name as their country: Misr. It has borne this name – which means "Egypt" but also means "metropolis", "capital", "that which is inhabited and civilised" – since the 7th century. In the 14th century, Italian merchants, mistaking a small walled enclosure called Al-Qahirah for the city as a whole but quite unable to pronounce it, invented the name "Gran Cairo," which was adopted throughout Europe.

Edwardian visitors to Cairo experienced a great deal more than most tourists can today: many more buildings and monuments were open to the public and many natural attractions had not yet been submerged in urban sprawl. In those days it took less time to cross Cairo by carriage that it does by car now. To experience as much as they did, we actually have to work harder.

A little labour is worthwhile, however, if it leads to knowing Cairo as it really is; and many a casual visitor still stays to become a life-long resident. One such was Ibn Khaldun, born in Tunis of Spanish stock. "Cairo," he wrote, "surpasses everything one may imagine."

Preceding pages: morning sun, At-Tahrir bridges; midday, looking south from Bulaq; evening light on the Radio and Television building; nightlife in Mayan Al-Husayn. **Left**, welcome to Cairo.

Prehistory to 3100 BC

Before 10,000 BC: Palaeolithic period: nomadic food gatherers.

c4500–3100: Neolithic remains at Maadi and in Wadi Hawf. Farming and domestication of animals. Simple pottery made; copper smelted, gold wrought. Local chiefs.

Early Dynastic Period, 3100–2649 BC

1st and 2nd Dynasties. Memphis founded as the capital of an Egypt united under one ruler. Tombs at Saqqarah.

Old Kingdom, 2649–2134 BC

c2649–2575: 3rd Dynasty. Zoser Complex at Saqqarah.

c2575–2465: 4th Dynasty. Strong centralised government; pyramids at Dahshur, Gizah, and Abu Rawash.

c2455–2134: 5th and 6th Dynasties. Pyramids and Sun-Temples at Abu Sir and Saqqarah. Tomb reliefs at Saqqarah and Gizah. Pyramid texts.

First Intermediate Period, 2134–2040 BC

7th–10th Dynasties. Collapse of central government; country divided among local rulers; famine and poverty.

Middle Kingdom, 2040–1640 BC

11th–13th Dynasties. Reunification by Theban rulers. Pyramids at Dahshur and Hawarah built by Amenemhet III (1842–1797). Pyramids at Al-Lisht, Mazghunah, and South Saqqarah.

Second Intermediate Period, 1640–1532 BC

14th–17th Dynasties. Country divided again. Asiatics ("Hyksos") rule in Delta.

New Kingdom, 1550–1070 BC

c1550–1307: 18th Dynasty. Period of Egypt's greatest prosperity, with Thebes (Luxor) as main royal residence. Pharaohs include Akhenaton (c1353–1335), Tutankhamun (1333–1323).

c1307–1196: 19th Dynasty. Ramses II (c1290–1224) embodies ideal kingship, builds many monuments, erects colossi.

c1196–1070: 20th Dynasty. Invasions by Libyans and "Sea Peoples". Series of weak kings rule from the Delta.

Third Intermediate Period, 1070–712 BC

21st–24th Dynasties. Tanis is capital, displaced as Egypt is divided among several rulers, threatened by Assyria.

Late Period, 712–332 BC

c712–657: 25th Dynasty from Kush (Sudan) unites country, begins revival of culture. Assyrian invasions in 667, 663.

664–525: 26th Dynasty rules from Sais in Western Delta. Continued rebuilding programme after Assyrian invasions. The first settlement of invading Greeks at Naucratis and Memphis.

525–405: 27th Dynasty (Persian). Canal linking the Nile with the Red Sea completed under Darius I (521–486). Fortress called "Perhapemon" (*Babylon* in Greek) built at the Nile end of the canal on the future site of Cairo. Memphis and Heliopolis visited by Herodotus.

404–342: 28th–30th Dynasties. Slow decline.

342–330: 31st Dynasty (Persian). Second Persian occupation.

Ptolemaic Empire, 332–30 BC

332–30: Alexander the Great conquers Egypt, founds Alexandria. Ptolemy I rules as governor after Alexander's death in 323 BC, then after 304 BC as first king of dynasty that ends with Cleopatra VII and her children. Decline of Memphis, dilapidation of Heliopolis.

Roman Period, 30 BC–AD 324
Rule from Rome. Fortress rebuilt at Babylon in AD 116 under Trajan (98–117). Visits to Egypt by emperors Vespasian, Trajan, Hadrian (twice), Septimius Severus, and Caracalla. Rapid spread of Christianity, despite severe persecution from AD 251 onward. Alexandria occupied by Palmyrenes under Queen Zenobia, AD 270–72. Monasticism begins.

Byzantine Period, AD 324–AD 642
Rule from Constantinople (Byzantium).
324–619: Christianity made state religion, 379. Coptic (Egyptian) Church separates from Catholic Church, 451. Last pagan temple converted into church, 527.
619–29: Third Persian occupation.
629–39: Re-establishment of Byzantine rule.
639–42: Arab conquest under Amr ibn al-

Preceding pages: wall relief from the Ptolemaic temple at Kom Ombo. **Left**, 18th-dynasty King Tuthmosis III. **Above**, dancing maidservants.

As, who founds new capital, Fustat, next to Babylon, builds first mosque.

Arab Empire, AD 642–868
Rule by governors on behalf of caliph.
642–58: The Rashidun ("Orthodox" or "Righteous") caliphs.
658–750: The Umayyad caliphs rule from Damascus.
750–878: The Abbasid caliphs rule from Baghdad. Al-Askar built. First Turkish governor appointed, 856. Nilometer built at Rawdah, 861.

Tulunid Period, AD 878–905
Ahmad ibn Tulun, Turkish governor, declares independence, founds Al-Qatai, builds great mosque, 876–79.

Abbasid Interim, AD 905–35
Reassertion of power from Baghdad.

Ikshidid Empire, AD 925–69
Turkish governor again creates independent empire.

Fatimid Empire, AD 969–1171
The city's first golden age, of which some 30 monuments and a vast number of objects (chiefly in the Islamic Museum) remain as evidence.
969: Al-Qahirah, royal enclosure, founded.
970–72: Al-Azhar built.
996–1021: Reign of al-Hakim, "The Mad Caliph". Mosque of al-Hakim completed.
1067–72: Drought, famine, and plague and revolt.
1085–92: Mosque of al-Guyushi, walls of Al-Qahirah, Bab al-Futuh, Bab an-Nasr, Bab Zawayla built.
1168: Frankish invasion, Fustat destroyed.

Ayyubid Empire, AD 1171–1250
Salah ad-Din and successors conduct campaigns against Franks and other invaders.
1171: Al-Qahirah opened to the populace, new fortifications added to extant walls.
1174: Crusader invasion repelled.
1176: Defensive wall begun enclosing all of Misr (i.e., sites of Fustat and al-Qatai, as well as Al-Qahirah). Citadel begun.
1187–92: Jerusalem and most of Palestine retaken from Crusaders.
1219–21: Frankish invasion by sea; occupation of Damietta and advance on Cairo culminates in Muslim victory at Mansura ("The Victorious") in the Delta.
1249: Frankish invasion under St Louis cul-

minates in second Muslim victory at Mansura. Murder of last Ayyubid ruler and brief reign of his widow Queen Sheger ad-Durr (mausolea of both are extant).

Bahri Mamluk Empire, 1250–1382

Era of expansion and prosperity, of which over 100 monuments survive.

1260–79: Reign of Baybars al-Bunduqdari ("The Crossbowman"). Defeat of the Mongols, reduction of Frankish states to vassalage, extension of empire from Sudan to Anatolia, from the Euphrates to Cyrenaica. Mosque of Baybars al-Bunduqdari.

1279–90: Reign of Qalawun. Mosque, Mausoleum, *Maristan* of Qalawun.

1293–1340: Three reigns of An-Nasir Muhammad ibn Qalawun. Period of great architectural splendour. Earthquake in 1303, followed by massive restorations. Buildings include: Mosque and Mausoleum of An-Nasir Muhammad at Bayn al-Qasrayn, Madrash and Mausoleum of Zayn ad-Din al-Yusufi. Mausoleum of Qarasunqur, Mosque of Salar and Sangar al-Gawli, Khanqah of Baybars al-Gashnakir, the Aqueduct, Qasr al-Ablaq (remains only), Mosque of An-Nasir Muhammad at the Citadel, Palaces of Qusun, Yeshbek (remains only) and Beshtak, Mosque of Maridani.

1340–82: Reigns of sons, grandsons, great-grandsons of An-Nasir Muhammad. Pillage and destruction of Alexandria by Franks, 1365. Gate of Mangak as-Silahdar, Mosque of Aqsunqur (Ibrahim Agha Mustahfizan, "The Blue Mosque"), Mausoleum and Mosque of Tatar al-Higaziyyah, Mosque of Mangak al-Yusufi, Mosque and Khanqah of Shaykhu, Mosque of Sarghatmish, Mosque of Sultan Hasan, Mausoleum of Tankizbugha, Mosque of Mithqal, Madrasah of Umm Shaaban, Mosque of Ylgai al-Yusufi, As-Sultaniyyah Mausoleum.

Burgi (Circassian) Mamluk Empire, 1382–1517

Continuation of massive building programmes (130 monuments survive) under 23 sultans. The most important are:

1382–89, 90–99: Az-Zahir Barquq. Mosque of Barquq at Bayn al-Qasrayn.

1399–1412: An-Nasir Farag ibn Barquq. *Khanqa* and mausoleum of Farag and Barquq.

1412–21: Al-Muayyad Shaykh. *Maristan* and Mosque of Muayyad Shaykh.

1422–38: Al-Ashraf Barsbay. Mosque, Madrasah of Barsbay.

1438–53: Az-Zahir Sayf-ad-Din Gakmak.

1453–61: Inal. The Inal Complex in the Northern Cemetery.

1461–67: Khushqadam (Greek).

1468–96: Qaytbay. Many buildings, including the Qaytbay Complex in the Northern Cemetery.

1501–17: Qansuh al-Ghuri. The Ghuriyyah Complex (Mosque, Mausoleum, Palace, *Hammam,* and *Wakalah.*)

Ottoman Period, 1517–1914

Egypt becomes a province.

1517–1798: Ottoman rule through 106 governors. Monuments (more than 250 extant) include Mosques of Sulayman Pasha, Sinan Pasha, Malika Safiya, and Burdayni, Bayt al-Kiridliyyah, Bayt as-Sihaymi, Bayt Zaynab Khatun, Bab al-Azab, Sabil-Kuttab of Abd ar-Rahman Katkhuda, Bayt Ar-Razzaz, the Musafir-Khanah.

1798–1805: French occupation.

1805–48: Muhammad Ali Pasha. Enormous programme of modernisation and creation of new empire, both thwarted by European intervention. Monuments: the Mint, The Gawharah Palace, Hawsh al-Basha, The

Harem Palace, the Shubra Kiosk, the Mosque of Muhammad Ali al-Kabir.

1848, 1849–54: Ibrahim Pasha, Abbas I. Abbasiyyah founded.

1854–63: Said Pasha. Suez Canal concession granted. Cairo-Alexandria rail link, Nile steamship service, telegraph established. Work begun on Suez Canal (1859).

1863–79: Ismail the Magnificent. New programme of modernisation, assertion of autonomy. Assembly of Delegates established (1866), principle of primogeniture accepted by Sultan. Title of "Khedive" granted (1867). Suez Canal opened (1869). Monuments of the era: Gazirah Palace, Abdiin

1922–36: King Fu'ad I. Sovereignty recognised by the British, constitutional monarchy established.

1936–52: King Faruq. World War II (1939–45), during which Egypt remained neutral, but reoccupied by Britain. Fires of Black Saturday (1952) lead to military coup.

1952–53: The July Revolution deposes Faruq in favour of his infant son, Ahmad Fu'ad, then declares Egypt a republic. All royal properties nationalised. Gamal Abd an-Nasir (Nasser) becomes leader.

1956: Nationalisation of Suez Canal. Tripartite Aggression.

1961: Introduction of Socialist Laws in July

Palace, Ismailiyyah.

1879–92: Khedive Tawfiq. British Occupation begins (1882).

1892–1914: Khedive Abbas II Hilmi. Monuments: Egyptian Museum, Museum of Islamic Art, Rifai Mosque.

Protectorate, Monarchy and Republic, starting from 1914

1914–17: Sultan Husayn Kamil. British Protectorate declared, martial law instituted.

1917–22: Sultan Fu'ad. Revolution of 1919.

Left, Muhammad Ali, father of modern Egypt. **Above**, digging the Suez Canal.

Ordinances, followed by further nationalisations, sequestrations.

1967: The Six Day War.

1970: Gamal Abd an-Nasir succeeded by Anwar Sadat.

1973: The October War.

1974–77: Open Door Policy, political liberalisation. Riots (1977) over removal of subsidies on food. Sequestrations ruled illegal.

1979: Camp David accords lead to peace treaty with Israel. Egypt boycotted by the rest of the Arab World.

1981: Sadat assassinated. Hosni Mubarak becomes president.

As the remains of thousands of monuments show, modern Cairo is only the latest in a 5,000-year succession of cities built in the same strategic position. Here Upper Egypt meets Lower Egypt. The narrow cliff-lined Nile valley broadens out into the flat fertile Delta, the river blossoming into several branches on the last stage of its northward course to the Mediterranean. The Nile provided an effortless harvest on which ancient Egypt could live well, and since the river was also the only highway in the country, the junction between its Delta and its narrow valley was the point from which the entire country could best be controlled.

When Upper and Lower Egypt were united by King Menes in about 3,100 BC, the first capital was established 15 miles (24 km) south of the future site of Cairo. It was called "The White Walls" after the name of the king's residence which was also the seat of government. A thousand years later the name of one of the capital's suburbs, Men-nefer, was applied to the whole city. This name was transformed by the Greeks into Memphis.

The successors of Menes in the Early Dynastic Period (3100–2649 BC) formulated much of the distinctive culture of the capital, which was to endure for over 3,000 years. Powerful gods in their lifetime and still divine after death, the kings of these early dynasties were interred in large mudbrick tombs at their ancestral burial ground at Abydos. For the nobility, *mastabah* tombs were built at Saqqarah on the desert plateau above Memphis, constructions that suggest a well-organised and confident administration. Unfortunately their dwelling places were built in the flood plain below and have effectively disappeared.

The Old Kingdom: The 3rd Dynasty saw the start of the Old Kingdom (2649–2134 BC) and a dramatic cultural flowering. Building a massive six-stepped pyramid at Saqqarah

Preceding pages: the Pyramids of Dahshur, photographed by Francis Frith in 1856. **Left,** the Gizah Pyramids, pictured more recently.

surrounded by a complex of ceremonial rooms, King Zoser started a new style in funerary monuments which continued for over 1,000 years. This pyramid building reached its apogee in the 4th Dynasty, when King Snofru built himself two pyramids at Dahshur to the south. Benefitting from the experience of predecessors, his son Khufu erected the largest and most perfect, the Great Pyramid at Gizah.

Each king probably resided near his pyramid. The 4th and 5th Dynasty pharaohs show a decided preference for the cult of the sun, centred at the sanctuary at Heliopolis, 20 miles (32 km) directly north of Memphis on the opposite side of the Nile, of which almost nothing now remains. The pyramids of the 5th and 6th Dynasties at Saqqarah and adjoining Abusir are poorly-built and the increasing size and complexity of the nearby tombs of the courtiers, with their wonderful reliefs showing scenes of everyday life, indicate that wealth and power were no longer concentrated solely in the person of the king.

The Middle Kingdom: The collapse of the Memphis monarchy at the end of the 6th Dynasty (2134 BC) was followed by a century of famine and trouble, known as the First Intermediate Period. Not until the country was reunited under a new line of kings from the South did the city regain its former prosperity. These kings of the Middle Kingdom built a new residence at Al-Lisht, 25 miles (40 km) south, and their poorly preserved pyramids are found there, at nearby Dahshur, and in the Fayyum, then a marshy basin upriver. Memphis itself seems to have been eclipsed during this period.

These 12th-Dynasty kings extended their control into Nubia (modern Sudan), subduing warlike tribes and securing lucrative trade in gold, ivory, and other African produce. The few Middle Kingdom monuments that have survived show a desire to emulate the great achievements of the Old Kingdom; the wonderful sculptured reliefs and statues of the 12th Dynasty are equal to anything from earlier periods.

The New Kingdom: This prosperity was interrupted again by the Second Intermediate Period (1640–1550), an era of trouble and fragmentation. Asiatics invaded to set up a separate kingdom in the Delta and Nubia broke away. Again, it was a powerful family from Thebes (now Luxor) in Upper Egypt who drove out the Asiatics and reunited the country, inaugurating the New Kingdom (1550–1070 BC), the period of ancient Egypt's greatest power and prosperity.

Early years of the 18th Dynasty were devoted to securing new frontiers. Strong warrior kings, notably Tuthmosis I and his grandson Tuthmosis III, not only drove back the

kept their main residence. The temple of Amun-Ra at Karnak, in particular, received much booty and tribute; and the power of its priests grew to such an extent that by the end of the New Kingdom they could challenge the authority of the kings.

Kings now chose to be buried not in pyramids, but under a pyramid-shaped mountain in the desert west of Thebes, the Valley of the Kings. The one royal tomb of this era that has survived almost intact to our own time, the tomb of Tutankhamun, displays the wealth with which they were interred. That a good proportion of the general prosperity also filtered down to the nobility is clear from

Asiatics, but extended Egyptian influence as far as the Euphrates, establishing a system of vassal states that paid handsome tribute to Egypt, but remained essentially self-governing. In the south, Nubia was annexed and administered directly, her gold being ruthlessly exploited.

Egypt grew fat on tribute and trade. Memphis remained the administrative centre of the country, the headquarters of the army, the main port, and the greatest manufacturing city. The new wealth of this period is most evident, however, in the building activity at Thebes in Upper Egypt, where the pharaohs

their beautifully decorated tombs, which stud the hillsides nearby.

Heresy: Towards the end of the 18th Dynasty, Akhenaton, the heretic pharaoh, tried to elevate the Aten, his personal sun-god, to pre-eminence within the Egyptian pantheon, creating a religious turmoil that briefly affected the whole country. It has been suggested that Akhenaton's ideas came from the ancient centre of the sun cult, the Temple of Ra at Heliopolis, but his successors of the 19th and 20th Dynasties, who tried to eradicate his memory as they restored the ancient cults, chose not to penalise the Temple of Ra, but to re-endow it lavishly. Memphis was likewise enriched with splendid buildings by the kings of the 19th Dynasty, who moved their residence northwards into the Delta in 1304, though they continued to be buried in the South.

Among these pharaohs of the 19th Dynasty, Ramses II so fulfilled the kingly ideal – a great warrior, sportsman, and statesman, an energetic builder, a superb propagandist and hence the willing model for a multitude of colossal statues, a doting family man who fathered over 100 children by several wives and concubines – that for subsequent generations his name was synonymous with king-

As the country once more fragmented, Memphis and the Delta came under Libyan rule, while the South became virtually independent under the High Priest of Amun at Karnak. Conflicts between these rival dynasties and the regions of Upper and Lower Egypt mark these difficult times, known as the Third Intermediate Period (1069–712 BC). Delta towns like Tanis and Bubastis grew in importance, while Memphis and the Nile valley became impoverished.

The Late Period: Even when the country was reunited under the Nubian kings of the 25th Dynasty, who inaugurated a cultural revival, foreign invasions continually under-

ship. Successors tried to imitate his achievements, but the later years of the New Kingdom were troubled by a new ethnic grouping, the "Sea Peoples", who disrupted trade and stability throughout the Eastern Mediterranean.

Their incursions in the 13th and 12th centuries BC were beaten off, but Egypt fell into decline. Control was lost over Syria and Palestine, Nubia became independent again, and within Egypt itself there was civil unrest.

Left, wall painting in Thebes. **Above**, King Tutankhamun's tomb.

mined its prosperity and stability. The Assyrians invaded twice, but did not stay. The Persians not only occupied the country, but remained for more than a century (525–404 BC), then left only to return three generations later. In the intervals between invasions, the country was independent under native rulers who embellished their hometowns in the Delta, but ruled from Memphis, attempting to carry on the revival begun in the 25th Dynasty.

A signal achievement of this period was the construction of a canal linking the Nile with the Red Sea. Begun under Necho II

(610–595 BC), it was completed by the Persians, for whom it facilitated communications and trade. At the point on the east bank opposite the island of Rawdah where the canal met the Nile a fortified settlement grew up called "Perhapemon" in Egyptian, which meant "the house of the Nile-God at On (Heliopolis)." The Greeks later transcribed this name as "Babylon".

The Ptolemies: When Alexander of Macedon arrived in 332 BC and defeated the Persians, he was seen as a liberator who would restore traditional cultural norms. With the foundation of Alexandria, however, a new capital manned by a Greek-speaking

tion from all sides of the Mediterranean. Egypt was transformed from a self-absorbed, self-regarding, and largely self-sufficient nation into a sophisticated extrovert, the greatest trader of the Mediterranean world, exchanging surpluses of grain, papyrus, and linen for the luxuries of East and West.

Resentment of the foreign élite encouraged frequent rebellions, however, supported and perhaps fomented by the Egyptian priesthood. The Ptolemaic administration consequently restricted temple privileges and wealth, thus undermining the mainspring of native culture. Memphis became chiefly a religious centre and its palaces were left to

élite, Alexander introduced radical change. Under his successors, the first two pharaohs of the Ptolemaic dynasty, Alexandria displaced Athens as the centre of Hellenic learning and became the cultural capital of the Mediterranean.

In the hinterland of this cosmopolis fiscal expertise was combined with the introduction of new agricultural techniques to bring vast acreages outside the Nile valley under profitable cultivation for the first time. Prosperity brought a rapid growth in population, which was further stimulated by the Ptolemies' policy of encouraging immigra-

ruin, though some of the Ptolemies were crowned in its chief temple. Heliopolis fared worse. Flourishing in Herodotus's day – he visited both Memphis and Heliopolis during the first Persian occupation, towards the middle of the 5th century BC – its priestly school had closed by the end of the 1st century BC, when the temple was being used as quarry and the town itself was in ruins.

Romans and Byzantines: As rebellions and wars weakened the country, Egypt became increasingly dependent upon Rome. Attempts by Cleopatra VII to recover sovereignty through politico-sexual alliances with Julius

Caesar and Mark Antony brought her four children, but no secure power; and after Antony's defeat at Actium in 30 BC, Egypt was formally annexed as a Roman province. For the next 300 years Roman governors systematically drained its wealth for the emperor's personal benefit, while it became increasingly rebellious and impoverished. A well-deserved reputation for revolt caused three legions to be stationed in the country, one of which was garrisoned at Babylon, to control traffic between Upper and Lower Egypt as well as the entrance to the Red Sea canal. Around the fortress at Babylon, which was rebuilt by the Emperor Trajan (AD 98–

eastern capital of the Roman Empire would ultimately diminish still further the declining importance of Alexandria, the country's only large city, and make Egypt a backwater.

When Christianity was declared the state religion of the Empire in AD 379, the ancient temples began to be abandoned, converted into churches, or destroyed, while the ancient religion – once regarded as the repository of all positive values – went underground, surviving after a fashion in alchemy, the practice of magic, local superstition, and various folk observances.

The fiscal policy imposed by Constantinople was as harsh as that of pagans had ever

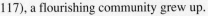

117), a flourishing community grew up.

Christianity spread rapidly, despite official persecution. Emperor Constantine's policy of toleration was promulgated in AD 313, but it was not until his accession as sole Emperor in AD 324 that the new religion was allowed openly in Egypt. It soon grew into a formidable political force. Meanwhile, however, the foundation of Constantinople as the

Left, hieroglyphs were not deciphered until the 19th century. **Above**, unflattering depiction of Cleopatra. **Above right**, portrait of the deceased on a mummy case, Roman Egypt.

been, but greater alienation arose from fanatical theological disputes, one of which led to a schism between the Coptic (from the Greek word *Aigyptios* = "Egyptian") Church and the rest of Christendom. In 617 Egypt was occupied for the third time by Persians. Recovered for Rome by the Emperor Heraclius, it was then invaded by an Arab Muslim army. The peace settlement negotiated in 641 was signed in the ruins of a palace in Memphis, the ancient capital, but it was near Babylon, now strategically far more important, that the Arabs settled to create the city we call Cairo.

THE COMING OF THE ARABS

In the early 7th century AD, while the Romans were engaged in their long and futile struggle with Persia, the Arabs were being united by the Prophet Muhammad under the banner of Islam. Following Muhammad's death in AD 632, the caliphs ("successors" of the Prophet) directed their tribal armies against the great empires to the north, targeting the Romans and the Persians.

The Fall of Babylon: One of the first Roman provinces to fall to the Arabs, Egypt was invaded by an army of 13,000 men under the command of General Amr ibn al-As, who captured Babylon in 641, then laid siege to Alexandria. When the whole country was firmly in his hands, Amr founded a garrison city he called *Al-Fustat* ("The Entrenched Camp"), just outside the Roman fortress of Babylon, which would serve as a Muslim stronghold in the Nile valley and a base for future expansion into North Africa.

His Arab soldiers were not allowed to settle outside Al-Fustat, but were assigned to tribal districts around the congregational mosque he built, the first Muslim religious building erected in Egypt. The original settlers were soon joined by their families and fresh tribal contingents from Arabia. Within 15 years of Al-Fustat's foundation, all the free space in the tribally designated districts had been occupied and the city began to expand to the north.

Fustat and Misr: As its population continued to increase and the borders of the Arab Empire were pushed further and further to the west of Egypt, Al-Fustat outgrew its role as a garrison city. Many of the descendants of Amr's army adopted civilian careers. After only a few generations, Al-Fustat had become a thriving centre of commerce and learning inhabited by several hundred thousand people. They commonly referred to their city as "Misr," the Arabic name for Egypt, since it was the seat of the country's government. And it has been called Misr – not Cairo – by Egyptians ever since.

Left, a Mamluk.

East of Al-Fustat beneath the Muqattam hills is the Qarafah, the city's vast medieval burial ground. Over the centuries, the cemetery grew steadily to the north, shadowing Cairo's own northern expansion. Today it stretches for over 3 miles (6 km) along the eastern flank of the medieval zone. The oldest section of the Qarafah, popularly known as the Southern Cemetery, was a renowned place of pilgrimage, filled with the tombs of miracle-working saints and members of the Prophet Muhammad's family.

For 100 years after the Arab Conquest, Egypt was ruled by a series of governors appointed by the Umayyad caliphs of Damascus. The governors lived in a palace in Al-Fustat, in close proximity to the common people. In 750, the Abbasid family seized control of the caliphate and transferred the capital of the Arab empire to Baghdad. Their first governor of Egypt decided Al-Fustat was too crowded for his comfort, so he settled his state officials and the army he had brought from Iraq outside the northern limits of the city. Here, he founded Egypt's second Muslim capital, called *Al-Askar* ("The Cantonment"). Although Al-Askar was never much more than an administrative suburb of Al-Fustat, the move established an important trend. Later Muslim dynasties would enlarge Misr by building new royal settlements away from their subjects.

The Turks: The most famous Abbasid governor of Egypt was a Turk, Ahmad ibn Tulun. His father was an officer in the Caliph's army of Turkish slave soldiers, referred to as *mamalik* ("those who are owned"; singular: *mamluk*), which in the early 9th century had come to dominate the Abbasid empire. Ibn Tulun took up his post in Al-Askar in 868 at the age of 33. By adroitly manipulating the rivalries amongst the Abbasid family and their Turkish generals, he was able to establish the first autonomous Muslim state in the Nile valley.

As a symbol of his independence from Baghdad, Ibn Tulun founded a new royal city to the north of Al-Askar, named *Al-*

Qatai ("The Wards") after its division into separate districts housing his administration and army of *mamluk* soldiers. Al-Qatai covered a square mile and contained palaces, government buildings, markets and a large hippodrome. In the middle of the city was the gigantic Mosque of Ibn Tulun, a masterpiece of Islamic architecture.

Ibn Tulun was an able ruler who brought prosperity and good government to Egypt, but his profligate descendants were too weak to resist the re-establishment of direct Abbasid rule in 905. As an example to future rebels against the Caliph's authority, all of Al-Qatai was demolished except the mosque of

Ibn Tulun. The Abbasids themselves were too weak to hold Egypt for long, however, and in 969 the country was conquered by the Fatimids of North Africa.

The Fatimids: As Egypt's only Shi'ite dynasty, the Fatimids claimed to be divinely inspired, thanks to direct descent from the Prophet Muhammad through his daughter Fatimah, and thus the only rightful rulers of the Muslim world. Their chief rivals were the Abbasid caliphs, the leaders of the majority Sunni sect of Islam, whom the Fatimids regarded as usurpers of their God-given royal prerogative. Shi'ite and Sunni enmity still divides the Muslim world; today Egypt's Muslim population is 99 percent Sunni.

After their victorious entry into Al-Fustat, the Fatimids constructed a new fortified royal enclosure, named *Al-Qahirah* ("The Subduer") north of the city. It was this name which was later corrupted by Italian merchants and travellers into "Cairo," the name by which Misr as a whole is known in all European languages.

Surrounded by high walls and separated from the predominantly Sunni Muslim population of Al-Fustat by two miles of wasteland, Al-Qahirah was originally forbidden to all but the Fatimid ruling élite. A segment of the city walls, rebuilt in the late-11th century, still survives. At the centre of al-Qahirah were two enormous palaces, the home of the Fatimid caliph, his harem and court bureaucracy. The city's religious and intellectual heart was the Mosque-college of Al-Azhar, which is today, ironically, one of the great bastions of Sunni Islam. The rest of Al-Qahirah's 300 acres (120 hectares) was filled with gardens, parade grounds and barracks for the Fatimid army.

The first Golden Age: The Fatimids were for the most part tolerant and easy-going monarchs. They made little attempt to convert their subjects to Shi'ism and freely employed Christians, Jews and Sunni Muslims in the running of their government. Their reputation as enlightened rulers was only marred by the antics of the unbalanced Caliph al-Hakim (996–1021), who managed to persecute just about everyone before mysteriously disappearing one night while riding his donkey alone in the Muqattam hills.

Under the Fatimids, Egypt became a major centre of artistic production, as well as an international trade emporium, where goods could be purchased from as far away as China and western Europe.

In a desciption of a Frankish diplomatic mission to the Fatimid court, the 12th-century Christian chronicler William of Tyre reports that the Frankish ambassadors saw wonders "such as the hand of the painter might depict or the licence of the poet invent or the mind of the sleeper conjure up in the visions of the night – such, indeed, as the regions of the East and the South bring forth, but the West sees never, and scarce hears of."

In Al-Fustat, an affluent middle class lived in five-storey buildings, complete with running water and sophisticated sewer systems. In Al-Qahirah, to the north, the caliphs lived in secluded luxury, preoccupied with court ritual and esoteric religious speculation. By the mid-11th century, the combined population of the two cities had already grown to half a million people, making Misr one of the largest urban centres of its day.

During the reign of Caliph al-Mustansir (1036–94), however, disaster struck. A sequence of seven low Nile floods between 1066 and 1072 destroyed the agricultural

the lawless troops and restored order. The very same year, a bountiful Nile flood ensured Egypt's return to prosperity. As a reward, Badr was appointed Grand Wazir with absolute powers. The Fatimids would never completely free themselves from the control of military men who ruled in their name.

As the prestige of the Fatimid caliphs declined, their state began to crumble. Fabulously wealthy and militarily weak, they became increasingly threatened by their more powerful neighbours. In 1168, Crusaders from the Latin Kingdom of Jerusalem (founded in 1099) invaded Egypt for the second time, violating a treaty and massa-

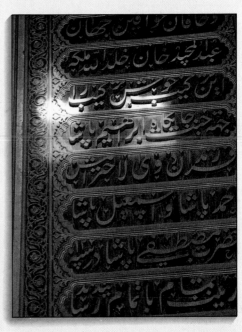

foundation of the Fatimid economy, bringing suffering of truly biblical proportions. The people of Al-Fustat were reduced to cannibalism as famine and plague spread throughout the Nile valley. In 1068, Al-Mustansir's starving soldiers revolted and sacked the Fatimid palaces, emptying the treasury and dispersing the library of 100,000 books. In desperation, the helpless Al-Mustansir called in his Armenian governor of Palestine, Badr al-Gamali, who suppressed

Left, drainage system at Al-Fustat. **Above left** and **right**, details from Ottoman tombs.

cring the civilian population as they advanced. Burned to prevent it from affording shelter, Al-Fustat never fully recovered and is today little more than a pile of rubble.

An appeal for help was sent to the Turkish sultan of Damascus, a devout Sunni, who had been ruling all Syria since 1154 with the blessing of the now powerless Abbasid caliph. The Crusaders were driven out of Egypt, but the Syrian army took control of Cairo. Two years later, in 1171, the Syrian army's Kurdish general, Salah ad-Din, deposed the last Fatimid caliph and reintroduced Sunni Islam as the official religion of Egypt.

The founder of the Kurdish Ayyubid dynasty, Salah ad-Din ibn Ayyub, known in the West as "Saladin," is remembered through the Scott novel *The Talisman* as the chivalrous opponent of Richard the Lion-Heart and other Crusaders. Reconquering Jerusalem in 1189, he re-established Muslim rule over most of Palestine.

During his 22-year reign (1171–93), Salah ad-Din was primarily concerned with build–ing an empire and waging holy war against Egypt from the Muslim East. Based on the *madrasah* ("school"), a state-supported institution for the teaching of Sunni Islamic law, this system remained the foundation of all higher learning in Cairo until the 19th century. Only *madrasah* graduates, well-grounded in Sunni legal practice and of proven loyalty, were allowed to fill the ranks of the Egyptian government.

Strengthening the city: To eradicate vestiges of Fatimid prestige, Salah ad-Din opened the

the Latin Kingdom. His long campaigns in Syria against both Christian and Muslim rivals left him little time for Cairo, where he spent only eight years. In this brief period, however, Salah ad-Din introduced changes that would permanently alter the social and topographic character of Cairo.

Before Salah ad-Din left Egypt to fulfil his destiny as one of Islam's greatest heroes, he first sought to protect Cairo against possible Fatimid resurgence and probable Crusader attack. As insurance that the Shi'ites would be excluded from positions of authority, he introduced a new educational system into private city of Al-Qahirah to the common people. Tens of thousands moved from Al-Fustat into what had been the restricted royal enclosure. The parade grounds and gardens of Al-Qahirah were rapidly transformed into neighbourhoods of irregular twisting streets, while the ceremonial highway between the two Fatimid palaces became the new centre of Egypt's commerce. Abandoned by its middle class, Al-Fustat began to decline and was soon inhabited only by the urban poor.

Preceding pages: *The Lion Hunt*, **by Vernet. Above,** *The Turkish Patrol*, **by Decamps.**

As defence against the Crusaders, Salah ad-Din began constructing the massive Citadel in 1176. Sited on a lofty outcrop of the Muqattam hills overlooking the deserted plane between Al-Fustat and Al-Qahirah, it dominated those two cities, which were eventually to be linked to the new fortress by a series of curtain walls. For the first time, the separate urban centres that made up the Egyptian capital of Misr were thus to be enclosed within a single defensive system, permitting its growth into one unified city. Salah ad-Din never lived in his great Citadel, but left Egypt for the last time in 1182, a year before it was completed. During the reign of his nephew, Sultan al-Kamil (1218–38), however, the fortress became the residence of Egypt's ruler and the centre of his government, a position it would continue to hold for nearly 800 years.

The Bahri Mamluks: Under the last major Ayyubid sultan, As-Salih Ayyub (1240–49), Egypt was threatened not only by Crusader attacks, but also by an invasion of the Mongol hordes under Genghis Khan. To defend his domain, As-Salih enlarged his army with extensive purchases of the Turkish slave soldiers, called *mamalik* or Mamluks. They were quartered on the island of Rawdah in the Nile, which gave them their regimental name, the Bahri (River) Mamluks. These military slaves crushed an invasion of the Nile Delta by the Sixth Crusade in 1250, but their victory proved a mixed blessing for the Ayyubids.

As-Salih died of fever during the hostilities, but his widow, a former slave named Sheger ad-Durr, kept the sultan's demise a secret until the Ayyubid heir could make his way from Anatolia. Two months after he arrived, however, the Bahri Mamluks assassinated him and seized control of Egypt. Wishing to legitimise their usurpation of power, they elected Sheger ad-Durr their queen, but intrigues soon led to her deposition and execution. But nobody questioned their right to rule: military prowess provided irresistible credentials.

The first great Bahri sultan, Baybars al-Bunduqdari (1260–77), established the political regime, based upon a self-perpetuating caste of military slaves, that would hold

sway over the Nile valley for 250 years. Under Baybars' system, all the resources and important governmental posts of Egypt were controlled by the reigning sultan and a council of great amirs ("commanders"). Each amir was responsible for the training and upkeep of a personal slave army. Since the children of Mamluks were forbidden to become soldiers, the ranks of these military households or *bayts*, had to be replenished by the annual importation of young Turkish slaves. When the Mamluks were at war, the *bayts* would unite under the sultan to fight against their common enemy. In times of peace, however, the amirs would use their private armies to further their own political careers. Rebellions were common.

Embellishing the city: The intense rivalry among the Mamluks was not restricted to the realm of politics. They also competed with each other in the construction of grand religious buildings, which were intended to serve as visible indices of their wealth, power, and piety. These mosques and *madrasahs* also fulfilled most of the social, educational and charitable needs of the medieval city. The enormous complex of Bayn al Qasrayn, for example, built by Sultan Qalawun (1280–90) on the site of the western Fatimid palace in Al-Qahirah, contained not only the mausoleum of its founder, but also a public hospital with an attached *madrasah* specialising in medical studies.

The political hub of Mamluk Cairo was the Citadel. Within its walls were the palace complex of the sultan and the headquarters of his army and government. Beneath the fortress was the city's most important square, Maydan ar-Rumaylah ("the sandy patch"), containing the major military markets and the training grounds of the Mamluk troops. The area west of the square grew into an élite residential district filled with palaces built by prominent amirs, who wanted to live as close to the Citadel as possible so that they could maintain their personal influence in the sultan's court.

Under An-Nasir Muhammad (1310–41), the most powerful Bahri Mamluk sultan, Cairo enjoyed one of its greatest eras of peace and prosperity. The sultan was a suspicious and despotic ruler, who loved horses, women and architecture. During his reign, the desolate region between the Citadel and Al-Qahirah was first developed as an urban area. The new district's main thoroughfare, the Darb al-Ahmar (The Red Road), became a popular site for Mamluk mosques and palaces. Linking Al-Qahirah with Maydan ar-Rumaylah and the Citadel, it was also an important processional route.

In the 41 years following the death of An-Nasir Muhammad, there were 12 Bahri Mamluk sultans. It was an age of great political instability, but cultural brilliance. The Mamluks' lust for power was matched only by their love of luxury, shown in the magnificent religious buildings, most of them funerary monuments, with which they continued to beautify the city of Cairo. The colossal Mosque of Sultan Hasan (1354–61), constructed opposite the Citadel during this period, is the grandest extant achievement of Mamluk architecture.

The Burgi Mamluks: The Mamluk army's insatiable demands for more slave soldiers so depleted the population of Turks in the steppes north of the Black Sea that Circassians from the Caucasus mountains were increasingly purchased as substitutes. By 1382, these new forces were strong enough to overthrow the last of the Turkish Bahris and establish a new dynasty, with Barquq (1382–99) as their first sultan.

The Circassian Mamluks followed the same cut-throat political system as their Turkish predecessors: only nine of their 24 sultans reigned for more than two years. They also inherited the Bahri love of architecture, but by the 15th century Cairo had become so heavily developed that Circassians who wished to build near the city's centre were forced to erect smaller mosques, often on irregular plots of land. Unwilling to cramp the style of their religious monuments, the sultans began constructing enormous funerary complexes in the newly opened and spacious Northern Cemetery, just outside the eastern walls of al-Qahirah, which became the most fashionable burial ground for Circassian Mamluk grandees.

The cost of financing such grandiose building projects and the expense of maintaining their huge army left the Circassian Mamluk rulers chronically short of money. To make ends meet, Sultan Barsbay (1422–37) resorted to grinding taxation, debasement of the currency, and the imposition of inefficient state-owned monopolies on local industry, all of which only made matters worse. Sultan Qaytbay (1468–96) managed to avoid financial ruin by controlling and participating in the profitable spice trade between Europe and the Indies. With profits and tax revenues from trade in eastern spices, aromatics, dyes, and drugs destined for the West, he was able to indulge his passion for architecture. Qaytbay's funerary complex in the Northern Cemetery is the finest of his many great works.

Exorbitant tolls on luxury items from the Orient, however, encouraged the maritime nations of Europe to seek ways of reaching the East that would simply by-pass Egypt completely. When the Portuguese discovered the sea route around Africa to India in 1498, Lisbon became the capital of the spice trade and the Mamluks were once again facing bankruptcy.

End of the Mamluk Empire: The fall of the Mamluk sultanate was not due to financial collapse, however, but to military defeat. Horsemen obsessed with their own prowess, the Mamluks refused to adopt modern gunpowder weapons, which allowed no scope to show off their equestrian ability or personal bravery. Their chief rivals in the early 16th century, the Ottoman Turks, had no such qualms. At the Battle of Marg Dabiq in 1516, Mamluk horsemen courageously but hopelessly charged batteries of Ottoman artillery. When the smoke had cleared, Cairo was the capital of a province in the Ottoman Empire. Its new ruler, the Ottoman Sultan Selim the Grim, had the last Mamluk sultan hanged above the southern gate of Al-Qahirah.

Surprisingly, however, the Mamluk role in Egyptian life was not finished. The Ottomans were engaged in a war against both Iran and western Europe and could spare neither the time nor the manpower to extirpate the Mamluks from Egypt completely. The surviving Mamluk amirs, now given the Turkish title of *bey*, were instead incorporated into the Ottoman provincial government as tax collectors and allowed to maintain reduced households of Circassian slave soldiers. They were held in check by a governor appointed from Istanbul and a crack regiment of Ottoman troops, the Janissaries, which was quartered in the Citadel.

Business as usual: Although Cairo was no longer the capital of a major world power, it remained an important commercial centre within the Ottoman Empire in the 16th century, inhabited by a quarter of a million people. The loss of the spice trade was compensated by the new global craze for coffee, which was shipped from the Yemen to Cairo, then distributed throughout the Mediterranean. The Cairene middle class, freed from west of al-Qahirah, stretching from the old Fatimid walls to Cairo's Nile port at Bulaq.

The gradual decline of the Ottoman Empire was mirrored in Egypt by the slow breakdown of the provincial administration. The governors became increasingly corrupt and inefficient, while the Janissaries were forced into local trade by the steady devaluation of their fixed salaries. Only the Mamluks, who lived away from the centre in such places as Azbakiyyah or even Gizah and kept armed households within their fortified *bayts*, were able to maintain cohesion as a military power. In the early 18th century the Mamluks emerged once again as the real

the exactions of the Mamluk court, could devote its energies to the profitable pursuit of trade and industry.

The prosperity of the times is indicated by the volume of the city's commercial traffic. In Ottoman Cairo there were 145 separate markets for locally produced goods, as well as 360 caravanserais (*wakalat* or merchant hostels) with facilities for selling foreign wares. Economic activity led to further urban growth. A new quarter developed to the

Flourishing trade within the stable Ottoman Empire produced lavish architecture in Cairo.

rulers of Egypt in the Ottoman Empire.

The Mamluk *beys* were prevented from exploiting their strength to the full, however, by an endless series of bloody feuds fought among their *bayts* for control of the country. By the end of the 18th century, one Mamluk faction had finally defeated its rivals, but the long years of civil war, coupled with repeated outbreaks of plague and a sequence of disastrously low Nile floods had brought Egypt to the brink of ruin. It was in this chaotic state that the country was invaded in 1798 by a French army under the command of General Napoleon Bonaparte.

On 2 July 1798, having evaded an English fleet under Admiral Nelson by sheer luck, Napoleon Bonaparte landed at what is now the resort town of Agami on the Egyptian coast just west of Alexandria with a force of 29,000 men accompanied by a team of 165 *savants*. Cleopatra's cosmopolis, now hardly more than a collection of hovels, was captured before nightfall. Proclamations issued the next day – printed in an Arabic font previously looted from the Vatican – announced that the French army had come to free the Egyptian people from the Mamluks, but Napoleon's real intention was to provide France with an overland stepping stone to British-occupied India.

The Mamluk *bayts* were courageous, but incapable of effective resistance to a modern army. Advancing on Cairo, Bonaparte shattered their headlong charges with caseshot at the village of Shubra Kit on 13 July. A week later, at the so-called Battle of the Pyramids, he routed what was left of their forces, then marched into Cairo, commandeering the newly-built house of Alfi Bey, a leading Mamluk, as his headquarters. Triumph seemed complete.

Early in August, however, the British fleet under Nelson annihilated the French fleet off Abu Qir, making it difficult for Bonaparte to communicate with Paris and impossible for him to strengthen his army or to withdraw.

To meet his pay-roll Bonaparte pillaged the Mamluk gentry, levied exactions from the merchants, and imposed heavy taxes. Though the Muslim élite of Cairo were told that he and his army were about to convert to Islam, he dealt with resistance mercilessly. Intimidation failed, however, and a general rising in October could be quelled only by a two-day massacre and a slaughter of prisoners. Mamluk leaders remained at large and conducted sporadic raids from Upper Egypt.

In July 1799 an Ottoman force landed near Abu Qir. Though they were easily re-

pelled, it had become clear that Egypt could no longer offer the glory that would serve Napoleonic ambition. In the last week of August Bonaparte therefore slipped away to France, so stealthily that his successor in Cairo, General Kléber, learned of his departure only from a hasty scribble left behind.

Kléber managed to defeat another Ottoman army and to persuade the most powerful of the Mamluks to collaborate with him, but local resistance continued; and in June 1800,

while taking the air in Alfi Bey's garden, he was assassinated. His successor declared Egypt a French colony, but was unable to impose French will. In the autumn of 1801 the remnants of Bonaparte's army – now numbering fewer than 7,000 – were transported back to France as prisoners in British ships. To succeeding generations they left the Rosetta Stone, specifically included in the terms of surrender, which was deposited in the British Museum, and the *Description de l'Égypte*, the vast study completed by Bonaparte's team of *savants*, which was published in a series of enormous volumes

Left, *Battle of the Pyramids*, **1798, painted by Lejeune. Right, the victor, Napoleon Bonaparte.**

between 1812 and 1829. But the Egypt surveyed by the *Description* had already begun to disappear and would in fact never exist again, thanks to the radical and irreversible transformations being created by one man, an certain Ottoman army officer called Muhammad Ali.

Founder of modern Egypt: Born in the Macedonian town of Kavalla in 1769, Muhammad Ali arrived in Egypt as second in command of an Albanian contingent in the Ottoman army. By the middle of 1805 the people of Cairo had turned to him to restore order and the Ottoman sultan duly confirmed their choice, naming him viceroy. On this basis

Bonaparte had been unable to do, putting a permanent end to Mamluk power.

Like Frederick the Great and Catherine the Great before him, Muhammad Ali saw that the rapidity and thoroughness of modernisation in the country he ruled would be directly proportional to the degree to which he could expand his own authority both within and beyond its borders; and that an efficient army, vital for this latter process, could also be a most effective instrument in carrying out the modernisation itself. The Pasha's first military ventures outside Egypt were a series of campaigns in the Arabian peninsula undertaken between 1807 and 1818 on be-

Muhammad Ali Pasha earned for himself the epithet "the Great", which was used even during his own lifetime, and founded a dynasty that ruled until June 1953.

Early moves consolidated his power. In 1807 he defeated a British attempt at intervention, destroying an expedition sent to support Mamluk leaders in opposition to the Ottoman sultan; and in 1811 a final campaign was undertaken against the remaining Mamluks. Members of a leading *bayt* were massacred in the Citadel and those who fled to Upper Egypt were hunted down and exterminated. Muhammad Ali thus achieved what

half of the Ottoman sultan of the time.

At home he established monopolies over the country's principal crops, then turned his attention to industry and trade, sending out missions to Europe to learn European expertise. In 1816 he opened a school of engineering in Egypt, the first secular institution to be founded since the Ptolemaic era, and in 1819 work began on the Mahmudiyyah Canal, which would link Alexandria with the Nile and make it once again a great port.

A new Empire: Successful campaigns headed by Muhammad Ali's three sons, particularly Ibrahim, created an Egyptian empire that was larger than those of the Ramessids, the Ptolemies, or the Mamluks, though Muhammad Ali himself was still officially an Ottoman vassal, ruling in the name of the sultan. The Egyptian army – which for the first time in history was mainly composed of Egyptian peasants – seemed invincible. In 1831 it challenged the sultan himself, marching into Syria and on into Anatolia. At this point the European powers became alarmed and in 1833 they intervened to force a settlement that left Muhammad Ali holding most of those conquests, but also kept the Ottoman Empire intact.

In 1839, however, an Ottoman army attempting to restore the sultan's authority was crushingly defeated by the Egyptians in Syria and shortly thereafter the entire Ottoman fleet defected to Egypt. This double exposure of Ottoman weakness led to a European crisis, as the British, Russian and Austrian empires hastened to prop up the Sick Man, while France continued to support Muhammad Ali.

Full-blown war was averted by agreement among the European powers to preserve the status quo. In 1841 they imposed a new settlement which asserted Ottoman suzerainty. The Egyptian navy, the strongest in the Eastern Mediterranean, was forbidden to build new ships and thus virtually abolished, while the Egyptian army was reduced from 200,000 to 18,000 men.

Concessionary trading terms that favoured the British were imposed, thus breaking Muhammad Ali's carefully protected commercial and industrial monopolies; these "Capitulations" meant that foreign nationals in Ottoman dominions were exempted from local taxation and from trial in any other than their own particular consular courts.

All the territories conquered by the Egyptians became Ottoman provinces, to be administered directly from Istanbul. For Muhammad Ali the only consolation in being thus stripped of power was that the office of viceroy was made hereditary in his line, devolving upon the eldest male.

Modernising agriculture: This European intervention that put an end to Muhammad Ali's empire-building also threatened the success of his programme of modernisation.

In 1820 a hired expert had developed the strain of cotton still known as "Egyptian",

Left, Empire-building British officers meet with the Ottoman Wazir. **Above**, *Interview with Muhammad Ali* by David Roberts.

which found instant favour with the spinners of Lancashire. From that time onward Muhammad Ali had given special attention to increased production of cotton, which required more water than could be supplied by traditional basin irrigation. Having already restored existing canals throughout the Delta, he had used draft labour (the *corvée*) to institute a system of irrigation that allowed as many as three crops annually and has remained the basis of all agriculture in Egypt ever since. The area of cultivable land in Egypt was increased by 25 percent.

Shipped out through the new Mahmudiyyah Canal, cotton created a renaissance in

Alexandria, which grew in population from 15,000 to 143,000, becoming not only Egypt's second largest city, but also its summer capital.

Another major enterprise founded by Muhammad was the printing works established in 1821 at Bulaq, Cairo's Nile port, where foundries, dockyards, and textile mills had already been built. By 1823 the Bulaq Press was in operation as the first publisher in the Arab world, producing not only pamphlets, manuals, and the official gazette, but also printed editions of Arabic, Turkish and Persian classics, which quickly found a ready market among Cairo's many booksellers.

Rebuilding Cairo: When Muhammad Ali came to power there were no roads. By his death Egypt had not only a system of highways, but also regular service by several of the earliest steamship lines, including one of its own, and there were plans to link the ports of Suez and Alexandria via Cairo by railway. The fleet of carriages he imported for his own use became the forebears of all the "traditional" carriages, carts, and barrows that have since been made in Cairo.

Since the city itself had few streets wide enough or uncluttered enough for wheeled vehicles, it was reorganised to accommodate them. Wholesale reconstruction was undertaken earliest at Azbakiyyah, where Muhammad Ali's family set up its first residence. Shari Shubra, a straight wide boulevard lined with sycamore trees, was built to connect Azbakiyyah with a new palace at Shubra. Shari Shubra later became a fashionable promenade for horsemen and carriages, the Cairene equivalent of London's Mall or Paris's Champs Elysées.

At the Citadel dilapidated Mamluk buildings were demolished, to be replaced with palaces, barracks, and administrative structures in the latest Istanbul style. The *mashrabiyyah*, the traditional oriel window with lattice-work or grilles of turned wood, built from upper residential storeys out over the city's streets from the 15th century onward and still common in its older quarters, was banned from all new construction, while the *mastabah,* traditional stone benches that obstructed every ancient thoroughfare, were removed.

Though there was no sewerage system, major steps were taken, after the establishment of the first medical school in 1825, to improve public health. One famous sanitary measure was the banishment of the city's celebrated dancer-prostitutes, who had fascinated European travellers, to Upper Egypt. Modern street-lighting was still to come, but Muhammad Ali's own palaces at Shubra and in the Citadel were all lit by gas before 1830.

Remaking society: Apart from such amenities, Muhammad Ali introduced many new strains of domestic animals and hundreds of species of plants, including most of those that currently gather dust in Cairo gardens or are grown throughout the rest of the country on a large scale for profit.

Muhammad Ali also abolished the Ottoman tax farming system and redistributed agricultural property, bestowing 10-year tax holidays and the outright ownership of large acreages upon anyone who would bring them under cultivation. In allowing proprietors not only to hold land, but actually to possess it in law, he created the first landed gentry, a class that had never existed before in Egypt, where all real ownership had immemorially been vested in the sovereign. At the same time he set up a consultative council, the first

use of land was extended even to non-land-owning peasants.

Ismail the Magnificent: Muhammad Ali the Great died in August of 1849, predeceased by his son Ibrahim, his heir designate, and was therefore succeeded by the eldest of his line, who happened to be a grandson. After ruling only five years, however, Abbas I was murdered by two favourites. More popular was the third viceroy, Said Pasha, a brother of Muhammad Ali best remembered for granting the concession to build the Suez Canal. The contracts based upon this concession made the fortune of his friend Ferdinand De Lesseps, but proved a disaster for the

such governmental instrument to exist in Egypt since the abolition of Alexandria's senate in 30 BC, which was intended to share his deliberations.

Such moves led to the emergence of a new secular élite. Before his death the right of landowners to dispose of their property as they liked was affirmed and the right to mortgage or transfer what was in effect the

country. Entitled to receive only 15 percent of annual profits, the Egyptian government nevertheless paid over 70 percent of capital costs, thus incurring debts to foreign money-lenders that the income from the canal itself could not possibly ever repay. This time-bomb was left ticking under the throne of Said's successor, Ismail, the third son of Ibrahim, who became ruler of Egypt at the age of 33.

In Ismail (1863–79) much of his grandfather Muhammad Ali's dynamism was re-born. Reform and rapid development once again became the order of the day. Massive

Left, 19th-century Cairo borrowed ideas from Paris. Above, Egyptian aristocracy – the young princes Abbas and Muhammad Ali (both seated) – on a visit to London in 1886.

bribes to the Ottoman court allowed him to raise the army's strength to 30,000 and thus to engage in imperialist adventures of his own. The same means secured him both an important change in the rules of succession – seniority was replaced with primogeniture – reserving power for his own descendents and the Persian title of Khedive ("Sovereign"), born by his heirs down to 1914, as well as the right to create institutions, issue regulations, and conclude agreements with foreign powers without consulting the Ottoman ruler. Among the institutions he created was an Assembly of Delegates, the country's first parliamentary body.

In 1867 Ismail opened the Egyptian exhibition at the Exposition Universelle in Paris. He had first known the French capital as a student in 1844, when it was still largely medieval. Dazzled by the transformation wrought under the Second Empire – Haussmann had created a new city, with broad straight avenues and parks – he set in motion a scheme for carrying out similar changes in Cairo. A master plan was drawn up that was never fully realised, but created the essential configuration of the city for the next hundred years.

The transformation of Cairo: The changes were unveiled to the world during the inauguration of the Suez Canal in November 1869; and the frenzied activity in Cairo itself during the last few months just before that event was merely the final phase in a programme of modernisation that had galvanised the whole country for five years. Monitored by telegraph, which now linked every population centre, other large-scale projects such as the digging of two further canals, the Ismailiyyah and the Sweetwater, which connected Cairo with the Great Bitter Lake and carried water for irrigation and drinking to the Eastern Delta and the desert areas along the Suez Canal, had already been completed.

Municipal water and gas companies had been set up in Cairo in 1865; and the city's main railway station, the centre of a system hundreds of miles long that included even the new cities along the Canal, had been symbolically illuminated two years later. A European-style commercial and residential quarter called Ismailiyyah was laid out between Azbakiyyah and the Nile, where a pontoon bridge was installed to provide access from the mainland to the new Gazirah Palace.

Azbakiyyah itself was transformed yet again, with a new park laid out by Barillet-Deschamps, one of Haussmann's landscape designers, who also conceived the original plans for virtually all the other green spaces that have remained in Cairo to this day. Surrounded by consulates and hotels, the park, which boasted its own opera house, was lit by 2,500 gas jets at night and was clearly the centre of the city, from which wide new streets would eventually radiate to all corners.

The British Occupation: Like his grandfather before him, however, Ismail had incurred the jealousy of the European powers, who had no wish to see either a strong or an independent Egypt and who therefore operated through the Ottoman sultan to insure his downfall. Citing Egypt's foreign debts, France and Britain imposed a receivers' commission, which forced Ismail to reduce his army and surrender both public and private property, including all of Egypt's shares in the Suez Canal. They then engineered his deposition by the sultan.

52

Ismail's son Tawfiq (1879–92) was unable to withstand either European pressure or the nationalist fervour that arose to resist it. Using an internal political crisis and the protection of foreign interests as their excuse, the British finally intervened outright. With the approval of the other powers, they bombarded Alexandria for 10 hours on 11 July 1882, landed an army of 20,000 redcoats and occupied the country. Although their presence was supposed to be temporary, it lasted more than 70 years.

When Tawfiq's European-educated elder son came to the throne as Abbas II Hilmi in 1892, he was therefore effectively power-

accounted for 90 percent of export earnings, real per capita income rose to levels during the 1890s that were not to be surpassed until the arrival of oil money.

To ensure their position the British had closed down as many educational institutions as they could and quashed attempts to rebuild an industrial base, but the landowning class created by Muhammad Ali and Ismail became extremely rich, as did the cotton brokers of Alexandria. Cairo underwent a building boom and several new suburbs were added. European immigration now accounted for as much as 50 percent of the city's annual population growth; and by 1914

less, a fact the British proconsul, Lord Cromer, made humiliatingly clear at once. His 22-year reign is nevertheless remembered as one of the city's golden ages. Completion of the Delta Barrages (begun under Muhammad Ali) and of a series of dams in Upper Egypt raised water levels, allowing production of cotton to be doubled, while its price on world markets tripled. Since cotton

Left, many of Cairo's streets have changed little since they were photographed in 1858 by Francis Frith. **Above**, Thomas Cook office in the grounds of Shepheard's Hotel.

more than 90 percent of the paid-up capital of firms registered in Egypt would be in European hands. Railways and steamship lines meanwhile brought aristocratic tourists, who could make the trip from London or Paris in only four days and were received in the city's famous luxury hotels.

The Protectorate and the monarchy: At the outbreak of war in 1914 the British suspended the Legislative Assembly they had allowed to be formed only one year earlier, declared Egypt a Protectorate, and deposed Abbas Hilmi, replacing him with his uncle Husayn Kamil, Ismail's second son, who was given the title of sultan. Egypt was thus informed that its 400-year-old role as an Ottoman province had come to an end. When Husayn Kamil died in 1917, the British chose Fu'ad, Ismail's sixth son, to succeed him.

Opposition to British rule crystallised among the élite during the war and had immense popular support, as well as encouragement from Sultan Fu'ad. To plead on behalf of the nation for an end to "protected" status, a delegation (in Arabic *wafd*, now the name of the major opposition party) was formed under the leadership of Saad Zaghlul, a prominent lawyer with much political experience. When Zaghlul was refused permis-

sion to take his delegation to London a crisis ensued that led to a mass uprising, usually referred to as the 1919 Revolution. Railway and telegraph lines were cut and 40 British soldiers and civilians were killed, while several hundred Cairenes were shot dead in confrontations with British and Australian troops, who had been unnerved by rumours and delays in their demobilisation.

Turmoil continued until the British High Commissioner, Field Marshal Lord Allenby, used his enormous prestige to bully Whitehall into submission, threatening to resign unless the Protectorate was terminated.

Allenby brought the proclamation recognising Egypt's independent status from London to Cairo in February 1922. In April Sultan Fu'ad was named King of Egypt; and the following year a new constitution based on that of Belgium was promulgated, as martial law, declared nine years earlier, finally came to an end.

The British had "reserved" four points in the 1922 proclamation, however, including the right to intervene on behalf of foreign interests. An attempt by King Fu'ad to establish a royal dictatorship ended with his death in 1936. Soon after the accession of his son, Faruq, a treaty was negotiated that abolished the High Commission, confined British military presence except in time of war to the Suez Canal zone, and promised British support in ending the old Capitulations (exemptions from local law and taxation for foreigners), which still pertained. Independence was never to be quite complete as long as the monarchy lasted.

When World War II broke out, the British reoccupied the country, as they were entitled to do under terms of the 1936 treaty, thus creating a most reluctant ally. Egypt did not actually declare war upon Germany until February 1945, nearly a year and a half after the surrender of Italy, when the defeat of Germany and Japan had long been clearly inevitable. In fact, during the North African campaigns of 1940–42, Egyptians of all types and classes publicly voiced hopes of a German victory.

On 4 February Sir Miles Lampson, the last British High Commissioner who had become the first British Ambassador, had the royal residence at Abdiin Palace surrounded by a batallion with armoured cars, then marched in to inform the young king that His Majesty would either appoint a government deemed favourable to British interests, as nominated by Sir Miles himself, or abdicate immediately, renouncing all claim to the throne for himself, and his heirs. Sir Miles had his way, but neither Anglo-Egyptian relations nor the prestige of the Egyptian monarchy ever recovered.

Left, street riots in the 1919 Revolution. Right, the British Residency.

In 1952 King Faruq was not given a choice: on 23 July, a date which is still celebrated as a holiday, a group of army officers seized power and forced Egypt's penultimate hereditary ruler to abdicate in favour of his baby son, Ahmad Fu'ad. On 26 July the ex-king sailed the royal yacht into exile, as his grandfather Ismail had in 1879. Eleven months later his heir was likewise dispossessed. Declared a republic, the country soon came to be headed by Gamal Abd an-Nasir, the most charismatic of the leaders of the officers' coup, who became known to the western world as Gamal Abdel Nasser.

Since then the monarchy's well-policed winter capital – with its trams and gharries clattering through uncrowded streets, its buildings restrained by a Paris-style six-storey limit, its parks and greenery, its up-to-date and functioning electrical, water, telephone, and sewerage systems, and its unamplified calls to prayer – has vanished except in memory, buried beneath today's cacophonous carcinopolis. The story of Cairo's latest transformation is complex, but there are clues to the puzzle in the city's monuments, which have always captured the moods and needs of changing times.

Black Saturday: Little archaeological evidence remains, for example, of 74 years of British domination. Cairo took its revenge on the unwanted *Ingleez.* even before their departure, during the undeclared war that marked the last years of the monarchy. On Black Saturday, 26 January 1952, crowds assembled in response to an incident the previous day in the Suez canal zone. Egyptian policemen and gendarmes had been ordered by the British commander in the zone to evacuate all government buildings, but were then counter-ordered by the Minister of the Interior on no account to leave their posts. During the subsequent bombardment

more than 50 of the policemen were killed.

In Cairo the next day mobs abetted organised teams of arsonists as they attacked and set fire to more than 700 of the architectural symbols of wealth, pleasure, and foreign rule: among them were the famed Shepheard's Hotel, the exclusive Turf Club (where 12 people died, many of them murdered, mutilated, then thrown into the fire), Barclays Bank, the Opera Casino, Groppi's, the Rivoli Cinema, Thomas Cook's, the Ford, Morris, and British Motors agencies, the British Council and the British Institute, all shops selling luxury goods, and many of the bars and nightclubs that had once been filled with rollicking Tommies and Anzacs on leave from the Desert War.

After the Revolution other British institutions were swept away. The Qasr an-Nil barracks were demolished, to be replaced by the Arab League building and a Hilton Hotel. Twenty years later the fortress-like Anglican Cathedral nearby, built to overlook the city from the west and strong enough to withstand a siege, was laboriously pulled down to make way for the 6th of October Bridge, now indispensable. Among the few reminders left by the British army are the homesick graffiti scratched alongside the inscriptions of French and Ottoman soldiers, who likewise suffered boredom far from home, in the towers of the Citadel.

Nasser seizes the canal: In 1956, to compensate for the abrogation of promises from Britain and the United States to help build the new High Dam at Aswan, the Suez Canal Company was nationalised. French-registered, but mostly British-owned, thanks to Disraeli's acquisition of Ismail's shares at bargain prices in 1875, the canal was a symbol of European power to Europeans as well as to Egyptians. The French and British therefore responded three months later by supporting Israel, which had already conducted raids within Egyptian territory several times, in a joint attack by land, sea, and air. Designed to topple Nasser, their Tripartite Aggression gave these accomplices con-

Preceding pages: the Revolutionary Command Council, with Nasser second left in the front row and Sadat far right. **Left,** the destruction of British interests on Black Saturday, 1952.

trol of Sinai and the canal zone, but American and Soviet military and economic threats forced them to withdraw before the end of the year.

The canal brought in 20 times more revenue annually as a state-owned enterprise than it had as a fee-paying private venture. Temptations were therefore great. In 1957 all commercial banks, insurance companies, and commercial agencies for foreign trade were "fully Egyptianised in management and capital." In 1960 there were further nationalisations and in 1961 still more, coinciding with a decree declaring Egypt "socialist". Large-scale sequestrations, which en-

tailed no compensation, began to be carried out against some 7,000 persons deemed to be enemies of the regime, chiefly because they were rich.

As a result of their Tripartite Aggression, British, French and Jewish interests had already come under attack. Other special targets were members of the Muhammad Ali family, the Muslim Brotherhood, or the Communist Party. As the Revolution marched leftward, however, Cairo's cosmopolitan élite in general found itself threatened. Rich Egyptians, as well as Turco-Egyptians, Armenians, Greeks, Italians, and Levantines, all found themselves stripped of their property and either expelled or placed on government living allowances. Townhouses and villas of pashas were taken over as schools and police stations, their factories and farms seized in the name of "the people". Non-Egyptian names have survived on a few shopfronts – Groppi, Weinstein, Mangozzi, Cicurel, Tseppas, Spathis, Ben Zion, Baijocchi – and some of the families attached to the names have remained, but most foreigners and many rich Egyptians took what they could of their wealth and went abroad.

The Nasser era: Ninety percent of Cairo's buildings during this period were designed, built, and used wholly within the public sector and might be expected to reject foreign influence. The new taste not only despised the old regime's Turco-European chic, however, but also disdained all native Egyptian tradition. The only architecture it approved thus clashed with the existing environment, making cultural and political statements that emerged as clear-cut, but negative. The Cairo Tower, raised in 1957, is a case in point. Resembling nothing else on earth, much less anything else in Egypt, it was erected with funds paid secretly to Nasser by the CIA. Its ugly purposelessness remains a standing rebuke to the Americans for their cynicism in attempting to bribe him. Amongst Cairenes its nickname varies between Kermit, the CIA Tower and Roosevelt's erection, in honour of the CIA's bureau chief in Cairo at the time.

Along the Corniche stand other grey concrete monuments, such as the huge Radio and Television Centre, from which the Egyptian leader's message of unity was broadcast to rapt listeners throughout the Arab world. South of Cairo, in the formerly fashionable spa of Helwan, rose belching smokestacks. Where little old ladies had once sat at tea, their corgis at their exquisitely shod feet, a giant industrial complex was built with Soviet help, the pollution-rich showcase of Egypt's expected great leap forward into the heavy industrial age. As Nasser imagined it, Egypt would soon be building "everything from a needle to a rocket."

Soviet-style visions show in the new suburbs designed for Nasser's Cairo. Apart from

20,000 cheap housing units for "the people", in the blocks of scabby concrete that are still visible on the city's down-market fringes, his planners laid out a new City of Engineers (Madinat al-Mohandisiin) for the technocratic vanguard of Nasserist Egypt. Their City of Journalists (Madinat as-Sahafiyiin) was supposed to house the propagandists for the Nasserist creed, whatever it might be. And most ambitious of all, their Victory City – Madinat Nasr – was to provide "modern" apartments for a class that did not yet exist, a new intelligentsia of managers and white-collar workers, in highrise breezeblock tenements laid out row upon row, as if they

clouded the city. Half a million refugees swarmed in from the devastated cities along the Suez Canal.

Within the city itself, the infrastructure had meanwhile broken down, largely as the result of neglect. The sewerage system, completed in 1914, when it was given a life-expectancy of 40 years, had never been updated or replaced. It had exploded in 1965 and was glued back together by the army. By 1970 the water system supplied only half the city, and leaked half of its load. The combined seepage had raised groundwater levels above buried electrical mains, including high-tension lines, and the foundations of most

stood in Volgagrad or Magnetogorsk.

Humiliation and decay: For most Egyptians the Nasser years were an era of optimism, which came to an emphatic end on the morning of 5 June 1967, when Israeli fighter-bombers demolished the Egyptian air force on the ground, the opening move of the Six-Day War that resulted in the humiliating loss of the Sinai Peninsula. For four years, even after the shock of defeat had passed, despair

buildings. The telephone system, which continued to be repaired after each breakdown single-handedly by an ageing English expert marooned in 1956, was later described by a German consultant as "not just moribund, but putrescent." To get a new phone was impossible and the last directory had been issued in 1961. No telephone directory has been issued for Cairo, in fact, since.

Nor was the war really over. Israeli aerial attacks were now directed at civilian targets: industrial plants were bombed and workers were strafed at precisely the times when shifts were changing, primary and secondary

Left, the Nasser era "disdained native Egyptian tradition". **Above**, factory bombed in war with Israel, 1967. **Above right**, Israeli tanks in Sinai.

schools were hit. Israeli planes were able to strike at will until 1970, when a truce allowed Soviet anti-aircraft missiles finally to be put in place. All available money was channelled into resistance, while the physical structure of the capital suffered still further: roads went unpaved, streets uncleaned, sewers, telephones, and electric lines unreplaced and unrepaired. Even after the October War of 1973, when commandos restored Egypt's honour by capturing Israel's supposedly impregnable Bar Lev line, there was not much left for binding the unfortunate city's wounds.

Anwar Sadat: The 1970s – the years of foreign immigrant to use the Open Door – could waste its value. Many of those who had benefited by becoming part of the apparatus of Nasser's all-powerful state may have suffered, but other people made fortunes.

All over Cairo a new architecture appeared to match the new mood. Flashy office buildings, hotels, and residential towers sprouted in the gardens of grand old villas or simply replaced them; and even the shabby fronts of shops were refurbished in neon and chrome. Every restaurant or food stall became a "cafeteria", every clothing shop a "boutique". Wimpy and Kentucky Fried Chicken became familiar landmarks by which taxi driv-

Anwar Sadat, who came to power after Nasser's death – were characterised by wholesale reappraisal of all that had gone before. Jilting its Russian suitors, the Egyptian leadership went off – without even a backward glance – to honeymoon with America. The dream of a socialist utopia was abandoned for the dream of a capitalist one, as Sadat launched his Open Door Policy. At the same time the heavy hand of the police lightened. The wraps came off after years of austerity. And money came out, as Egyptians say, "from under the tiles", to be invested with the utmost rapidity, before inflation – the first ers navigated (street names play little part in orientation around the city) and establishments with names like Uncle Sam Bazaar, Up Pop or Bony M multiplied. With the Aswan High Dam holding back the annual late-summer flood, which normally created ponds in Cairo, scoured out the sewers, and turned Gizah into a single enormous lake, the city's area expanded as never before.

Building fever: Corruption and laxity both allowed a boom in unlicensed construction; and while new blocks of jerry-built "luxury flats" for the rich shot up in violation of building ordinances, whole districts of "informal sector" housing for the poor appeared overnight. Until laws forbade it, irreplaceable topsoil was converted into bricks. Speculators were encouraged to gobble up the few remaining patches of green, while billboards for toothpaste and aftershave lotion covered every other available space.

Car ownership, once the privilege of the rich, was suddenly within the means of many middle-class Cairenes, especially those who had worked a stint in the rich countries of the Arabian Gulf. But there were also more of the rich: Egypt became the leading importer of Mercedes cars in the world and the city's new BMW dealer exceeded his sales target by 50 percent in the first year of operation. Television aerials grew into thickets on rooftops as the new generation sat down to digest a diet of hard-sell jingles and weepy melodramas. Tinny synthesised pop replaced the emotive ballads of Umm Kulthum, Farid al-Atrash, and Abd al-Halim Hafez, superstar singers whose deaths in the 1970s marked the end of an age of innocence for many Egyptians.

Peace with Israel was ratified in the Camp David accords, signed under American sponsorship in 1979. The settlement was greeted with euphoria in Egypt, but led to immediate isolation from the rest of the Arab world, the country's major source of foreign exchange. As soon as it became clear that Egyptian and Israeli interpretations of the terms of the accord were at odds, relations chilled, but not before Sinai had been recovered and the refugees from the canal zone had begun to take up residence in rebuilt cities. The Open Door policy meanwhile collapsed.

Hosni Mubarak and the future: On the 6 October 1981, at a military parade celebrating Egypt's storming of the Suez Canal, President Sadat was shot dead, the fatal bullet entering between two gold lotus blossoms embroidered on the collar of his Cardin uniform. The flamboyant leader was succeeded by the stolid, dependable figure of President Mubarak, who quickly declared that he would avoid the excesses of his predecessor, then

set about attempting to rebuild both his country's infrastructure and its relations with the rest of the Arab world.

Once again it became possible not only to place a call without infuriating delays, but even to get a new phone. Decaying medieval and pharaonic monuments received some attention. A metro system, highways, flyovers, and parking garages eased traffic. Cleaner streets and thousands of newly planted trees gave the city a healthier look. And many of the largest projects are the result of foreign aid, for Cairo has received generous gifts: the city's new Opera House and children's hospital are Japanese, for ex-

ample, while its new underground transit system, airport, and university-connected research hospitals are French. It has a Franco-Japanese phone system, a British sewage system, an American power plant, Chinese conference and business centres.

But as the city nears the 21st century its problems are far from solved. Since 1952 the population has grown from less than two and a half million to more than 15 million; and despite vast new satellite suburbs like Madinat as-Salam, at 15 May City and 6 October City, there remains insufficient space for what will soon be 20 million.

Left, Port Said on the reopening of the Suez Canal, 1978. **Right**, Sadat shortly before his assassination in 1981.

MOTHER OF BUREAUCRACY

Few other countries are so utterly dominated by their capitals. Cairo is the focus of state-owned or private industry, production, and commerce, government, entertainment, fashion and communications. Small wonder that the traditional name for Cairo – *Misr* – is also the Arabic word for Egypt or that two epithets have become attached to it: "The Well-Guarded" and "The Mother of the World".

For most of the past three millennia the peasants of the Nile Valley have laboured for foreign rulers. And throughout the last 1,000 years, some would argue, the most arrogantly oppressive of alien presences has been none other than the Mother of the World. Not a few Cairenes, moreover, would confess that they see the rest of Egypt as merely the hinterland of their own great city.

Centralisation: From time immemorial to the reign of Muhammad Ali the sovereign – whether Pharaoh, Roman emperor, caliph, Mamluk sultan, or Ottoman governor – used his power over all of Egypt's agricultural land to hand out exploitation rights to cronies, who generally plundered the peasantry for all they were worth. Any surplus was sent back to the capital, where the ruler lived on this "taxation" like a kind of god.

The foundation of Cairo merely exaggerated the parasitic relationship between the seat of central government and the rest of the country. It was axiomatic that control of the head of the Delta gave control over the whole of Egypt, and after the Muslim conquest nothing could move up or down the Nile without passing "The Well-Guarded". Far enough inland to be relatively safe from seaborne invaders, it was protected by the desert from provincial uprisings or overland incursions. Once ensconced in the Citadel a ruler could ignore nearly every threat except intrigue inside his own palace – of which there was usually plenty.

In recent times the predominance of the capital has only increased. Between 1835

and 1956 Alexandria's control of shipping and the all-important cotton trade made it a serious commercial rival, and the government's habit of moving there in the summer to enjoy the more clement Mediterranean weather momentarily diminished Cairo's ascendancy. After the Tripartite Aggression of 1956, however, foreign communities were expelled and business went into a decline. The end for Alexandria came in 1961 when the cotton industry was nationalised and all

private commercial activity was radically curtailed, with ceilings placed on incomes. Most economic power – and with it all political power – moved back to Cairo.

Arab socialism: As the state's grip tightened around the economic and social life of the country, the importance of the provinces declined. Like other revolutionary governments Nasser's based its economic policies on the supposed needs of an urban industrial working class. Since in Egypt's case this class did not exist, it had to be invented, mainly at the expense of the rural population. *Fellahin* (peasants) were given land owner-

Left, sign welcoming the liberation of Kuwait, 1991. **Right**, President Mubarak.

ship, but had to sell their produce to state monopolies, as in the middle years of Muhammad Ali, at compulsory prices. The state would use its profits from agriculture, the rest of the theory ran, to build an industrial base, thus bringing a working class into being. The trouble was that the prices paid to the peasants were well below the level at which real costs could be recovered.

As the countryside was being almost systematically impoverished, the cities – chief among them Cairo – enjoyed subsidised food, subsidised housing, subsidised education, subsidised transport, subsidised medicine, and subsidised entertainment. Officially rec-

ognised as supplements for otherwise inadequate salaries, subsidies often made the crucial difference between mere poverty and destitution; and once city dwellers got used to them, it became dangerous for any government to speak of their abolition. Unrest in the provinces was easy enough to quell by a show of force, but riots in Cairo, like the ones over subsidised food prices in 1977, could prove seriously destabilising.

Security fears thus provided another excuse for pandering to the urban population. And the one-party state needed the support of Cairenes who, by virtue of their ideologi-

cal value and their potential riot power, became its major constituency. Showcase industries, like the iron and steel complex at Helwan, were built to impress this urban populace. It was to nourish their dreams that new universities were built and it was to give them a sense of being employed that new jobs were created, by the simple expedient of expanding the bureaucracy.

The overwhelming disadvantages of living elsewhere than in Cairo pushed professionals to abandon provincial towns. By the early 1960s there were few medical specialists and even fewer qualified engineers or lawyers to be found outside the capital. Land reform and sequestration had meanwhile already uprooted rural aristocrats, seized their properties, including libraries, and forced them to move to Cairo or Alexandria, if not abroad. Whatever refinement there had been in the Egyptian countryside vanished.

Over-concentration: During the 1960s Cairo thus emerged as the centre of Egyptian industry. Plants for steel, cement, cars, pharmaceuticals, electronics and household appliances were set up by the state. Industrial zones, complete with workers' cities, sprouted at the northern and southern ends of the city in Shubra, and the old summer resort of Helwan. This concentration meant that in later years other industries chose Cairo in order to be close to supplies, but even companies with plants elsewhere had to maintain Cairo offices or risk falling out of touch with the bureaucracy and its ever-changing whims.

By the 1980s concerns about over-concentration grew and the government began offering incentives for firms to move elsewhere. Billions were invested in new satellite cities built from scratch in the open desert. But the attractions of Cairo, with its ready-made workforce, market and communications, meant that much of this effort went unrewarded; people with jobs in the new cities still preferred the long commute from the capital to living in unaccustomed quiet and solitude. The satellite cities thus had no perceptible effect on Cairo itself.

The radical imbalance in living standards, in fact, had meanwhile encouraged thousands of peasants to migrate to all of Egypt's cities, where the population was already exploding: the number of Cairenes, for example, grew from 3.5 million in 1960 to 15 million or more in 1990, but 70 percent of the increase was due to internal growth, not migration from the country. In 1960, when two-thirds of the populace were *fellahin*, only one out of every nine or 10 Egyptians lived in the country's capital. Nowadays more than 80 percent of Egyptians are urban folk and nearly one out of every three is a Cairene.

Links with the world: Before 1970 most tourists coming to Egypt still disembarked at Alexandria or Port Said. Pilgrims to Mecca sailed from Suez; travellers from Sudan still

tion of state-owned radio and TV thus gave the city a total monopoly of mass entertainment. There are one or two printing presses in Alexandria, but the publishing and information industries have also become exclusively Cairene, thanks in part to the Revolution, which abolished private ownership of major publishing houses, newspapers, and magazines to create what was called a Press Sector. The four national newspapers – without exception now all headquartered in the capital – carry skimpy columns in their inner pages titled "The Provinces" or "Beyond the City Limits". The implication is that everything happening in all the other pages of the

arrived by boat or camel caravan. Now that air traffic has superseded virtually all other forms of transport, however, Cairo has become Egypt's bridge to the world. Nearly 3 million tourists, diplomats, businessmen and refugees pass through the city every year, bringing with them foreign ideas and tastes, to which inevitably Cairo adds its own touches before passing them on to the hinterland.

The Egyptian cinema industry has always been concentrated in Cairo and the introduc-

newspapers is therefore happening in Cairo.

Behind such attitudes are millennia of cultural centralisation. Seekers of knowledge from all corners of Islam were trained at Al-Azhar, the university-mosque founded by the Fatimids in 970, not only in exegesis of the Holy Qur'an and the Traditions of Islam, but also in such subjects as higher mathematics and astronomy. After the capture of Córdoba by Christians in 1236 and of Baghdad by the Mongols in 1258, refugees from Andalusia and Mesopotamia fled Western or Eastern terror, bringing skills and knowledge with them. The Ayyubids opened

Left, Foreign Ministry building. **Above**, Tomb of the Unknown Soldier at the Sadat Memorial.

madrasahs offering free instruction in the *Sharia,* Islamic law; the Mamluk sultans, amirs, and beys who succeeded them adorned the city with a multitude of such schools, as well as with houses of worship, mausolea and private palaces. Medieval Cairo was not only the intellectual centre of Egypt, but the cultural capital of the Islam. It was the Mother of the World.

Communications and the media: In the 20th century the broadcast media have spread Cairo's cultural influence even further and wider. Long-isolated villages have grown thoroughly familiar with city ways. *Fellahin* who used to build their houses of cheap and

their teary tribulations have fans from Marrakesh to Muscat. From Mosul to Mauritania, Arabs sing along to Cairene music, the wailing lovesongs of the 1960s or the synthesised pop of the 1990s. There was a time when the political messages broadcast from Cairo likewise had a Pan-Arab audience; and the ideal of nationalism propagated by the Nasser regime reverberates to this day in virtually every Arab country, even in those where overt political expression of all other ideas is suppressed.

Paper-pushers: But Cairo's most enduring cultural export is also its least endearing. The governmental style that now infests the Arab

energy-efficient mud-brick now prefer urban-style concrete, cold in winter and hot in summer; and the crowded living conditions of the capital, its hectic moods and fashions and its middle-class mores, have become universally the Egyptian norm. The drama and excitement of Cairo as shown on TV, the variety and richness of its life, have added to its magnetism for rural immigrants.

It is not just inside Egypt that the Cairo lifestyle, as conveyed by the airwaves, has had such an impact. Egyptian stars and their scandals, Egyptian tele-*shaykhs* and their sermons, Egyptian soap opera families and

world, a combination of inanity and repression, was introduced into the rest of the region's administrative blood-supply by the Cairo-trained clerks who created all its bureaucracies. Inheriting the worst vices of their ancient ancestors, the scribes of the Pharaohs, they have infected everything they have laid their hands upon.

Clearly designed – as a cynical Frenchman once said in regard to the institution of marriage – solely to solve problems that it has itself created and which would not otherwise exist, Cairo's bureaucracy is famous. The dismal shabbiness and dirt of over-crowded offices, the unfathomable complexity of procedures, the mind-boggling pettiness of the officials who administer them, their callous contempt for the public that feeds them and their blatant corruptibility – all these things have enriched a Kafkaesque reputation. There are occasional miracles, such as when the required file is found at first attempt without money changing hands, but the rule is that any single task requires at least two visits from the petitioner on two different days, a dozen signatures, a half-dozen fiscal stamps, and the help of a paid scribe.

Between 1952 and 1978, while the Egyptian population nearly doubled, the number the Mugamaa or Central Government Complex in Maydan at-Tahrir. It is within this grey 14-storey Stalinist hulk that foreigners strive for visas and that Egyptians from all over the country attempt to obtain identity papers, permits, licences and other documents. Until a recent cleaning, one of the building's light shafts was filled with waste paper up to the third floor. The main stairwell is a choice spot for frustratees to commit suicide, driven to despair by merciless pushers of paper.

One reason Cairo's bureaucracy is so pernicious is that officials are so badly paid. Most government employees have to sup-

of public-sector employees multiplied 13 times. Attempts since then to streamline procedures have made some headway, but getting a passport or a birth certificate still requires running the gauntlet of scores of officials. And many such bureaucratic chores require unfortunate residents of the rest of Egypt to make several trips to Cairo. Of the hundreds of offices where heavy-lidded functionaries hold court, the most classic are in

Left, election banner with camel symbol for easy party identification. **Above**, political trials and tribulations: a cinema poster.

plement their income by either lining their pockets at taxpayers' expense or taking a second job. A good percentage of taxi-drivers hold government positions that require little more than a sign-in every morning. In this manner nearly one in three working Cairenes has cleverly made his way on to the state payroll.

Complaining and cracking jokes about the *Saidis* (Upper Egyptians) affords the only balm most Cairenes have for their daily frustrations. History has convinced them that there is little they can do that will change the nature of things.

THE ECONOMICS OF GETTING BY

You are young and in love. Your parents, your friends – indeed everyone – expects you to marry. But where on earth are you to find the 25,000 Egyptian pounds you need – LE 10,000 to make the down-payment on a two-room flat, LE 10,000 to furnish it, LE 5,000 for the wedding itself – when you and your fiancée together take home less than LE 250 a month?

Such is the dilemma faced by thousands of young Cairenes every year. The miracle is that so many manage to get over life's hurdles – marriage, birth, education, disease, death – even when the numbers make no sense at all. And not a few do very well for themselves, too.

Classic salesmanship: Cairenes are past masters at getting by, as any fresh arrival at the airport, assailed by fixers, hawkers and taxi drivers, can testify. Nor is Hard Sell the only method of separating money from wallets. Consider this scene witnessed on a Cairo bus: one vendor of plastic combs gets on at the front, another at the back door. "A comb for only 50 piastres," cries the first. "Forty piastres a comb," the second calls out, pushing his way up the aisle. A few customers stir. One buys a 50 piastre comb. But as the hawkers draw closer they overhear each other. "Only 30 piastres, my combs only 30," shouts the first. Not to be outdone, the second shrieks, "Two combs for half a pound."

As the vendors' bidding drops still further in a frenzy of competition, more and more buyers snap up the combs thinking they are getting the bargain of their lives. Just as the early customers begin to grumble that they have paid too much, the comb sellers crash together in the centre of the vehicle. "You want my seven children to starve, you son of a whore," snarls the first, grabbing his competitor's collar. Fists fly and the conductor intervenes. "Both of you, off my bus." The two are roughly pushed off. But as the bus

pulls away a glance backwards reveals the tousled pair collapsing with laughter on the sidewalk: their flimsy combs are not worth more than a "*bariza*" – 10 piastres.

Poverty as a norm: The good old days – when there were a tenth as many Egyptian mouths to feed and private-sector exportation of long-staple cotton was the mainstay of the economy – are certainly over. During the past 25 years remittances from individual Egyptians working abroad have clearly

emerged as the single most important source of foreign currency and of investment capital, as well as of personal, private-sector income. Revenues from sales of armaments and petroleum and from Suez Canal tariffs, earned solely in the public sector, have some significance, as well as income from foreign tourism, which funds enterprises ranging from five-star hotels to sweatshops mass-producing tacky souvenirs.

Next to remittances, however, major importance has become attached to aid from other countries. Donors include the US most significantly, followed by the Soviet Union and nearly every other country in Europe, as well as Canada, Japan, China, and the Arab OPEC members. Such indispensable fixtures as Cairo's sewers, telephones, and power plants, not to mention its Metro, its new Opera House, its luxurious Conference Centre at Madinat Nasr, and several well-equipped hospitals, owe their existence to foreign generosity. As in sub-Saharan Africa, foreign taxpayers are very rarely thanked, even perfunctorily, for their largesse, while senior bureaucrats routinely take not only the credit for having initiated and carried through any project that is a success, but also whatever is going in the way of substantive rewards.

Such good fortune, however, is not the lot of everyone: very little of the foreign aid bonanza seems to trickle down to the streets, where most Cairenes have to scrimp and save to get by, doing without such luxuries as holidays or meat. Thousands of daytime petty bureaucrats work at night in second and even third jobs. Other breadwinners travel abroad, usually to the Gulf, to win enough to support their families and, if they are lucky, come home with a car or cash to buy property or start a business. The normal diet is based almost exclusively upon starch and a few vegetables.

Relatives up from the country may contribute an occasional chicken and a pair of rabbits may be kept in hutches on the roof, but eggs, fish, beef or lamb are apt to appear, if ever, only on major feast days. To pay for private lessons, the sole guarantee that children will even learn to read, additional sacrifices are made. For the very poor, however, there is often no alternative to sending the children off to work. The garages, ateliers, and small-scale factories or *warshas* of Cairo employ hundreds of thousands of boys and girls, sometimes no older than eight or nine years old.

Networking: Some Cairenes have other mechanisms for coping. Family networks spread their influence far and wide. A cousin in the army can either secure exemption from compulsory service altogether or fix things so that the draftee is stationed close to Cairo, reports briefly once a week, then returns home to work at another job. A cousin in the police can smooth out bureaucratic problems and arrange to have enemies officially threatened or legally persecuted. If a cousin happens to be a professor, no need to worry about exams, written or oral, about the children's standing in their class at graduation, or consequently about their finding an appropriate nest in the bureaucracy, where the pay may not be much, but is at least secure.

For those whose demands are modest, Cairo's cost of living is low. Government subsidies keep flour, rice, sugar, and cooking oil – if not meat – affordable. Transport is cheap. State hospitals offer low-cost – if risky – health care. The flea markets of Wakalat al-Balah, Imbabah, and Imam ash-Shafii provide worn but usable goods at rock-bottom prices. Membership of a *gamaiyya* or savings pool gives many otherwise poor Cairenes periodic access to lump sums of money. And at the very worst, Muslim or Christian charity can be relied on to keep beggars alive. Legend has it, indeed, that many a Cairo panhandler is the secret master of millions.

Special hazards: The life of the city's poor – its vast majority – is neither painless nor picturesque. Though public health improved radically under the Revolution – it virtually eliminated such scourges as trachoma, for example, which had been endemic under the old regime – the dark hair of many children still has the beautiful coppery tinge that is symptomatic of serious malnutrition. Longer-range effects of a diet based on bread are evident in the figures of girls and women and the bow-leggedness of more than half of all adult men.

Hazards unheard of in richer countries – bilharzia, polio, cholera, open manholes, uninsulated electrical cables, collapsing buildings, exploding gas cylinders, bizarre industrial accidents – take a frightening toll. And the pervasive crowding – more than 100,000 people, for example, live in the square kilometre or so of the Bab ash-Shaariyyah district, averaging four persons per room – creates infrabiological tensions that are frequently uncontainable, though most victims cannot even begin to trace them to their source. Cairenes have the ability to feel cosy in conditions of noisiness and overcrowding that a Westerner would regard as completely intolerable.

But life in Cairo, even for the very poor, has always had its brighter side. Excluding *crimes passionnels*, for example, violent crime is almost negligible by Western norms. Recent years have seen the first reports of armed robberies, however, and instances of petty theft have increased markedly. Decline of oil prices has meant that many of the city's thieves and prostitutes, who were the first to seek their fortunes abroad, have returned. The city they left has meanwhile grown so much and so uncontrollably that it now provides them with the cloak of Western-style before being shattered by the Revolution. Ill-gotten gains therefore translate rapidly into respectability. Not a few of the flashy Mercedes cruising the city belong to black marketeers, smugglers, and the like. Their sequinned, feathered and painted consorts, two or three at a time, can be seen at the great wedding receptions held in five-star hotels. Meanwhile, thanks to influences from the Gulf and the Arabian Peninsula, manners have tended to become self-consciously vulgarised. There is a new conspicuous consumption. One recent private event created a scandal when the society press revealed that several hundred guests had received their

anonymity. Harder stuff, sad to say, has increasingly supplanted traditional stimulants like hashish, bringing with it all the usual problems of addiction and organised crime. And meanwhile copious corruption lubricates all the wheels of government – even quite big wheels.

High society: Cairene society is upwardly mobile, fiercely materialistic, and has no landed aristocracy or patriciate of the European or even the American kind. Such a social class had only just begun to exist

Craftsmen working brass.

invitations engraved on solid silver trays.

Given the general poverty, wealth has an almost magical cachet, which is perhaps why so many Cairenes strive so heedlessly to attain it or to seem to have attained it. Almost as a matter of habit people in Cairo dress, act and talk above their stations. But the smiling affability, the Armani suit, the Turnbull and Asser shirt with the dazzling collar and cuffs, the Rolex watch, the Dunhill or Cartier lighter, the Mont Blanc pen, the second-hand BMW or Mercedes, and the talk of projects and plans are as often as not a mask concealing hunger for escape.

God, in His wisdom, has bestowed upon the Egyptian capital a population that is not only abundant, but prolific: more than 15 million people reside here and an additional 3,000 newcomers join the crowd every day, arriving at the city's bus and train stations, as well as by way of its overflowing maternity wards. It contains several of the most densely populated spots on earth.

Along with over-population, Cairo has by no means been spared the same grinding poverty and ravaging social dislocations that the modern age has brought to the rest of the developing world: it suffers from such ills to a degree that in any other Third-World carcinopolis would long ago have produced soaring crime rates and explosive political instability. But God, in His mercy, has endowed Cairenes with the strength of character to endure all hardships with grace and equanimity. They cope and they persevere, much to the disbelief of most foreign visitors, who routinely forecast convulsions of revolutionary violence – which never, of course, take place.

For an accurate understanding of what Cairenes are "really" like, in fact, the traveller would have to sample daily life in a dozen different neighbourhoods, each of which has its own history and has evolved its own unique personality, manners, and customs. Cairenes cultivate a talent for understanding such uniqueness and for drawing exquisite distinctions between themselves and their neighbours.

A son of the city: The highest compliment one Cairene can pay another is to call him an *ibn al-balad,* literally a "son of the city, the homeland" (or *bint al-balad* – "daughter of the city" – if the other Cairene is a woman), a true Cairene. The *ibn al-balad* embodies the special combination of shrewdness and generosity that distinguishes a native resident of the capital city from a country bumpkin, an effete bourgeois, or a foreigner. More

distinct as a species than the Cockney or Carioca, he also has a far longer history. A typical *ibn al-balad* is usually a resident of a *baladi* ("indigenous", i.e., working-class) quarter, such as Darb al-Ahmar, Gamaliyyah or Sayyidah Zaynab, where medieval monuments overshadow twisting alleys and streets. So strong is likely to be the allegiance he feels to the old neighbourhood that he may spurn the company of any former resident who has rejected it by moving to one of the

new, affluent, and quite characterless middle-class suburbs like Mohandisiin or Duqqi, which sprawl over what used to be agricultural land on the other side of the Nile.

As Nobel laureate Naguib Mahfouz shows so touchingly in his novels, an *ibn al-balad* is most at home when he is not actually at home, but sitting in his favourite teashop in the *harah* or alley where he lives, well out of earshot of wife and family, surrounded by friends. Though born in such a quarter, Mahfouz himself lives in a comfortable 12-storey high-rise overlooking the Nile in Duqqi, as befits a successful *littérateur*. But

Preceding pages: Cairo's nautical aspect. Left and right, sons of the city.

Mahfouz is supremely an *ibn al-balad*, a fact that demonstrates how the term has risen above social classes. The medieval quarters were not always so exclusively working-class as they are today and *awlad al-balad* (plural of *ibn al-balad*) may be found in several social strata, among casual labourers or the bourgeoisie. "Whoso would know what the townsfolk of Egypt are like should make acquaintance with the Cairo shop-keeper," remarked one turn-of-the-century English traveller. And certain it is that many a Cairene shopkeeper, member of a class identified with the city since the golden era of the Fatimid caliphate, nine centuries ago,

presence in Cairo of several million *fellahin* (peasants), especially *Saidis*, who pour into the major cities to escape a farm-bound economy that can no longer sustain their way of life. They are forced to seek employment at the very bottom of the ladder, as teaboys in downtown offices or manual labourers on construction sites. When they acquire enough capital they may become *bawabs* – porters or doormen – either in the up-market apartment blocks of Zamalek, Mohandisin, Garden City, or Duqqi or in the older buildings of Ismailiyyah, between Azbakiyyah and Maydan at-Tahrir.

Saidi jokes: If the *awlad al-balad* consider

is a perfect *ibn al-balad*: affable but acute, hospitable without pretentiousness and polite without servility, straightforward, but extremely knowing – and though serious in his business, equipped with a savage sense of humour.

The targets of Cairene humour seem invariably to be either the hapless *Saidi* (Upper Egyptian), whose legendary backwardness makes him the perfect victim, or the President of the Republic, whose putative deficit in intelligence earns irreverent comparisons with cows or donkeys. Decades of poorly managed agricultural policy account for the

themselves shrewd and savvy, they view the *Saidis* as exactly the opposite: credulous, gullible, and maddeningly simple-minded. A typical *Saidi* joke usually depicts the luck-less victim trying to adapt a piece of modern equipment – a computer terminal, say, or a vacuum cleaner – to some obscure and vaguely idiotic rustic purpose. Sometimes the target is not just stupidity, but blind traditionalism, as in the tale of the newly married *Saidi* who murdered his wife a mere two nights after the wedding celebration. When asked what his motive was, he declared that he was acting in defence of his honour, having discovered that his bride was not a virgin. "Why then," said one of his interrogators, inclined to be sympathetic, "did you wait 24 hours? Why did you not cut her throat on your wedding night?" "How could I?" said the *Saidi*. "On that night she *was* a virgin!"

Cairene attitudes are perfectly reflected in a popular television show that makes use of hidden cameras to film unwary victims as they are put into ridiculous situations, a sort of Egyptian *Candid Camera*. In one particular episode an unwitting young female job applicant, fashionably attired and clearly middle-class, arrives at a well-appointed denly an inner door opens and out shambles a tall, unshaven *Saidi* clad in a tattered *gallabiyya*, a sodden cigarette dangling from one corner of his mouth, who is introduced as "the company president". To capture the look on the young lady's face – an expression of total horror – was, of course, the point of the stunt.

Out of Africa: If Cairo derives its cultural identity from the Arab world, its demographic character is distinctly African. This character is most obvious and visible in the city's Nubians, the custodians of a proud civilisation that historically has exercised power from deep in what is now the Sudan north-

downtown office for an interview with a "senior company representative". The interviewer is stiffly formal, even severe, warning the young lady that the president of the company, a very important man, is extremely demanding, that his employees must speak perfect English, be absolutely punctual and obedient, and work industriously. Intimidated and impressed, the applicant recites her qualifications, smiling nervously. Sud-

ward as far as Aswan and sometimes throughout the whole of Egypt. The pharaohs of the 25th Dynasty (772–664 BC) were Nubian, Nubian mercenaries fought under the Fatimid caliphs, and every ruler from Ibn Tulun to Faruq employed Nubians in his palaces, not as slaves, but as paid servants famed for their honesty. Latecomers to Islam – Nubia did not begin to be converted from Christianity until the 14th century – they were absorbed within Muhammad Ali's Egyptian empire and now form an important minority in Cairo.

Taller, darker and finer-boned than most Egyptians, Nubian men frequently work as

Left, education unlocks the middle class. **Above**, new city dwellers who come in from the country are sometimes the butt of Cairene jokes.

cooks or *bawabs*, though universal education has combined with their own enterprising spirit to give them a marked upward mobility. A growing number of Nubians thrive among the ranks of Cairene businessmen and civic leaders.

Bureaucrats: The elephantine governmental bureaucracy created under Gamal Abdel Nasser (1953–70) and expanded under Anwar Sadat (1970–81) employs so many Cairenes – more than a million by some estimates – that they form a class (called *muwazzafin*) in their own right. To encourage the lower economic strata to seek higher education, Nasser promised lifetime employment to

universities dump over 40,000 new graduates on to the job market. Among those who do find employment, many are working in jobs quite unrelated to their training: house-painting veterinarians and taxi-driving engineers abound. But almost 4,000 annually are unable to find any work at all and nearly a quarter of all unemployed Cairenes are university degree-holders. This segment of the population is rightly viewed by the government as the most volatile, apt to provide eager recruits for religious radicals and other malcontents. The neighbourhood around Ayn Shams University, where hordes of poor and unemployed university graduates reside, is

anyone capable of graduating from university. As a consequence, the ranks of government administration are swollen with diploma- and certificate-laden paper-pushers, over-qualified for what they do, but under-educated for anything better and notoriously underpaid: their penury, in fact, is almost as legendary as their torpor. Male *muwazzafin* beguile away hours each day in the local *qahwa* (coffe house) alongside their more entrepreneurial – and prosperous – *ibn al-balad* friends, while their drab spouses toil at odd jobs in a losing battle to make ends meet.

Every year Cairo's three large national

considered by security forces to be the most explosive quarter in the city and is therefore carefully monitored.

New Rich versus Old Money: The economic reforms introduced by Anwar Sadat in the mid-1970s not only brought foreign capital into Egypt, but also brought hidden Egyptian capital into the open, thus creating what was recognised as a new class of middlemen, fixers, company representatives, managers, and agents for foreign corporations. During the day their new Mercedes clog the streets in front of private schools as their drivers arrive to pick up or deliver Benetton-clad charges. At night the chic bars of Zamalek teem with their teenage issue. Some 200,000 of Egypt's 250,000 millionaires reportedly live in Cairo; and to serve their needs, clusters of boutiques and gourmet food stores have sprung up alongside expensive beauty parlours and pastel-painted pre-schools. They are referred to derisively as the "parasitic bourgeoisie" by those less fortunate and scorned as upstarts by the old privileged class, the families of the pashas and beys whose property and power were liquidated by the Nasser regime.

It is far easier, of course, to be an Egyptian millionaire these days, when a million Egyp-

To be rich meant being very rich indeed.

It was said then that the country was still run by the same 40 families who had allegedly controlled it under King Faruq. The following year the Revolution began systematically sequestrating the wealth of the *ancien régime*, seizing all the moveable and immoveable property that belonged not just to these 40 families, but to a total of more than 4,000: land, bank accounts, houses, flats, furniture, cars, jewellery, art objects, clothing, and even books. To provide an example in central Cairo, the great houses of Hoda Shaarawi, the feminist leader, and her neighbours the princely Zogheb family were

tian pounds is actually worth only 300,000 devalued and depressed US dollars, than it was in 1960, when the Revolution had not yet decided to dismantle the economy and to start all over again. In 1960, the last year during which Old Money remained more or less intact, £1million was worth eight times as much as it is now – nearly two and a half million – in US dollars and probably 30 to 40 times as much in real terms, after inflation.

Left, the smart eat-out in the big five-star hotels. **Above**, a local *mawlid* is a more traditional form of celebration.

seized and demolished, leaving spaces that stood vacant for more than 25 years. The aim of such moves was to strip the old upper classes of their capital assets, their power, the culture that had set them apart from the masses, and thus to eradicate them.

Since 1977, when the sequestrations were finally declared by the courts to be illegal, Old Money has re-established itself, but in nothing like its old position of influence. Many Cairenes who had gone abroad returned to claim their property, joining those who had been unable or unwilling to leave. Some settled down again to stay, but others found the country too changed to be endurable. A whole cultural and social substructure had disappeared. A new Opera House has finally been built – by the Japanese, not the Egyptian government – but private orchestras, private collections of art or antiquities, and private libraries, even small ones, no longer exist. The Muhammad Ali Club survives, under a different name, only because it was taken under the wing of the Foreign Ministry. There are no great banquets or balls, no large parties at all except wedding receptions, which are given with elaborate buffets, but without champagne: even the rich find the cost too high and the

dreary spectre of Muslim fundamentalism too daunting. The Gazirah Sporting Club, once the watering hole of a small élite, has served no alcohol since 1980 and is increasingly full of people who are strangers to one another: with well over 20,000 memberships on its books, it cannot keep up with the demand from *arrivistes*.

The new poor: The spectacle of a shiny new Mercedes Benz sharing a street with a decrepit donkey cart has become such a familiar motif in the capitals of the Third World that it no longer inspires comment. Far more glaring contrasts, symptomatic of a widening gulf between the living standards of rich and poor, will confront the visitor who leaves his luxury hotel and wanders around other parts of the city. Day and night, the streets of the older quarters teem with young children at work, holding aloft trays of tea, bicycling precariously through traffic on delivery missions, or scampering barefoot over piles of garbage. Almost half the population of the city is below the age of 18. This fact alone would betoken a bleak future, but combined with rising unemployment, severe shortages of housing and inadequate medical care, it creates a mixture that is explosive.

Poverty has many faces in Cairo. Hospitals, for example, report a steady rise in the incidence of childhood malnutrition and preventable diseases. The state's overcrowded school system, to which only the children of the poor are condemned, already teaches its pupils in two abbreviated shifts per day and is considering squeezing in a third. Meanwhile as many as a fifth of all Cairenes live without ready access to clean water and electricity. The most recent newcomers to Cairo, *Saidis* and Lower Egyptian *fellahin*, many of them transient, tend to settle at the city's margins, in the "informal sector" shantytowns that sprawl along the base of the Muqattam Hills and into the desert beyond. These settlements not only lack electricity, piped water, and drains, but are also far removed from schools and clinics, markets, bakeries, shops, and pharmacies. Malnutrition and disease thrive, and local authorities, charged with providing municipal services but lacking the means to keep up with the need for them, have largely abdicated responsibility.

All this overwhelming evidence of poverty and neglect exists in a city that remains one of the world's most voracious consumers of European luxury cars, where a year's tuition at the American University in Cairo exceeds the combined annual income of 10 wage-earners. And while the appetite of the moneyed classes for trendy imported goods grows increasingly insatiable, the diet of the poor is being reduced to ever more meagre portions, quite literally: since international lending agencies began to pressure the government to devise subtle ways of reducing subsidies for essential foodstuffs, the size of a five-piastre loaf of bread, the staple food of the poor and the working class, has shrunk by over a third.

The influence of Islam: But the prevailing mood on Cairo streets is one of contented bustle, not depression. Rarely does the visitor encounter the sort of hopeless resignation characteristic of cities in the West. A partial explanation for such extraordinary morale lies in Islam, the religion of almost 90 percent of Cairenes. A powerful unifying force, it may in large part account for Cairo's social cohesiveness and its relatively placid political climate, as well as its low rate of violent

the meantime he is encouraged to accept his earthly lot as God's will.

Western visitors believe they see evidence everywhere of "fatalism". Nowhere else in the Arab world, certainly, is the word *insha'Allah* ("God willing"), accompanied by a resigned shrug of the shoulders, used so frequently: a taxi driver will utter it quietly when you tell him your destination; a travel agent will use it a dozen times in a brief conversation ("When you arrive in Luxor, *insha'Allah*"), and a government minister announcing next year's budget will repeat it after every item in his speech. But this verbal tic is very far from being the whole story. As

crime. It is Islam's insistence on the equality of all male believers before God that strengthens the status quo. At the popular mosque of Sayyidna Husayn, for example, a beggar can pray alongside the President of the Republic – after passing through a security check, of course – assured that in the eye of the Almighty they are brothers and that if he remains free of envy he too will be given his due when heavenly accounts are settled. In

Left and above, tradition, religion and superstition work together to make a surprisingly safe and stable city.

Edward William Lane observed of the Cairene Muslim in the 1840s: "His belief in predestination does not prevent his taking any step to attain an object he may have in view, nor does it make him careless of avoiding danger."

Indeed, Cairenes are renowned for their street savvy, their ability to bend seemingly inflexible rules and install themselves up front ahead of everyone else. This trait is most dramatically on display at the bus terminus in crowded Maydan at-Tahrir as boarding passengers refuse to queue and jam both exits and entrances in a frenzied rush to

FIVE-STAR WEDDINGS

A visitor can hardly spend more than a couple of nights in any of the city's smart hotels without encountering a wedding celebration. Festivities commence with a *zaffa*, a musical parade, in the lobby, featuring minstrels in "Oriental" costume. Trumpets blare, drums beat, and tambourines chatter, as the happy couple is ushered through the throng to a banquet room by a belly-dancer with finger-cymbals or a prancing youth in pantaloons, puff-cheeked as he blows on a rude instrument called the *muzmar dakar*, a baritone-range or "male" pipe.

Although getting married is regarded as the fulfilment of a man's religious duty, Islam prescribes no ceremony, much less a lavish celebration. Egyptian tradition is older than Islam, however, and without a proper party for their children, families have no status at all. Since 1962, when the Nile Hilton was first hired as the venue for a reception given after the wedding of a Coptic couple, the custom among more moneyed families has been to hold the traditional party in a five-star hotel. The family of the groom will foot the bill, which may well be equivalent to US$30,000 or more; the family of the bride will already have

paid out an equivalent sum for the reception that announced the engagement.

Sitting in gilded thrones on a dais, the lucky couple greet well-wishers. They will have been dressed to look like the plaster figurines on the wedding cake: he will wear a dinner jacket, she will be dressed in a white Western-style bridal gown complete with veil, wreath, and bouquet. As she and her new husband confront legions of well-wishers, the blush on her cheek may begin to look a little hectic.

These days, most weddings – even five-star affairs – remain alcohol-free out of respect for Qur'anic injunction. Everyone except the bride and groom will nonetheless be in perfect humour, elbowing for space at the buffet, simpering at acquaintances not seen since the last such reception, scintillating for the video, and chuckling at the antics of children who are lavishly and ornamentally dressed specially for the occasion.

An Egyptian wedding reception, whether it is staged in a five-star hotel or some hashish-fumed back alley, typically incorporates a belly dancer. Fees for the most famous start at the equivalent of around US$400 for a 10-minute display. The tone is normally none too refined. Coy to begin with, the belly dancer will first only flutter lashes at rows of seated matrons. As the music quickens, however, she will warm to her task, bumping what is nominally private towards the bald heads of retired bankers and government officials (in whom she arouses perhaps no more than nostalgia), shaking secondary sexual characteristics in the blushing face of the groom (with whom she may have better luck), and offering blunt and telegraphic advice to the bride.

The belly dance – euphemistically called "Oriental" dancing – has provided entertainment at private parties, especially wedding parties, throughout Egyptian history. It may be seen any night of the week in the supper clubs of the five-star hotels, but is also performed by ordinary Egyptian women and girls in the privacy of their own homes for audiences of other women.

In its professional form the phases of true belly dance are closely related to music, which is typically played by a small ensemble on the *ud* (lute), flute, zither, and violin, with a drum, tambourines, and a double-bass to provide percussion. Tomb paintings from the 15th century BC show women performing movements resembling those of the modern belly dancer and musicians playing the ancient forerunners of these same instruments.

The art of the more respected – i.e., older and less athletic – dancers is said to lie in their relationship to the music. Others use the techniques of the sex show, addressing themselves to an audience of men with money to burn: their movements create an aura of erotic promise, which the dancers themselves have long had the reputation of readily fulfilling. It is not surprising that they should have become targets for fundamentalist violence. To society at large, however, despite a widespread religious revival, they continue to represent a beloved and ineradicable tradition.

secure seating before departing riders have even had a chance to get off. An Egyptian sociologist has observed that his compatriots, like most of the rest of the Third World, "have a low empathy quotient." If Cairo once enjoyed the world's highest per capita motor vehicle fatality rate (the grim statistics have improved somewhat in recent years), the distinction could certainly be attributed to drivers' customary disregard for anyone else on the road.

Driving is one of the few activities not explicitly governed by religious stricture, which reaches out in every other direction to make Cairene behaviour surprisingly con-

among the young on the streets of any Western capital seem almost shockingly obscene.

The Christian minority: As befits a city renowned for religious tolerance, Cairo can also lay claim to a multifarious and thriving Christian community. The overwhelming majority of Christians residing in Cairo belong to the Coptic Orthodox Church, founded in Alexandria, according to legend, by Saint Mark and today still presided over by a Patriarch of Alexandria. The word *Copt* derives from the Egyptian word *Kuptaios*, which in turn derives from the Greek *Aigyptios*, and means simply "Egyptian". Many of the city's million or more Copts live in Gizah, Shubra,

servative. Public contact between the sexes, for example, is so strictly circumscribed that even a middle-aged and obviously married couple who hold hands as they ride the Metro or stroll a downtown street will draw stares of opprobrium from tradition-minded onlookers. Young Cairene couples in lovers' lanes along the Nile or on the Muqattam are rarely seen to touch each other because such areas are patrolled by "morals police". Compared with their decorum the varieties of physical intimacy ordinarily observable

Above, football unites young Cairenes.

Daher, Heliopolis (Misr al-Gadidah, "New Cairo") or Misr al-Qadimah ("Old Cairo"), where in some areas church steeples outnumber minarets. The list of Christian persuasions represented in Cairo offers a capsule history of the schisms and infighting that has plagued Christendom since its birth; apart from the Coptic Orthodox, some 150,000 members of the Greek Orthodox church live in Cairo, as do smaller numbers of Coptic Catholics, Armenian Catholics, Maronites, Melkites and other followers of the Syrian or Latin Rites. And some 500 Jews remain in Cairo, having resisted for decades the lure of Paris, Geneva, or Tel Aviv, to which most of their co-religionists migrated after the Tripartite Aggression (Britain, France and Israel) of 1956.

The shifting tides of history have deposited a rich cultural sediment along the banks of the Nile. Medieval Cairo always welcomed refugees and, as one of the freer and more open capitals in the Middle East, the modern city has been a magnet for dissidents from less tolerant regimes throughout more than a century and a half. Syrian Christians founded the city's newspapers; Armenians and Kurds, who fled genocidal pogroms in their homelands earlier this century, were for

years fixtures of the Cairo merchant class, alongside expatriate Greeks and Italians, Sephardic and Ashkenazi Jews, Levantines, Maghribines and, of course, native Egyptians. Nasser's nationalisation campaigns, which expelled most foreigners, robbed Cairo of much multicultural charm.

Refugees and exiles: Today the city plays host to a staggering number of refugees from south of the Sahara and elsewhere in the Arab world. Escapees from the bloody and protracted conflicts around the Horn give the city an increasingly African character, as Sudanese, Ethiopians and Somalis arrive by

the planeload to form a new underclass, a reserve of casual labour. Already overburdened with the impossible task of providing a minimum standard of living for its own people, the Egyptian government regards this influx warily. Many refugees are supported by agencies of the United Nations, but allowances are so small that immigration to Europe or the Americas becomes the only conceivable goal.

Exiles of an altogether different variety also proliferate in Cairo, drawn from abroad by governments, petroleum companies, construction firms or news services, by their surrender to the lure of travel, or by some inscrutable summons of the Nile. Cairo is thus home to more than 100,000 foreigners from the West. They tend to cluster in enclaves in suburbs like Maadi and Zamalek, which are quieter and cleaner than the rest of the city and offer schools where their children can be taught in familiar languages. Chic clubs, embassy receptions, and charity balls have given way to more mass-produced remedies for boredom; expats now typically seek such diversions as are offered by the Hash House Harriers, who run footraces around pharaonic monuments, or organisations for "petroleum wives".

As in any city with a glorious past and an apparently dismal future, the present day in Cairo is viewed by many inhabitants as offering a sad contrast with times gone by. While an *ibn al-balad* recalls with regret an era when tradesmen and craftsmen lived well and were esteemed as pillars of a real community, there are ex-pashas and expats who have wistful memories of a sophisticated allure that revolution, over-population, and uncontrolled development seem to have obliterated. But such nostalgia itself is not really new – European travellers in the 1830s customarily deplored the changes made by Muhammad Ali, lamenting the disappearance of "Oriental" charm – and 100 years hence, visitors may well look back upon this epoch, with its traffic, deafening noise, horrific poverty, and unimaginable pollution, and pronounce it a Golden Age.

Left, *fellah* **in the city selling his vegetables. Right, university student.**

The jostling crowds in central Cairo at night, especially when the cinemas turn out, is evidence that birth control has been fervently eschewed. The fact that these multitudes are composed exclusively of young men, however, may make a visitor wonder if Egyptians practise clandestine female infanticide. Why are there so many men?

Public pleasure at night is reserved, on the whole, for the male. Women of most sorts stay home after sundown. Not that the films the ladies miss – locally-made comedies and gangster flicks, re-runs of beefcake epics (Maciste), spaghetti Westerns (Bud Spencer), and martial-arts Easterns (Bruce Lee) – are anything to rave about. Tickets are cheap, however, and a visit to the cinema allows young men to get away from home for a few hours, leaving oppressive interiors to the women already condemned to sit out entire lives within them.

In striking contrast with the restrictiveness that seems to wrap the second sex in drabber concealment as the years wear on, the young men of Cairo – hundreds of thousands of them – indulge in a lively nocturnal *paseo*, parading the city's major streets to show off clothes and grooming.

Male supremacy: A man's freedom of movement and display reflect his freedom of decision and hence his maleness. That the masculine sex is superior and should be specially privileged is automatically presumed by all men, acceded to by nearly all women, supported by a millennium of precedent, and sanctioned by the dominant creed, which authorises the Cairene male to do more or less what pleases him. As for women, the unmarried ones must be fearful lest they displease their fathers, while the married ones had best be strictly attentive to their husbands' needs, though also mindful of the fact that no matter how scrupulously and submissively they behave, they may still be divorced at whim. A good Muslim wife

Left and **right**, many male Cairenes lead lives – both at leisure and at work – in the street.

certainly has no right to complain when – after the fourth or fifth child that such men seem to require to advertise their potency – she has grown fat, wrinkled, and dull and her hubby decides to insert a younger, sexier woman into his happy household.

Between 1910 and 1970 polygamy was unfashionable among the middle and upper classes and it has remained unthinkable still in many Muslim families. With the new millionaires, however, it has made some-

thing of a comeback; and the right to have up to four wives at a time has always been enjoyed in any case by prosperous Muslim peasants, urban businessmen, and even senior bureaucrats, regardless of upper-class fashion, whenever they thought they had enough money. Among respectable people the male's special sexual privileges are not exercised without the theoretical assumption of financial responsibilities: wives and children, however many, must be clothed and fed; and in such families the women are not expected even to be educated, much less to go out to work. Though it is never poverty alone that prevents multiple marriages, not many Cairene men, in fact, can really afford even the time to think about having more than one wife.

A man's life: If it is the aspiration of most Egyptian men to be successful, it is their misfortune to see success in unambitious forms – a job, a flat, a wife, a car, kids, electric appliances, pampered retirement. To acquire these things a man should have at least a secondary-school certificate and preferably a university degree of some sort. Such pieces of paper complete his education. Having acquired them he will rarely read anything thereafter except an occasional news-

but unlike those who went to the old Opera House, they do not own or read books.

A richer or more ambitious man will go into business, opening an office from which he can exploit relatives and family to offer the services of paid minions to a growing network of contacts. He will buy a Mercedes on the company account. The more money he makes the more deference he will enjoy from staff and relatives. As time passes and official contacts mature he will perhaps complete a project – a chicken farm, a ready-to-wear clothing factory, an agency for a foreign firm – then raise an apartment block. Leaving the building unfinished will sub-

paper. To foster an air of sophistication and appear "in the know", however, he may pepper his conversation with hackneyed formulæ, both pious and impious, and unsubstantiated political rumours, which will suggest, if only to the equally uninformed, that he has an intelligent interest in matters other than the purely financial or domestic.

Such crassness should not be surprising. Since 1952, after all, formal culture has almost disappeared, having been abandoned by the state as even a minor element in education. The crowds that flock to the new Opera House do so because they love ballet,

stantially reduce his tax bill. Incorporating a wayside mosque into the structure will lower it still further; and as middle age sets in and he becomes increasingly religiose, he may well have platters of food sent there during the month of Ramadan, from which poor worshippers may eat before the commencement of the daily fast.

He will already have grown increasingly indolent. Only perhaps a pose at first, assumed in order to appear respectable or business-worthy – since anyone who displays energy is regarded as eccentric, an object of puzzlement and pity – his lassitude will have grown into a habit, fed by the universal and deep-seated belief that a man's inner self yearns to return to pampered babyhood and that the purpose of life is to fulfil this yearning. Once re-achieved, at "retirement", the state of infantile idleness will be regarded with deep satisfaction. In the rosary beads that dangle from fingers resting lax upon the mounded belly will be told, in fact, the same litany of fatuity that has mesmerised middle-class Cairene males for generations: the great-grandfather of this flaccid oaf may not have worn trousers, but he certainly knew the pleasures of being a man and therefore himself undoubtedly wound up in pretty much

either group really liked it that way or not.

Take falling in love, for instance, as reflected in mainstream Egyptian pop songs, such as those of the Nightingale of the East, the late Umm Kulthum, or her male counterpart, Abd al-Halim Hafez. In these songs the sweetness of ideal love never cloys or enervates. Girls (preferred soft and plumpish) are sugar, honey, cream, sweetness, strawberry syrup – all that little girls used to be made of in the cheap European or American serial fiction of, say, the 1880s or '90s. Like the heroes and heroines of late-Victorian romance, Cairenes go in for lengthy courtships, modesty, old-fashioned compliments,

the same shape at pretty much the same age.

Victorian values: To the Westerner, the social conventions of Egypt are at once reassuring, being still vaguely familiar from our own receding past, and disturbing. It's as if one were trapped in a time-warp, transported back to unspecified days of old located somewhere between the late Middle Ages and 1939, when men were men and when women were women – regardless of whether or not

Left, the cotton industry is a substantial employer. Above, Friday, a non-working day, is for backgammon with male friends.

and wildly possessive jealousy. They believe that a woman's role is not to compete with a man, but to "tame" and "purify" him through noble self-sacrifice, that personal happiness in a woman therefore not only does not matter at all, but is sinful even to contemplate.

The lives of men are likewise apt to be unfulfilled. Most young men dream of a period of freedom away from domestic supervision and sanction, but this longed-for golden age rarely materialises. Seeing the world – outside the Arab world – is for the determined and lucky few. The typical man will live in the bosom of his family or toil in the spartan and unromantic Gulf until he has saved enough to put down the deposit on a flat, having planned for years with his fiancée to set up home together. By this time he is likely to be in his late twenties or early thirties and in dire need of release from an unnatural celibacy. Once the money is in the bank, he has, in any case, no alternative to getting married. In a society where offspring increase a couple's status and contraception is deemed unnatural, children automatically follow. So ends the dream of freedom.

Forbidden love: Other less openly acknowledged liaisons occur, of course, as they do far beyond the average Cairene's means or inclination.

If opportunity knocks, on the other hand, no young man is likely to be deterred. Religion may frown, but once he has made up his mind to sin, he will enjoy himself thoroughly. Though circumscribed by formulaic self-images – the *geda* (regular guy) must have gusto and guts and Devil take the hindmost! – what goes on behind closed shutters may thus be infused with real passion and joy. Unaccustomed to introspection, Egyptians suffer little from Western-style sexual guilt, but see carnal pleasure as a gift to be much relished, if a suitable place can be

even in the most repressive societies, but Cairo scarcely lives up to its pre-World War II reputation for lurid licence and wild abandon. Even during the puritanical Nasser years, when the unaesthetic requirement (again in force) that belly-dancers cover their navels was first instituted, districts like Aguza or Zamalek were famed for the furnished premises they offered on a short-term basis to Arab visitors. Seedy down-town hostess-bars and cheap nightclubs in Shari al-Haram (Pyramids Road) still offer the *fantasiyya* – whisky and flesh in full measure – to the same Arab visitors, but such distractions are

found and a willing partner is at hand.

The *geda* has hair on his chest, which he displays, with or without a gold medallion, according to his income and social origins. He dresses more nattily, class for class, than his Western counterpart and takes better care of his appearance generally. Until he gets married he will probably do some kind of sport, though the long-term benefits of exercise are likely to evaporate in idleness and cigarette smoke. Since his contacts with girls

The art of bellydancing is practised largely for the benefit of men.

of his age must be relatively clandestine, a strong male bonding – which can last a lifetime – is the norm. From early schooldays, youths regularly study together, go on holiday together, sleep together. Sexual experimentation is a natural development out of companionship and is considered part of what kids do together – not worth talking about, since they'll grow out of it soon enough anyway. Most do.

Homosexual sex has its aficionados, rules and roles. That Egyptian men – even policemen and soldiers – kiss when they meet or hold hands in public, however, is no indication whatever that there is a homosexual relationship between them, conscious or unconscious; and homosexuality is far less acceptable in Cairo, where the word *khawal* ("fag", "pervert") is the commonest insult, than in any city in the West. Gay consciousness is therefore quite out of place, as many a Western tourist – expecting to encounter temptations like those he succumbed to last year in Tangier – has discovered much to his chagrin.

Sex/power relationships between Cairene men are a subset of the general sexual consciousness, with its strong emphasis on hierarchies. In a society where role-stereotyping is so widespread and absolute, men who take an active role in homosexual acts thus see themselves as men and only the passive are regarded as *khawalat* ("queers", "catamites"). It doesn't mean you're gay – God forbid! – if you seek sexual release in your buddy, but if you let him do it to you, your honour is gone for ever.

Friendship and the group: Camaraderie, however, of a kind that long ago disappeared everywhere in the West – except, of course, in Hollywood movies of the "male-bonding" type – remains one of the many positive features of Egyptian society. It binds men together at all levels and they have no reason to be afraid to show their feelings in this regard. Camaraderie is reinforced by the required period (up to three years) of military service, in which young men learn to abase themselves in the face of arbitrary and often irrational authority. Such humiliations are best endured in groups.

Military service prepares a young man for the insults he will receive from his superiors if and when he gets a job: there is nothing subtle about the relationship between the weak and the strong, but strength is seldom appreciated until it is exerted in threats and bullying, which are therefore expected. Men compensate for humiliations at work both by playing the tyrant at home and by insulting each other playfully in their leisure time. In any café at night, for instance, the noise level is phenomenal: shouted profanities fly while backgammon tiles or dominoes are slapped down with aggressive *joie de vivre*. Cairenes are certainly among the rowdiest and most sociable people on earth.

Group activities, such as spectator sport, are taken very seriously and international football matches or such major local ones as the clashes between the Ahli and Zamalek teams are followed by maniacally honking, flag-waving cavalcades that last well into the small hours. Soccer is also fought out with fervour in suburban streets and in every available car park. The rich and lucky few frequent their sporting clubs, where they meet friends to play squash, tennis and the mating game.

In Egypt privacy is nearly as suspect as freedom. Virtually everything important, especially among men, is always done in groups. Groups, by their nature, are susceptible to control; and through them it is easy to exert pressure, to enforce and reinforce a given set of norms in attitudes and behaviour. The norms of Egyptian society all centre on the high value given to social cohesion and continuity and hence to social conformity, which is consciously sought and achieved at the expense of personal space, personal growth, and personal self-fulfilment. Authoritarianism, moreover, the use of outright repression to achieve such social conformity, is not only not regarded negatively, but much admired. As all women are subject to men, so are all men thus subject to the powers that be.

Egyptian society therefore controls and conditions its young. This does not often result in individual happiness, which is not after all its aim. It does, however, frequently result in a deep-seated but ill-understood sense of frustration.

WOMEN, WORK AND THE VEIL

Married women in ancient Memphis had far more rights than married women in ancient Athens – far more, for that matter, than married women in mid-Victorian London, despite the fact that a rather formidable woman sat on the British throne. In the latter half of the 20th century, however, Egyptian women still have not achieved equality with men, neither in law nor by custom; and no matter how much they may rule within the bedroom, the kitchen, the shop or even the office, the public places of Cairo, including streets, coffee-houses, and popular cinemas, have remained fundamentally male preserves. Women's status since 1970, in fact, has probably declined.

The first steps towards modernising the rights of women were taken by the Muhammad Ali family. The Khedive Ismail himself had 14 wives, but in 1872, instead of presenting four eligible princes of the family with Circassian concubines, as had been the custom, he married them to four of their cousins, their equals in rank, thus signalling the end of the harem system in the ruling family. This example rapidly filtered down, as did the indomitable ways of some of the family's women, who refused to be treated as less than equals.

Princess Nazli Fazil, for example, eldest of the daughters of Mustafa Bahgat Fazil, brother of Ibrahim Pasha, kept a *salon* under the British Occupation that mixed sexes as well as nationalities and consistently took public political positions of her own in opposition both to Khedive Tawfiq, her first cousin, and to Khedive Abbas II Hilmi. Sir Ronald Storrs, a diplomat whose memoirs are an excellent record of the period just before World War I, describes her as being then "a once beautiful and still brilliant sexagenarian, keeping, and using, fiercely interested eyes."

By the time Princess Nazli died in 1913, Egyptian women were at least as cultivated

Left, four women teachers in Zamalek. Right, and a student at the university.

as Englishwomen of comparable background. Describing the behaviour of the wives of British officials under the Occupation, for example, Storrs comments sardonically: "Nor was there, save for one or two notable exceptions, the faintest effort on the part of the official's wife to make the acquaintance, still less cultivate the friendship, of the wives or daughters of her husband's colleagues or subordinates; and it was with an air of virtuous resignation that she steeled herself to

sacrifice an afternoon for a call upon an Egyptian or Turkish lady, as likely as not better born, better bred, better read, better looking and better dressed than herself."

Removing the veil: Egyptian women of all religious faiths and social classes took active part in the 1919 Revolution and there are photographs of them marching in veiled ranks to confront British troops. The veil quite clearly had no particular religious significance. It was worn by all respectable middle- and upper-class women, Christian, Muslim and Jewish, whenever they appeared in public, much as Western women of the same era wore large ornamental hats (often with veils) and gloves, as well as some sort of symbolic wrap, even in mid-summer, and were obviously corseted. When the famous Egyptian feminist Hoda Shaarawi deliberately removed her own veil in 1923, however, the example was rapidly followed and by 1935 veils were a comparative rarity in Egypt, though they continued to be worn as an item of fashion in neighbouring countries like Syria and Jordan for 30 more years, while complete concealment has remained obligatory to this day for women in the Arabian Peninsula.

During the same era Egyptian women be-

tinue to make up a third of registered students. A quarter of the graduates working in professional and technical fields are now women.

The return of the veil: The Revolution has also severed Egypt from its past, however, and as the 1970s arrived, wore on, and turned into the 1980s the continuing decline of older cultural values and their liberalising influence was underlined by a return to the veil, though in a new form that is exclusively Muslim in meaning. Visible in the streets of university districts like Ayn Shams or Gizah are scores of women of all ages wearing the *higab* – a wimple-like headcovering made of

gan to enter into businesses and professions. There were female doctors, dentists, lawyers, engineers and university professors in Cairo a decade and a half before Women's Liberation made its appearance at cocktail parties in New York: by 1965, in fact, thanks to the additional impetus given to social change by the July Revolution, Egypt could boast a far higher proportion of women in these professions or working as diplomats or high officials than might have been found in any Western country outside Scandinavia. The Revolution encouraged a massive influx of women into universities, where they con-

lightweight material – which hides the hair and neck. Such women are called *muhagabat*. ("those who wear *higab*").

Critics of the *higab* say that to wear it represents a step backward for women. What baffles American feminist commentators, however, who have been taught to put a high value upon wage-earning, is that its emergence has not been accompanied by obvious efforts to confine women to their homes or to prevent their taking jobs. On the contrary, the typical adult *muhagabah* is a working woman and dresses as she does in order to be able to go to work. A major reason often given for wearing the *higab*, in fact, is that it tends to discourage male advances, either physical or verbal, to which women would never be subjected if they were not out working themselves.

Women at work: The media never tire of observing that Egyptian women have become parliamentarians, ambassadors, even ministers, but the lot of most working women is a far cry from such shining examples. Almost 70 percent of the women working in the formal economy are employed by the government and the public sector. A typical habitat for the *muhagabah* is thus governmental or public-sector offices, which are

often filled wall to wall with *muhagabat*.

Forced on to the labour market by need more than inclination, they generally come from the lower middle class, a social stratum in which wives and daughters traditionally stayed home and never saw strange men. The economic situation continues to make it impossible for such families to survive on one income, however, and to keep one's womenfolk at home is a luxury few men can afford. Among city people the ideal of seclusion

Left and **above**, the various and varied faces of women in Cairo.

traditional among the Cairene middle classes is thus being rapidly discarded: a working woman is considered far more desirable as a wife than one who is unemployed.

Low pay, dead ends: Holding for the most part low-paying dead-end positions for which they have to commute long distances on overcrowded public transport, many *muhagabat* know that their jobs represent neither career paths nor routes to a better life. Their work at best is merely paper-pushing, their offices are so overstaffed that on some days there is hardly an hour's worth even of paper-pushing to do, and they have little job satisfaction. They carry the double burden, moreover, of a job outside the home and another within. A recent study showed that in urban areas husbands and male children may help with shopping, but that all other household chores are performed by the households' women, whether they hold jobs or not. Men therefore have twice as much leisure time as women.

Because of high unemployment, appeals are frequently made in the press and in the National Assembly for women in the public sector to surrender their paid positions to men and stay at home, where they would receive subsidies from the government. The fact that these appeals are welcomed by many women working in the public sector reflects the steadily worsening conditions of state employment far more than it does any sense that they are neglecting their family needs at home.

The *higab*: The act of wearing the *higab* headcovering may make transitions easier for such women. It declares that in spite of changed conditions the cultural value implied by their lost seclusion – feminine modesty – is being reaffirmed. It also saves the expense of maintaining a stylish appearance; some women may wear the *higab* to veil a lack of means as much as anything else. Sociologists additionally cite the vagaries of fashion and peer-group pressure as reasons why women choose to don the *higab*.

It is probable that the majority of women in Cairo occasionally put on some sort of shawl, as most women in most of the countries around the Mediterranean have throughout most of civilised history. The constantly changing traditional styles evolved by both Muslim and Christian *banat al-balad* or village women – typically based upon *gallabiyyas* of various cuts, with coloured headscarves – are often worn under shawls or transparent black veils. The *higab*, however, has nothing whatever to do with such folk practice or tradition. It was deliberately begun among educated Muslim city women in a conscious effort to innovate, to create something quite different: a "truly Islamic" mode of dress. But even the most casual observer cannot fail to notice that there is no consensus as to what may properly constitute "truly Islamic" attire.

A head covering or *higab* of some sort and a long dress seem to be the minimum. Apart from this, however, minimum *muhagabat* garb varies, reflecting a range of attitudes. At one extreme, for example, are the *munaqabat*, who wear tent-like floor-length dresses in sombre colours and *higab* reaching below the waist that conceal not only the hair but the entire face, leaving only the eyes uncovered. The outfit is completed with gloves and often with dark glasses, so that even the eyes are hidden. Mostly university students or professional women in their twenties and thirties, *munaqabat* never use old-fashioned veils, which nowadays in Egypt are worn only by Bedouin women, heiresses of the urban fashions of a century ago.

Munaqabat are the subject of much controversy. Their way of dressing creates problems of identification for official purposes, such as university examinations, and is alleged to go far beyond what is required by Islam. Another group of women adheres to an interpretation of religious stricture that defines Islamic attire in a way that is similar to what *munaqabat* wear – their dresses are wide and shapeless, so as not to reveal the body's contours, and their *higab* are hip-length – but the face is left uncovered. These garments, they claim, represent the attire actually prescribed in Islam.

Most *muhagabat*, however, work out a compromise between Western fashion and Muslim modesty. They see no need to forego entirely the fetching styles they see in fashion magazines. To cater specifically to their wishes, shops specialising in *muhagabat* apparel have sprung up in Cairo and elsewhere. Though the clothes sold in these establishments have long sleeves and hems at ankle height, they are otherwise cut along the latest Parisian or Milanese lines. Eye-catching prints in bright colours, jackets with padded shoulders, and narrow skirts with saucy-looking flounces or pleats are very much in evidence. Headgear comes in a variety of shapes from the pill-box to the sugarloaf and in shades ranging from pastel pinks to electric purples. Surmounting the headgear and completing the outfit are the point of the whole thing: colour-coordinated *higab*, which are often embellished with beads, sequins, braid, embroidery, and tassels. The costume is sometimes so elaborate that it prompts an obvious question: "Don't these women realise that they are attracting more attention – not less – than they would by not wearing the *higab*?"

The meaning of the veil: The 1970s brought a new economic system. Anwar Sadat promulgated what was called an "Open Door Policy", loosened restrictions on both imports and emigration and invited foreign capital into Egypt, which suddenly discovered itself to be a consumer society. To earn the money to satisfy new tastes, hundreds of thousands of Egyptians were able to take advantage of a favourable labour market in the oil-rich Arab countries. Between 1974 and 1984, 16.5 percent of the Egyptian labour force migrated to work in neighbouring Arab countries, where they could earn in a year or two what it would take a lifetime to earn in Egypt.

For the vast majority who did not migrate, however, conditions failed to improve and by the late 1970s it had become clear that Sadat's Open Door policy could never bring economic salvation. Its benefits had gone to a handful, inflation was out of control, economic crimes – fraud, bribery, embezzle-

Communists – took on a Muslim religious colouration.

To what extent is wearing the *higab* a political act today? To interpret it as merely a declaration of the desire to live in a rigorously Muslim society is probably wrong. The government, however, which is fighting a battle against Muslim fundamentalism, may well believe it veils an adverse political message, as well as the facial features of the wearer, and so may be keeping *muhagabat* off television screens deliberately.

What should also be observed, however, is that so far there has not been the least whisper of a request from Egypt's TV-addicted

ment, extortion, and prostitution – had all increased, and the gap between poor and rich had widened alarmingly, creating much economic hardship. This hardship combined with social dislocation, it is claimed, to trigger a "reassertion of puritan values". And the spread of *higab*, sociologists say, was a symptom of this reassertion, which in some instances emerged as radical political sentiment. During the Sadat years, in any case, all effective political opposition – even from

Left, street market girl. **Above**, public-sector office staff take the Metro.

public for the authorities to put the *higab* on any actresses or female presenters, who continue to be elaborately coiffed and made-up. In television advertisements blonde girls recruited principally from the resident expatriate community in Cairo continue to dance to jazzy jingles extolling the virtues of locally-made import-substitutions, while in soap operas, which are enormously popular, actresses wearing dressing gowns and flashy evening wear play the roles of career girls and working mothers. Only villagers and grandmothers, it would seem, ever bother to cover their heads.

The month of Ramadan in Cairo, just before sunset. The street is hushed, deserted except for a single car that careers heedlessly past, engine roaring, carrying its famished driver homeward. Hot cooking-oil palls the air.

A cannon shot, no more than a pop in the distance, is heard from the Citadel; and suddenly a thousand loudspeakers crackle into action with the call to prayer. The clatter of spoons and cutlery hitting bowls and plates can be heard from every direction. Millions of believers, most of whom have not swallowed a bite of food or a drop of drink – not even their own saliva – since sunrise, pounce upon loaves of bread, heaps of vegetables, meat, fruit and holiday delicacies.

The fasting and feasting that take place during the Muslim holy month of Ramadan are a dramatic manifestation of religiosity. But neither fasting nor religiosity is confined to Islam. Many Coptic Christians, who make up 10 percent or so of Cairo's population, actually fast nearly half the year: they abstain from meat, eggs, and dairy products on Wednesdays and Fridays all year round, with the exception of the 12-day festival of Christmas and Epiphany and the 50 days between Easter and Pentecost. They also observe more rigorous additional fasts for the entire period between Pentecost and the Feast of the Apostles on 12 July, for two weeks before the Feast of the Assumption on 22 August, for 43 days before Christmas, and of course throughout Lent. For Copts, moreover, there is no feasting at night.

Universal piety: Among innumerable other indicators of piety, some are subtle and some – like the screech of a neighbourhood mosque's *mikrofun* (loudspeaker) – are definitely not. Television programming, for example, is routinely interrupted by each of the four daily prayers prescribed in Islam that take place during broadcast hours (there is a fifth at dawn). Soft zither music, a bass voice

with an echo chamber, and stock footage of the wonders of creation are followed by panning shots of an incalculable multitude at Mecca, all bowing inwards toward the Kaaba, as if to form a single huge satellite dish designed to receive an earthbound signal from the Almighty.

"I rely on God," say stickers plastered over taxis. On the upper floors of high-rise office-blocks cutthroat lawyers flipflop across their wall-to-wall carpet clutching limp towels,

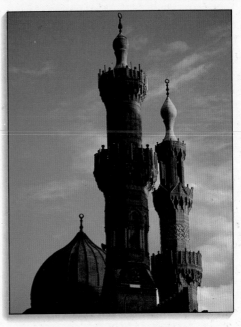

having just performed ritual ablutions in preparation for prayer between lucrative appointments. In the popular shrines of Muslim saints like Sayyidah Zaynab, whose mosque is near the city's centre, supplicants press little bits of paper into the wooden grilles surrounding draped cenotaphs. At any Cairo bookstall half the goods are sure to be works of popular Islam by famous *shaykhs*. On Arabic typewriters, the words "Allah" and "Muhammad" have single keys to themselves, so frequently are they used in writing.

Day-to-day language resounds with appeals to and praise for the Almighty: should

Preceding pages: praying in a shrine. Left, Bohra devotees debate in Al-Hakim Mosque. Right, minarets fill the city skyline.

anything go wrong it is because "God is all-knowing." Should anything go right it is "thanks to God." Religious rules – as well as many traditional misinterpretations of dogma – carry weight. Despite the all-too-evident need for birth control and the fact that it has the blessing of respected religious figures, millions of families reject it on vague grounds of piety: "God knows best." Alcohol and premarital sex are almost universally deplored as wicked and even inanimate things are touched by heavenly sanction: bread must never be thrown away, shoes must never be left with their soles upwards, a speech, an essay or a book must begin with

it is illegal, to the extent that even a marriage between a Muslim woman and a non-Muslim man contracted outside Egypt is not valid in Egyptian law. Proselytising by anyone other than Muslims is a criminal offence. Conversion from Islam to any other faith, though not absolutely forbidden under Egyptian law – as it is in Sharia, where the penalties are extremely severe – is officially and heavily discouraged. Small wonder that "What is your religion?" is one of the first questions a stranger is asked.

Islamic orthodoxy: For most of the past 1,000 years Cairo has been the largest city in Islam. The stamp of the Faith in medieval

the words, "In the name of God the Merciful, the Compassionate ."

For the Muslim majority marriage, divorce, and inheritance are all governed by the prescriptions of Sharia, Islamic law. Under the Egyptian constitution, Christians are likewise subject to religious rule, the canon law of their churches; and thus for Copts divorce is impossible, while for Muslims – for Muslim men, at least – it is very easy. Intermarriage between religions, though by no means infrequent among the pre-Revolutionary élite, is frowned upon by both Christians and Muslims; and in the case of Muslim women

times is still visible in the domes and minarets of hundreds of mosques and *madrasahs*, many of them magnificent, which make Cairo a veritable museum of Islamic architecture. Dozens of *sabil-kuttabs*, two-storeyed buildings that house a public fountain below and a Qur'anic school above, dot the core of the city and testify to the power of a saying of the Prophet Muhammad's: that the two greatest mercies are water for the thirsty and learning for the ignorant. One of the major surviving monuments is the Mosque of Al-Azhar.

Founded in the 10th century and sometimes described as the world's oldest university, Al-Azhar ("The Resplendent") has been the champion of Muslim orthodoxy and the great conservator of Islamic traditions for much of the past millennium. It has always attracted scholars from throughout the Muslim world and has therefore been continuously expanded and embellished by every Egyptian government up to the present day. Now subsumed into the larger university that bears its name, which offers scientific as well as religious training, Al-Azhar continues to wield power. Its graduates preach from pulpits not only in Egypt, but in every city in the world that has a Muslim population of any appreciable size, from Bradford

continues to be forbidden in his homeland, thanks to an Azhar-ordained ban imposed in 1960. Sale of a study of Muslim painting published abroad by a former Minister of Culture is prohibited because the book contains a reproduction of a well-known miniature – typical of many, all painted by Muslim artists – depicting the Prophet. The reprinting in Egypt of a well-known collection of major Muslim texts translated into English has been banned because the editor is foreign and a Catholic. Production of desk calendars printed with Qur'anic quotations was forbidden in 1990 for fear lest used leaves drop on to some unseemly surface and

to Brunei and from Timbuctoo to Toledo, Ohio. Azhari *shaykhs* pronounce irreversible judgements – which are often regarded with dismay by many of their compatriots, both Muslim and Christian – on all manner of issues.

Every book sold in Egypt, for example, is subject to Azhari censorship and may find itself placed on an index from which there is no appeal. A major work by Egypt's Nobel-prize winning novelist Naguib Mahfouz thus

thus profane the Word of God.

Mysticism and ultra-orthodoxy: Al-Azhar is the repository of Islamic conservatism. Outside its authority is the tradition of Muslim mysticism, known as Sufism, which was first introduced into Egypt by Salah ad-Din, who also built the first *khanqah* (Sufi hostel or convent), a building designed to house his imported mystics. By 1952, eight centuries later, Sufism had become the form of faith that was probably most typical of Cairo: more than half of all adult Muslim males belonged to one or more of the Sufi orders, called *turuq*. To the new Revolutionary gov-

Left, fine screen in the Maridani Mosque. **Above**, Al-Azhar, the centre of Muslim orthodoxy.

ernment, however, any organised group was suspect. It banned two of the most interesting Sufi orders, the Mevlevi and the Bektashi, because of their international connections and forced others to suspend traditional observances, which include periodic meetings, *dhikr* (rhythmic utterance of the name of God), contemplative retreat, and a great parade on the eve of the Prophet's Birthday. It was not until the 1970s that the *turuq* began to reappear in public and to reclaim something of their old popular position,

Even before the Revolution, however, both orthodoxy and the mystical tradition had been challenged by interpretations of reli-

gion that see it as a revolutionary force. Finding fertile ground among generations alienated by life in a society that is heedless of its future, greedily materialistic and yet poverty-stricken, ultra-orthodox movements, some of them violent, have gathered many adherents. They offer utopian programs for reform, based upon the creation of a theocratic state in which strict adherence to an austere version of Islam would be uniformly imposed by a central authority. Only change of this kind, they believe, can save Muslims from Western degeneracy, corruption, and self-doubt.

The most militant of these so-called fundamentalists have been responsible for much political violence, including the dramatic assassination of President Sadat in October 1981. Their condemnation of Egyptian society as "infidel" – which means that it is legitimately open to displacement by a "correct" government, to be installed by "true Muslims" using any methods available – is nothing less than a blatant call for revolution and has therefore brought them into open conflict not only with the current political regime, but also with the state-sponsored religious apparatus.

Revivalism: Most Egyptians dismiss the ultra-orthodox as misguided fanatics. The fact is, however, that they represent the headline-catching tip of a quiet and deeply rooted religious revival. Modern technology has enabled mass religion to increase its audience ten-thousandfold and hence to multiply its power, which depends upon being able to mobilise social attitudes and behaviour. Electric amplification and prime-time tele-*shaykhs* spread the heavenly message both locally and across what used to be prohibitive distances. The twin dislocations of rapid urbanisation and Western cultural penetration have meanwhile created confusions to which for many people the absolute certainties of religious faith are the only positive alternative.

Public displays of religious piety are most definitely on the increase. The number of middle-class women who have taken to wearing a wimple or head-veil (*higab*), either voluntarily or at the insistence of a male relative, has by all accounts risen dramatically since the early 1980s, even while the number of lower-class women wearing genuinely traditional clothing has declined. The contrast of such new fashions in attire with the Western-style feminine modes of, say, the 1950s or 1960s is certainly striking.

What was modish for women then is clearly visible in documentary footage of audiences at concert performances, which shows chic Cairo dames wearing deep décolletage, or in the imitation-Hollywood movies of the period, in which preposterously pneumatic starlets sewn into satin dresses alternatively wriggle their bits and simper for the leering lens. These norms have totally disappeared.

Men whose foreheads bear the dark bruise referred to as a "raisin", which is earned by many hours of enthusiastic prayer, are a common sight; and some high government officials are said to cultivate theirs in advance of public appearances. During the holy month of Ramadan, when the faithful are expected to fast by day, it is a badge of zeal to behave with particular – and uncharacteristic – ill-temper, especially toward those who are clearly not observing the strictures, despite the fact that actual anger would invalidate the entirety of one's fast. Even today it would be difficult to contest the observa-

United States, where it has become clear that some self-serving cynics are manipulating the credulous fanaticism of the masses. Its success may be based upon the same causes – ignorance, emotional deprivation, a longing for authority – and could conceivably produce the same effects.

Egyptians, however, have far more experience with the varieties of belief than Americans do. Genuine saintliness among the living, for example, is an everyday phenomenon; and even ordinary people enter regularly and as a matter of course into states of contemplative purity that have long been forgotten in the West. Nor does the current

tion of the early 19th-century Arabist and ethnographer E.W. Lane, who remarked: "It is considered the highest honour among the Muslims to be religious; but the desire to appear so leads many into hypocrisy and pharisaical ostentation."

The current religious revival is not so different from the waves of religiosity that periodically sweep the West. In its use of technology it is no different at all, in fact, from the televangelism prevalent in the

Left, theological discussions at Al-Azhar. **Above**, quiet contemplation at Ibn Tulun.

revival by any means represent the first time Egypt has gone through religious fires.

Tolerance: Before the Arab conquest the country was torn by disputes between pagans and Jews, between pagans and Christians, between Christians and Gnostics, and – finally and most bitterly – between various Christian factions. Under Islamic rule the Coptic Orthodox Church was made paramount and the inter-religious rumpus ended. During these early years, contrary to Western legend, conversion to Islam was not encouraged, since to be Muslim meant to be exempt from taxes; and there is good reason

SHAYKH CULTS

Shabaan, the eighth month in the lunar Muslim calendar, is *mawlid* season in Egypt. The night sky over the older quarters of Cairo glows with a green smoky luminescence: neon lights hang from dozens of minarets, each announcing the celebration of a *mawlid*, a religious festival that honours a *shaykh* or saint revered for his great wisdom or miraculous power. Hundreds of thousands of people will have come on pilgrimage from all over Egypt to participate in these festivals, camping out in every available space around each shrine.

Shaykh cults are a peculiarly Egyptian marriage of Islam and ancient beliefs and forms of worship. As recently as 1940 more than 100 *mawlids* were celebrated annually in and around Cairo, which has always been a Muslim city, but historically the preserver of much pre-Islamic tradition. Many traditional observances survive and are maintained – in somewhat muted form – to this day.

In Egyptian folklore, saints can contact the living by sending out *ishara* (signals), such as dreams or omens, to set the terms for a *nadr*, or bargain, by which the petitioner can see his wishes fulfilled. If the saint already has a shrine, he (or she) may require that a sacrifice

should be made near it. If he does not have a shrine, he (or she) may require that one be built or that another structure be adapted for use as a shrine. The shrine will invariably take the form of a mausoleum. According to Cairene tradition, it must therefore have a dome and will contain a *tabuut* or cenotaph, which will be covered with a cloth that is replaced annually. Many a Mamluk cutthroat has been elevated to sainthood simply because his last resting-place fulfilled all the requirements for a shrine.

Though some saints had historical existences and therefore have actual burial places, no grave is necessary either for sainthood or a shrine. How could one bury someone, after all, whom one has only seen in a dream? It is irrelevant and confusing, moreover, to ask whether or not the saint in question "really" lived. Reality is defined in this context not by its contrast with unreality, but by its contrast with appearance. What modern Westerners and educated Egyptians think of as the real world is regarded as merely appearances (phenomena), completely different from the "real" real world, the one to which the saint belongs, an esoteric realm where far more important business is carried on.

The most favoured way to honour a saint – and earn the benefit of his or her *baraka* (grace, ability to grant blessings) – is to hold a *mawlid*. *Mawlids* normally take place on the putative birthday of the *shaykh* and entail a visit by the faithful to his shrine, accompanied by performance of the *dhikr*, a devotional dance whose repetitive movements and chanting of the word *Allah* induce a trance that is thought to testify to direct communion with God. The ostensible purpose of *mawlids*, as an experienced participant puts it, is "to glorify God by venerating one of his favourites."

Saints inhabit a recognised hierarchy. The four great saints of Egypt are Sayyid Ahmad al-Badawi, Sayyid Abd al-Qadir al-Jilani, Sayyid Ahmad ar-Rifai al-Kabir and Sayyid Ibrahiim ad-Dasuuqi (Al-Metwalli), who are said to hold up the corners of the world.

Until the 1970s the *mawlid* of Sayyid al-Badawi is reported to have attracted more pilgrims annually to Tanta than the *Haj*, which is incumbent upon all Muslims to complete as part of their belief, brought to Mecca.

The great saints of Cairo include Sayyidna Husayn, Sayyidah Zaynab, Sayyidah Nafisa, Sayyidah Ruqayya, Sayyidah Sakkinah, and Imam ash-Shafii; they share their responsibilities with dozens of *shaykhs* that are local to particular quarters, such as Sidi al-Bayyumi in the Husayniyyah and Sidi Abu Suud, patron saint of lovers, whose shrine can be found on the edge of the site of Fustat.

Belief in the powers of saints and their ability to banish evil spirits, *afariit* or *jinn*, has persisted in Cairo despite the spread of secular and scientific thought. Far more fatal to such traditions are Islamic orthodoxy and Sunni fundamentalism, which have already succeeded in stamping out some of the more interesting features of several of the cults.

to suppose that the country as a whole remained more than half Christian for seven more centuries. Numerous Muslim rulers staffed their governments with non-Muslim functionaries, including even viziers.

The mad 11th-century caliph Al-Hakim, who persecuted everyone, tried to impose Muslim strictures and once banned the sale of women's shoes to prevent the fair sex from venturing outdoors. Travellers from the mid-14th century onward describe seeing Christians and Jews being obliged to wear distinguishing turbans and forbidden to ride horses. More often than not, however, relations between faiths have been charac-

northern extremity, while most of the major Christian monuments are concentrated at its southern edge – in Misr al-Qadimah ("Old Cairo") and especially around the Coptic Museum in the Mar Girgis (St George) quarter, which lies within the remains of the Roman fortress of Babylon (Qasr ash-Sham).

The current religious revival is by no means limited to Muslims. The Coptic Orthodox have likewise turned with renewed fervour to their church, which is one of the world's oldest. Miraculous visions of the Virgin Mary – first seen by two Muslim workmen – brought huge crowds to the Cairo districts of Hilmiyat az-Zaytun in the late 1960s and

terised by tolerance. In the countryside Muslim peasants have customarily celebrated local Christian and Jewish festivals as well as their own and they continue to do so today.

Cairo itself is dotted with churches of every denomination: contrary to what is sometimes naively claimed, there is no "Christian quarter". Districts with large Christian populations, for example, include Daher, Shubra and Heliopolis (Misr al-Gadidah, "New Cairo"), all of which are at the city's

Shubra in the mid-1980s. Some of the many sites in Upper Egypt where the Holy Family is said to have rested during its flight from Palestine count hundreds of thousands of pilgrims every season, as do many monasteries. In Wadi Natrun and the Eastern Desert, monastic foundations dating from as early as the 4th century – two 4th-century Egyptian Christians, St Paul the Theban and St Antony, are venerated as the actual founders of monasticism – have been revived, modernised, and expanded after years of decline.

Saints, voodoo and magic: Islam specifically condemns any kind of worship that

Left, horse-dancing in the *mawlid* season. **Above, Coptic Christians in Old Cairo.**

might deflect consciousness from the Oneness of God. Only God is worshipped and nothing else that lives is venerated. To the embarrassment of their stricter coreligionists, however, millions of Egyptians regularly appeal to the spirits of Muslim saints to intercede with the Creator on their behalf; and in Cairo alone dozens of neighbourhood festivals celebrate the presumptive "birthdays" of such saints.

Some of them are real historical figures, such as Sayyidna (Our Lord) Husayn, the martyred grandson of the Prophet, Sayyidah Sakkinah, his daughter, Sayyidah Nafisa, his great-grandaughter, Imam ash-Shafii, the 9th-

century founder of one of the four rites of Sunni Islam who accompanied Sayyidah Nafisa to Egypt, and Sayyidah Zaynab, who may have been either Sayyidna Husayn's sister or a companion of Sayyidah Nafisa.

The historical existence of other kinds of sanctity may be more problematical, either because the person now regarded as a saint is established from other records to have been far from saintly in his or her behaviour, or simply because he or she seems unlikely ever to have existed in reality at all. For the purpose of intercession, acknowledged sainthood is arrived at, by consensus among believers, regardless of other considerations.

The "birthday" or *mawlid* of each saint is celebrated annually on a specific date. The biggest of these *mawalid* is that of Sayyidna (Our Lord) Husayn, the martyred nephew of the Prophet whose severed head is said to be buried at his mosque in the heart of the city. Whole families of country folk, as many as 2 million of them, flock to the city annually for the occasion, pitching tents in back alleys or on plots of wasteland set aside by the governorate, camping out on rooftops, or dossing down inside many of the larger mosques. The sophisticates of Cairo may frown on such doings, but the hypnotising energy of the *dhikr*, in which entranced devotees sway to the beat of drums with increasing rapture until all hours, testifies not only to the power of God, but also to some of the innocent joys of living.

Even more unorthodox and quite unrelated to the cults of saints is the voodooistic or *macumba*-like ceremony of exorcism called the *zar*, which is supposed to have been imported into Egypt from sub-Saharan Africa through the Sudan. Popular among working-class women, the *zar* is based upon the idea of possession by mischievous (but not evil) spirits and is widely regarded as a form of folk psychotherapy.

On the far periphery of religion is magic. Belief in other supernatural agencies than God or His angels has survived repeated orthodox purges and infuses much Egyptian religiosity. So closely has Egypt been associated with the practice of magic since ancient times that the Talmudic expression for a futile act, approximating "Bringing coals to Newcastle," is "Bringing magic into Egypt." Rites to induce fertility are still conducted by peasant women in the ruins of pharaonic temples; and in the heart of the city, as not a few charlatans have discovered, both black and white magic, with their stock of spells, rites, charms, amulets, and prescriptions for the future, can still provide a lucrative, ego-aggrandising, and even sexually satisfying trade.

Left, Greek Orthodox pilgrims at St George's Church in Old Cairo. **Right**, the Church of St Sergius, Old Cairo.

Cairo

800 m / 0.5 miles

PLACES

When London and Paris were hardly more than towns and when Rome had declined to the status of a ruined provincial capital, Cairo was a great city several times the size of all three combined.

The historic zone created during that period of expanding Arab power occupies approximately the area running eastward from Shari Port Said to the Muqattam and southward from Bab al-Futuh and Bab an-Nasr to Fustat and Old Cairo. Though it is larger by 50 percent than the historic zone of Venice, street patterns and the scattering of monuments to the north and west show that this represents only a fraction of the city as it was at, say, the end of the 15th century. The zone includes the great cemeteries, the cities of the dead, where people have always lived. The historic zone's most impressive buildings are those medieval Muslim religious structures which date from the 7th to the 16th centuries.

The present-day city's Nileside glamour and glitz are deeply rooted in these same narrow, winding, crowded, dirty, noisy and wonderful streets, where the smells of incense and attar of roses remind the senses of still another world beyond this one, outside either Christendom or Islam.

Preceding pages: ceremonial funeral tent in construction; camel caravan; morning calm at the Mena House Hotel; the mosque of Sultan Hasan.

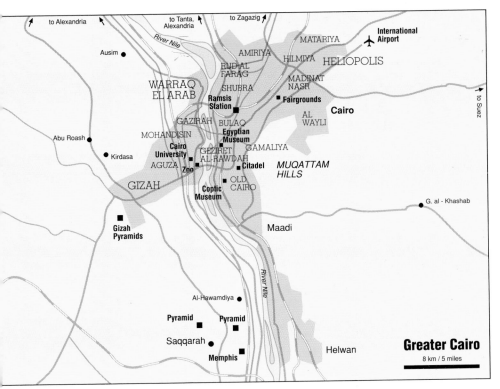

DOWNTOWN AND GARDEN CITY

In 1865, when the Khedive Ismail ordered the region stretching west from Azbakiyyah to the Nile to be drained and demarcated for development, it was on the western periphery of the city. Named "Ismailiyyah" after its founder, it became a luxurious residential neighbourhood, with tree-lined streets, large villas and and a few grand houses or palaces. Now far more commercial than residential – the change was taking place even before World War I, as the villas began to make way for hotels, apartment blocks, shops, banks, and diplomatic missions – it is generally referred to as the centre of town. Distances throughout Egypt are measured from **Maydan at-Tahrir**, formerly Maydan Ismailiyyah, which marks the southern boundary of the district.

Just like Paris: A visitor standing in the middle of Ismailiyyah – outside **Groppi's Corner House** in Maydan Sulayman Pasha (Talat Harb), for example – might almost believe he was in Paris. Three wide straight streets pass into and through the *maydan* to make a six-pointed *étoile*, which is flanked by six-storey apartment buildings with shops on the ground floors, balconies above and French windows. Some of them even have mansard roofs, like the one on the opposite corner, formerly the Savoy Hotel. A glance into their entrance halls would reveal rows of enamelled plaques advertising *médecins* and *avocats* and antique lifts that would not be out of place in the inner *faubourgs*. To give more substance to the delusion, newspaper stalls display *Le Monde*, *Libération*, *Point de Vue/Images du Monde*, *L'Equipe*, *Paris Match*, *Le Figaro,* the Café Riche is down a street to the right, the Rue de la Bourse Khédiviale is down a street to the left (within a stone's throw of the French Consulate), and almost facing are the offices of Air France.

Both **Maydan Sulayman Pasha** and **Shari Sulayman Pasha**, the street running north-south through it, were named after Colonel Anthelme Sève, the French-born veteran of the Napoleonic wars who trained Muhammad Ali's armies and accompanied Ibrahim Pasha as an adviser on every campaign. His statue remained in the square until 1963, when it was carted off to adorn the garden of the Military Museum in the Citadel. But taxi drivers are still as likely to respond to a call of "Sulayman Pasha!" as they are to shouts of the name of Talat Harb, the nationalist banker whose statue was brought out of storage to displace Sulayman Pasha's. In his business suit, Talat Harb actually looks more European than the Frenchman.

A tour of the district's commercial life, however, shows its essentially non-European character. Portions of each street are specialised, bazaar-fashion, in a single kind of merchandise. On Shari Sulayman Pasha (Talat Harb), miscellaneous cheap imported goods – pocket

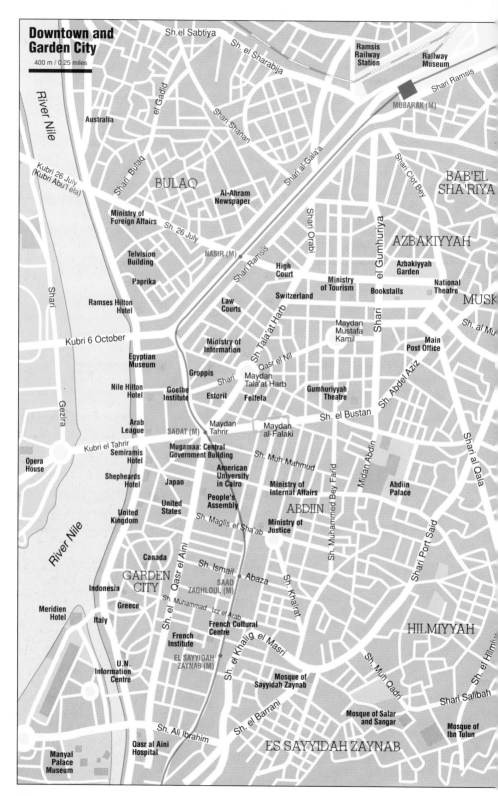

Downtown and Garden City

400 m / 0.25 miles

River Nile

Sh.el Sabtiya

Sh. el Sharabja

Ramsis Railway Station

Railway Museum

Shari Ramsis

MUBARAK (M)

el Gadid

Shari Shanan

Shari al-Gala'a

Shari Clot Bey

BAB'EL SHA'RIYA

Australia

Kubri 26 July (Kubri Abu'l ela)

Shari Bulaq

BULAQ

Al-Ahram Newspaper

Ministry of Foreign Affairs

Sh. 26 July

AZBAKIYYAH

Shari Orabi

el Gumhuriya

Azbakiyyah Garden

Television Building

NASIR (M)

Shari Ramsis

High Court

Ministry of Tourism

Bookstalls

National Theatre

MUSK

Paprika

Ramses Hilton Hotel

Law Courts

Switzerland

Maydan Mustafa Kamil

Sh. al Mu

Shari

Kubri 6 October

Ministry of Information

Sh. Tala'at Harb

Qasr el Nil

Main Post Office

Sh. Abdel Aziz

Egyptian Museum

Groppis

Shari

Maydan Tala'at Harb

Gumhuriyyah Theatre

Nile Hilton Hotel

Goethe Institute

Estoril

Felfela

Sh. el Bustan

Arab League

Maydan Tahrir

Maydan al-Falaki

Gezira

SADAT (M)

Kubri el Tahrir

Semiramis Hotel

Mugamaa: Central Government Building

Sh. Muh Mahmud

Shari al Qala

Opera House

Shepheards Hotel

American University in Cairo

Ministry of Internal Affairs

Abdiin Palace

Japan

People's Assembly

ABDIIN

Midan Abdin

United Kingdom

United States

Sh. Maglis el Sha'ab

Ministry of Justice

Shari Port Said

River Nile

Canada

Qasr el Aini

Sh. Ismail

Abaza

Sh. Muhammed Bey Farid

Sh. Khairat

GARDEN CITY

SAAD ZAGHLOUL (M)

HILMIYYAH

Indonesia

Greece

Sh. Muhammad

Izz el Arab

Sh. el Hilmi

Meridien Hotel

Italy

Sh. el Khalig

Sh. el Aini

French Cultural Centre

el Masri

Sh. Muh Qadri

French Institute

EL SAYYIDAH ZAYNAB (M)

Mosque of Sayyidah Zaynab

Shari Safibah

U.N. Information Centre

Qasr al Aini Hospital

Sh. Ali Ibrahim

Sh. el Khalig el Masri

Sh. el Barrani

Mosque of Salar and Sangar

Mosque of Ibn Tulun

Manyal Palace Museum

ES SAYYIDAH ZAYNAB

128

radios and cassette players, trinkets, aftershave lotion and sometimes clothes – are displayed together in crowded windows. Cutting through the *maydan* from southwest to northeast, **Shari Qasr an-Nil** offers high-quality fabrics and shoes, while **Shari Sherif**, which crosses Qasr an-Nil, specialises in foreign-language bookshops, office supplies, artists' and draughtsmen's equipment, and stationers' goods. **Shari Tahrir,** which runs through Shari Sulayman Pasha, sells electrical appliances and **Shari Hoda Shaarawi,** parallel to it, has up-market fast food and antiques. Scattered Western-style among all these enterprises are smart new clothes shops, airline offices, travel agents, and many banks.

Social centre: Established by an Alexandrian Swiss family in 1924 and designed to cater for the city's Egyptian and foreign rich, Groppi's was one of the foci of the pre-1952 social world. It sold silver, porcelain and crystal as well as afternoon teas, apéritifs, confectionery, pâtisseries, and delicatessen. In the rear were a garden and a rotunda with a stained-glass ceiling where concerts and dinner-dances or supper-dances took place on alternative nights during the winter. Though the fires of Black Saturday destroyed the rotunda, Groppi's survived later political changes. As the Revolution veered further left, however, it became less glamorous, and old Turkish ladies in fur coats were increasingly replaced by students, whores, and racketeers. Purchased in 1983 by a teetotal Arab who immediately closed the restaurant and bar, its style is now typified by black plastic chairs and waxy croissants. Upstairs in the same building is the **Greek Club**, whose gilt-framed pier-glasses, oil paintings, card tables, dance floor and predominantly octogenarian membership are far more faithful to the way things used to be.

Founded the same year Groppi's Corner House was built – and still occupying its original premises just around the corner at number 10 Shari Qasr an-Nil – is the *siège social* of the **Automobile**

Club, formerly the Royal Automobile Club. It became one of the favourite haunts of King Faruq, who liked playing poker for high stakes. The elegant building of the **Muhammad Ali Club** in Shari Bustan, erected in 1907, likewise still stands, thanks to intervention by the Foreign Ministry, which operates a **Diplomats' Club** in the premises. Designed in the Beaux-Arts style by Alexandre Marcel – he had worked on the Petit Palais in Paris seven years earlier and was executing major work for the new suburb of Heliopolis at the time – it has provided a temporary home for 16 Orientalist paintings from the Khalil Collection, which could not be hung with the rest of the collection in the Amr Ibrahim house in Zamalek.

Other pre-revolutionary institutions survive in Ismailiyyah. **Shari Muhammad Farid**, for example, could well be described as the city's City, its Wall Street, or perhaps simply as the **Bank Misr** quarter. The earliest of the three Bank Misr buildings in this street – all worth looking into – is a masterpiece of neo-Islamic design by Antoine Lasciac Bey, who had previously been Court Architect to Abbas II Hilmi. It was built in 1922. The **Stock Exchange** inhabits premises in Shari Sherifayn built 10 years earlier. Elevated by the circumstances of World War II into the third largest in the world, it was destroyed by the Revolution, but now shows signs of revival: 1980 saw a turnover of only LE 9 million, but in 1990 the Exchange did about LE 500 million worth of business. Across the street from Bank Misr, **St Joseph's Catholic Church**, the city's largest Catholic church, dates from 1904. On Shari Adli (Maghrabi) is the **Shaar Hashamaim Temple**, built in 1905, one of the 29 synagogues that existed in pre-1956 Cairo.

The character of Ismailiyyah began changing rapidly after 1956, when all resident Britons and Frenchmen and many Jews suffered the consequences of the Tripartite Aggression. It changed again after 1961, when large-scale

Stylish downtown wedding.

sequestrations began: most of the remaining foreign communities either left while the going was good or were effectually expelled, stripped of all their Egyptian assets. The names of members of the Muhammad Ali family were expunged from every street, square, or monument that had been named after them, even those they had built; and historical figures associated with them were consigned to oblivion, no matter how noble their services to the nation. It was then that **Shari Fu'ad** became **Shari 26 July** and **Maydan Ismailiyyah** became **Maydan at-Tahrir**.

New life: The name Maydan at-Tahrir has stuck, possibly because the *maydan* is far larger and more important now than it was before the Revolution. The statue of Ismail in the southeast corner was removed and hidden, though it was not until 1988 that its massive pedestal was finally taken away. On the western edge of the *maydan* had stood the Qasr an-Nil barracks, built under Viceroy Said and occupied by British troops from 1882 to 1954. Torn down after the Revolution, they were replaced by the present vast open space, edged at one side by the **Arab League Building** and the **Nile Hilton**, the first luxury hotel built in Egypt since 1910, which opened in 1959. Among older buildings only two palaces remain: the palace of Khairy Pasha, built in the 1870s, is occupied at present by the **American University in Cairo**; the other is owned by the Foreign Ministry. Everything in the square is dwarfed by the monstrous **Mugamaa**, one of the world's most depressingly ugly buildings, run up in the 1950s to house those portions of the Egyptian bureaucracy that deal with the public. Its huge stairwell echoes to the sound of shuffling feet as the country's innocents are mercilessly sent from one office to another, day after day, in pursuit of more pieces of paper. At the northern end, opposite and in complete contrast with the Mugamaa, is the **Egyptian Museum**.

Treasure-house: Before 1858, when

Auguste Mariette became the first director of the Egyptian Service des Antiquités, most important Pharaonic antiquities went abroad: in 1855, for example, with typical expansiveness, Said Pasha had simply given the entire national collection to Archduke Maximilian of Austria, brother of the Emperor. Mariette had all new finds stored in a warehouse in Bulaq; and in 1863 Khedive Ismail built the first museum for them. The four decades that followed were the heroic period when most of our present-day picture of ancient Egypt was put together. The collection rapidly outgrew its quarters in Bulaq and was moved to the Gizah Palace, the grounds of which later provided the site for the Cairo Zoo, but by 1895 it was clear that a large purpose-built structure would be required and accordingly an international competition was held for the best design.

Completed in 1902, the Egyptian Museum is an elegant structure worthy of the riches it contains. In normal seasons, however, it is filled all day every day by hordes of tourists, on whose list it has been put second only to the Pyramids. Displays on the ground floor are arranged clockwise more or less chronologically. Thus Pre-Dynastic and Old Kingdom objects, such as the famous greywacke triads of Menkaura, are left of the entrance; and beginning from there the conscientious visitor can work his way round to the statue of Alexander the Great in Room 49, past Ptolemaic and Roman period objects, and finally to a replica of the Rosetta Stone (the real one is in the British Museum) next to the entrance on the right.

The **treasures of Tutankhamun**, found in 1922, occupy two large galleries on the floor above, but the queue to see them often extends down the stairs to the ground floor. Among cabinets packed with gold are cases containing the young king's bows and arrows and boomerangs, his chariots and the wilting bouquets of flowers that were put in his tomb. Other galleries on the first

Maydan Sulayman Pasha show distinct French influence.

floor are worth seeing. In Room 27 are models found in an 11th-dynasty tomb showing life as it was in 2000 BC. In Room 53 are mummified baboons and cats. In the foyer at the head of the stairs is Case H, containing delicately-crafted statuettes, most of them made famous from postcards and photographs in books that give no idea of their diminutive size: the ivory statuette of Khufu from Abydos; the black steatite bust of Queen Tiyi; the statuette of a Nubian girl with a single earring; the gilded statuette of Ptah; dancing pygmies carved from ivory; and blue faience hippopotami.

Urban garden: South of the Ismailiyyah district beyond the Mugamaa is **Garden City**, which was laid out in 1904 on the sites of two palaces: Qasr ad-Dubarah, which had belonged to Ibrahim Pasha and the enormous Qasr al-Aliy, the property of Hoshyar Kadineffendi (the Princess Dowager Khushyar), the mother of the Khedive Ismail. It was conceived as a "garden city", along the lines of Bournville,

Letchworth and similar experimental towns in England, and was designed on principles derived from Ebenezer Howard's classic *Tomorrow: A Peaceful Path to Social Reform* (1898). Howard's special concern was the use of design to counteract the effects of industrialisation and overcrowding upon the working classes. Though the Cairene version is meaner in its use of space than European "garden cities", it has the same greenery and the same arcing, interlacing, thoroughfares, which provide vistas, inhibit heavy traffic, and discourage crowding. But Cairo's Garden City was never intended to house "workers".

Its earliest inhabitants were quiet and rich; and Garden City remained quiet and rich for decades. Then in the 1970s it was rediscovered – by international banks in search of exactly such dignified premises. The result has been disastrous. Never designed to absorb the high densities of building, population, and traffic that accompany commercialisation, Garden City in the daytime is

The Egyptian Museum.

stuffed far beyond capacity. Cursing drivers at the intersections of its narrow, curving streets may find themselves sitting in exhaust fumes for hours, as one-way and no-entry signs, arbitrarily placed, are ignored or not, depending on what seems possible. Garden City's design has kept it one of the few places in Cairo where walking can be fun, especially when one has no expectations of getting anywhere. The challenge is merely to try not to get lost.

Like other expensive districts, Garden City has long provided sanctuary for diplomatic delegations. Between Shari Qasr al-Aini and Shari Amrika al-Latiniyya, for example, stands the **American Embassy** compound. Dubbed "Festung Amerika" because of its elaborate defences against terrorism, it is not easy even for US Marines to enter these hallowed premises.

On the opposite side of the same street is the British Embassy compound, dominated by the **British Residency**, built in 1893. Before the new Revolutionary government constructed the Corniche, the Residency's gardens ran right down to the Nile – as described in *Mountolive*, the third novel in Lawrence Durrell's *Alexandria Quartet* – presenting a barrier of diplomatic privilege between the ends of two Nile-side streets.

South of Garden City, occupying land between the Corniche and Shari Qasr al-Aini, is **Qasr al-Aini Hospital**, now the teaching hospital attached to the Faculty of Medicine at Cairo University. It was originally established in 1837 on this site in the palace of a 15th-century amir by Antoine Clot Bey, Muhammad Ali's chief medical adviser, as an adjunct to his 10-year-old School of Medicine and Pharmacy. The palace, which gave its name not only to the hospital but to the entire Nile-side district that surrounds it, as well as to the major road passing through the district, survived in part until the 1980s, when final demolitions were carried out to prepare for the present French-built structures.

Sarcophagi the Egyptia Museum.

134

BARS AND NIGHTLIFE

To some visitors the City of 1001 Nights beckons with glamorous images of decadence. In the heyday of smart Euro-American tourism – from 1896 until 1914 and again perhaps from 1922 to 1939 – Egypt tried hard and with some success to live up to the fame it had somehow acquired as a fleshpot. Thousands of Tommies and Anzacs (British, Australian and New Zealand troops) enthusiastically embroidered the reputation during two world wars and popular Western legend still peoples the city with non-existant hawkers of smutty postcards and virgin sisters.

The fact is, however, that the overwhelming majority of Cairenes lead modest, even humdrum existences, sparing no thought at all for the city's tiny demimonde, with whose hedonistic ways of living their own have nothing whatever in common. The clientèle in any typical Cairo nightclub is therefore almost certain to be largely foreign – Gulf Arabs, for the most part, who have the time, money and lack of imagination to spend lugubrious evenings being rooked by old-fashioned pros.

Once in a while it may be fun, though, to take a table in a nightclub along the fabled Shari al-Haram (Pyramids Road). Apart from paying an entry fee, the customer will be expected to order an extremely expensive bottle of whisky for his table and to tip the hostess who pours it generously. The cabaret at the venerable Auberge des Pyramides normally features leggy European dancers and has an "international" flavour. More "Oriental" fare, with *takht* band and moodier belly-dancing, can be sampled down the road at the Arizona. The Sahara City club, sited in a tent, offers family-style entertainment, with juggling, "dancing" horses (dressage), and legerdemain.

The Salt and Pepper and the Cave du Roi, both in Zamalek, cater for a more Egyptian crowd and connoisseurs prefer them. Grander entertainment is offered in the city's four- and five-star hotels. All clubs offer food, often without prices on the menus. Most nightclubs begin serving food at 9 p.m.; cabarets or shows begin after 11 p.m. and all

clubs stay open until the morning. Expect to spend about LE 150 a head. Other establishments, more raucous and much less stylish, may be found in the area of Shari Alfi Bey, downtown. Here one usually pays a small entrance fee. The service is cheaper, the tips smaller, and the entertainment, featuring superannuated belly-dancers, is dull.

Young Cairenes much prefer discotheques, which have been a distinctive feature of the city's night life since the late 1950s. The most popular are probably Régine's in the Gazirah Sheraton, Jackie's at the Nile Hilton, and The Saddle at the Mena House Oberoi, near the Pyramids. More down-market, but with an occasional live band, is the Longchamps Hotel in Zamalek.

Old Cairo hands wax wistful over memories of the vanished Cecil Bar, the Aladin, the Strand, the Turf Club, and the bars at the National Hotel and Groppi's Corner House. Most surviving bars are in the larger hotels. It is possible for a single woman to visit Cairo bars other than the ones in five-star hotels, but not advisable; and even in hotel bars a male sidekick can be helpful.

For tête-à-têtes, the Safari Bar on the first floor at the Nile Hilton or the Library in the Marriott are good. A splendid night-view of Cairo may be had from the Club 36 at the top of the Ramses Hilton. The new bar in the mezzanine of Shepheard's Hotel has been given lots of brown leather and exactly the right meditative atmosphere for a spot of serious imbibing.

Other respectable watering holes, all in Zamalek, are Pub 28 in Shari Sheger ad-Durr, the noisy and yuppie-smart Cellar Bar at the President Hotel in Shari Taha Husayn, or Bee's Corner, with a younger crowd, practically next door. Down-town and further down-market is the bar upstairs at the Windsor Hotel, off Shari Alfi Bey, which still has hints of former cachet as a British officers' club.

For those determined to pub-crawl, small and insalubrious establishments cower in the alleyways off Maydan Atabah. You could do worse, however, than the Tout Va Bien. And just off Maydan Ahmad Urabi, the Ana W'inta Wa Cairo (You, Me and Cairo) bar upstairs is open 24 hours a day, while the diner downstairs offers nice hot snacks all night long.

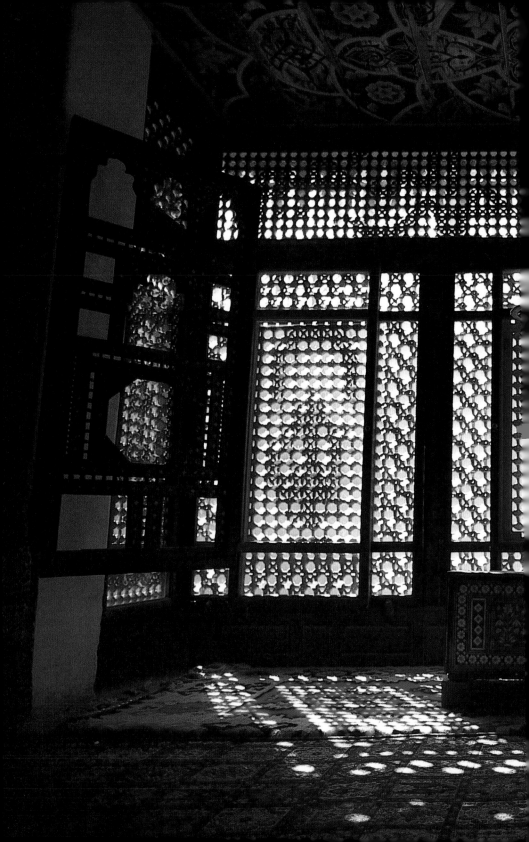

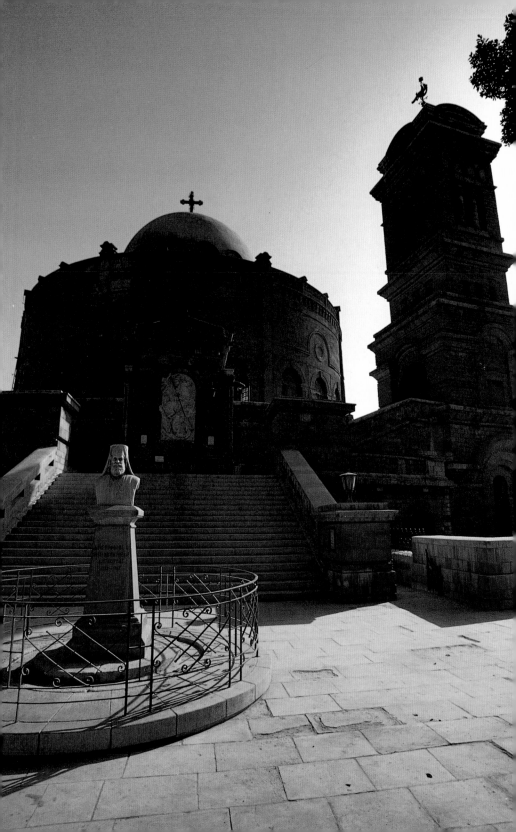

OLD CAIRO

Misr al-Qadimah, or "**Old Cairo**," as it is confusingly called in English today (it existed long before Al-Qahirah, of which "Cairo" is a European corruption, had ever been thought of), was originally a settlement on the east bank halfway between Memphis and Heliopolis where a branch of the Nile went off to the north-east towards Heliopolis.

The easiest way to reach Misr al-Qadimah is by the Metro: the station called **Mar Girgis** (Saint George) stands opposite the Greek Orthodox church of that name, which is built on one of the great circular towers of **Trajan's Fortress**, called **Qasr ash-Shamah.** The alternating layers of brick and rubble masonry typical of Roman architecture have been imitated in the church, which dates from 1909, an older structure on the site having been destroyed by fire in 1904, when only the icon of St George and the relics survived.

When Trajan (AD 98–117) cleared the canal that linked the Nile with the Red Sea, he refortified its entrance on the Nile by building the present fortress around it. The Nile ran just under its walls, approximately where the Metro line is now, and the two enormous circular towers on the western side between which one presently enters the fortress may well have flanked the canal, which flowed through the fort. By the time of the Arab invasion, the new Babylon had already eclipsed Memphis in practical importance and the Arab settlement of Fustat established next to it rapidly became the capital city of Egypt, referred to as Misr.

As it was no longer viable for military purposes, Trajan's fortress evolved into a Christian and Jewish enclave. Many churches were built inside the walls, several of which are still in use. All have been rebuilt several times, however, preserving little of their original architecture or decoration; and most important items have been removed to the Coptic Museum, leaving only a few medieval icons still in place, next to modern ones that often show strong Western influence. The use of pews and vestments is also the result of recent foreign influence.

Icons and writings: The entrance to **The Coptic Museum** lies between St George's church tower and the ruined south tower. Founded by private benefactors in 1908, the Museum became part of the national heritage by royal decree in 1931. Its purpose was to salvage objects of early Christian art, which were being destroyed or leaving the country. Objects from Saqqarah (Apa Jeremias) and Bawit show pervasive Hellenistic inspiration: ancient Egyptian influence is minimal. Occasional early stelae contain both Christian and pagan deities, but only one or two uniquely Egyptian symbols – the *ankh* sign, used as a cross, for example, and the motif of Isis suckling Horus, which

becomes the Virgin nursing the Baby Jesus – were incorporated into Coptic iconography. The icons collected in the north wing are mostly of late date and show strong Byzantine influence, but in the south wing 4th-century painted panels are close to the famous Roman-period mummy portraits from the Fayyum in technique and style.

Also in the museum is a fine collection of manuscripts, including the earliest known copy of the Book of Psalms, found in a Coptic grave, and nearly 1,200 papyrus pages of Gnostic writings in Coptic, bound into books called *codices*, the earliest leather-covered ones known. The Gnostics were considered heretical by the Church, which succeeded in suppressing them and their writings. Hidden in a cave at Nag Hammadi in Upper Egypt in the 4th century, the Nag Hammadi Codices have shed much new light on Gnostic doctrine and its sources – a mixture of Jewish, Christian, Zoroastrian, Hermetic and Platonic teachings – and have re-opened the question of how the authenticity of biblical texts was decided.

Pious places: On the south side of the Museum garden is the main southern gate of the fortress, a magnificent piece of Roman architecture. A portal in the south wall of the Museum garden leads up to the **Church of the Blessed Virgin Mary, Al-Muallaqa,** ("The Suspended"), built atop the bastions of this gate. Tradition gives this church a 7th-century foundation but, like all the churches in Old Cairo, it has been repeatedly rebuilt up to modern times. Much old furniture has been preserved, however, including a particularly fine marble ambon or pulpit (11th century) and a screen of ebony inlaid with ivory (12th/13th-century).

Like all other Orthodox churches, the Coptic church screens off altars with an iconostasis, the main door of which is open only during services. To the right of the iconostasis, behind another very fine screen, are a small chapel of St Tekla and a baptistry, built over the

Left, the B
Ezra
Synagogue
Right, the
Coptic
Museum.

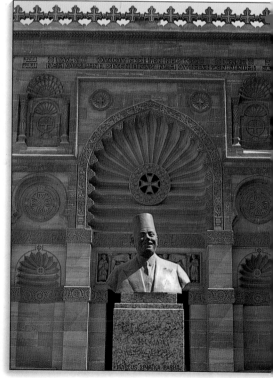

eastern bastion of the gate. From the small window of the chapel there is a good view of the western bastion.

A stairway near the ticket office leads from the Museum gardens down to the narrow stone-paved alleys of the settlement within the fortress. To the right is the **Church of St Sergius**, traditionally regarded as the oldest in Misr al-Qadimah, said to have been built in the 5th or 6th century over a cave where the Holy Family stayed during their sojourn in Egypt. It has a basilica plan, with aisles divided by marble columns reused from older sites, which support an upper gallery. Rebuilding of the church has continued to the present day and the oldest portable fittings are presently in the Coptic Museum.

The **Church of St Barbara** is further down the main alleyway, then left. Like St Sergius' church, it is entered by a flight of stairs descending below street level. Continuously rebuilt, it has a fine inlaid medieval iconostasis. On the left is one of the few surviving medieval icons of St Barbara. On the right is a beautiful 13th-century icon of the Virgin with Child Enthroned, set within a 14th-century frame, which was restored in 1990 by Zuzana Skálová, the leading expert in the field. A door on the left leads to the tiny **Church of SS Cyrus and John**, whose relics are contained within a case on the south wall below a triptych so covered with the smoke of incense and candles that the images are scarcely visible. The bare concrete walls here are covered with pious graffiti – "Remember me, O Lord."

A few steps from St Barbara is the **Ben Ezra Synagogue**, in use as a church of St Michael from the 8th century onward, closed under the fanatic Caliph Al-Hakim (996–1021), then sold to the Sephardic community. For centuries it served as a *geniza*, a repository for documents made sacrosanct by being sworn under oath, which could not be casually discarded without sacrilege. Since these documents include such mundane items as contracts, bills of sale, and letters of

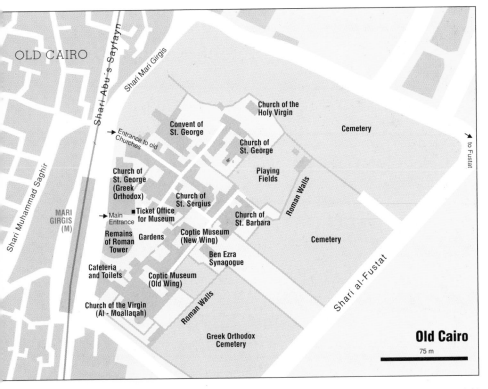

OLD CAIRO

Shari Abu's-Sayfayn

Shari Mari Girgis

Shari Muhammad Saghir

Church of the Holy Virgin

Convent of St. George

Cemetery

Entrance to old Churches

Church of St. George

Church of St. George (Greek Orthodox)

Playing Fields

Church of St. Sergius

MARI GIRGIS (M)

Main Entrance

Ticket Office for Museum

Church of St. Barbara

Roman Walls

Remains of Roman Tower

Gardens

Coptic Museum (New Wing)

Cemetery

Cafeteria and Toilets

Ben Ezra Synagogue

Coptic Museum (Old Wing)

Shari al-Fustat

Church of the Virgin (Al - Moallaqah)

Roman Walls

to Fustat

Greek Orthodox Cemetery

Old Cairo

75 m

credit, they constitute an extensive record of medieval Mediterranean life. The present structure is the result of heavy rebuilding, expecially in the 19th century. Behind it the ruined walls of the eastern gateway of the fortress are visible.

The shortest route back to the main road outside the fortress returns past the Church of St Sergius, then goes around a corner to the **Convent of St George**, which contains a remarkable Fatimid or Ayyubid reception room with wooden doors 23 ft (7 metres) high, the remains of a house, though both its use and origin are now shrouded in legend. The exit from the fortress is just beyond the convent.

Among the seven other early churches outside the fortress in Misr al-Qadimah, the most interesting is the **Church of Abu's-Sayfayn** (**St Mercurius**) in Shari Ali Saalem, which was the cathedral church of Misr and became the seat of the Coptic Patriarchate when it was moved to Fustat from Alexandria in the

11th century. It contains several 18th-century icons.

Ruins and reconstruction: North of the fortress is a famous Muslim site, the **Mosque of Amr ibn al-As,** built in 641 or 642, rebuilt in 688, 710, 750, and 781, doubled to approximately its present size in 827, restored in the 13th century, rebuilt again after the great earthquake of 1303, partially rebuilt again near the end of the following century, then massively rebuilt just before the French invasion. The latest renovation work, carried out between 1980 and 1983, has sought to recreate its appearance as it might conceivably have been in 827, though the style employed is neo-Fatimid, belonging to a period 150 years later. Only an expert could now pinpoint original construction, but the site is important as marking that of the first mosque in Africa.

Directly east are the **ruins of the city of Fustat**, which became modern Cairo. Among thousands of important archaeological finds made on the site the most

A funeral at Amr Ibn al-As, the first mosque buil in Africa.

beautiful, mainly ceramics, may be seen in the Museum of Islamic Art.

In the alluvial area between the Metro line and the Nile opposite the southern end of the island of Rawdah are a half dozen other Muslim monuments dating from the 14th century to the 18th. A significant later monument is the **Tomb of Sulayman Pasha**, which stands in the centre of a small square and is visible from the Corniche, looking rather like a creation of mid-19th-century Orientalist fantasy.

Born in Lyon in 1788 and originally known in France as Anthelme Sève, Sulayman Pasha had an extraordinarily colourful career. A veteran of both Bonaparte's navy and his army, he had been present – by some savage quirk of fate – at every great Napoleonic defeat, not only the Russian débâcle and Waterloo, but also the disastrous battle of Trafalgar.

Hired at the rank of colonel by Muhammad Ali's agents, he served as the architect of the new Egyptian army, converted to Islam, and took the name Sulayman al-Faransawi ("The Frenchman"). Ibrahim Pasha's great victories in Arabia, Morea, Crete, Syria, and Anatolia made Sulayman's fortune. When he died in 1860 he was a very rich man and a pasha, whose blue-eyed descendants would eventually be allied to the royal family.

The architect of the tomb was Karl von Diebitsch, who also designed an enormous palace for Sherif Pasha, Sulayman Pasha's son-in-law, a Turco-Circassian grandee. It was Sherif Pasha who paid for the tomb, a pavilion constructed of cast-iron modules, like the arcades of Ismail's Gazirah Palace, which von Diebitsch also designed.

In the building nearby is interred the body of Lady Maryam, Sulayman Pasha's wife, a beautiful Greek whom the young and dashing colonel had rescued from among a boatload of captives being borne off as booty by the victorious Egyptians during the Morea campaign in 1824.

quiet corner
Old Cairo.

RAWDAH

The island of **Rawdah** – the name means "garden" – is separated from the rest of Cairo by an arm of the Nile no wider than a canal and from Gizah by the river's main channel. Its northern end is dominated by the huge glass-and-steel curve of the **Meridien Hotel**, a monument to the tastes and aspirations of the 1960s that took more than 15 years to build. Apart from the Meridien, this quarter of the island has been occupied since 1928 by buildings belonging to Qasr al-Aini Hospital, which stands on the mainland just opposite Rawdah. From the Meridien the island stretches southward past Garden City to end opposite Misr al-Qadimah ("Old Cairo") some 2 miles (3 km) to the south. The cone-shaped wooden structure that roofs the Rawdah Nilometer marks the island's southern tip.

Two main roads, Shari Rawdah and Shari as-Saray – which becomes Shari Sayalat ar-Rawdah – cut straight across the island and thus divide it into zones. Four short bridges on the east join Rawdah to Cairo; two on the west span the main channel of the Nile to connect it with Gizah. The southernmost of these two large bridges, the **Kubri Abbas** (Abbas II Bridge), affords one of the best river prospects in Cairo. It carries Shari Rawdah, leading eventually to Shari al-Haram (Pyramids Road) and the Gizah Pyramids. The northern bridge, the **Kubri al-Gaamah** (University Bridge), carries Shari Sayalat ar-Rawdah, which is transformed on the Gizah side into Shari Nahdet Misr, the main approach to Cairo University.

Unlike Gazirah, the island to the north, which was formed alluvially less than a millennium ago, Rawdah is composed of bedrock and has been where it is since before Egypt existed. Its influence on the history of Cairo has been substantial. The recognised bounds of Memphis, the country's capital throughout much of the Pharaonic era, ran right up to include what is now Gizah, on the west bank of the river, while the eastern bank, the site of modern Cairo, was recognised as territory belonging to Heliopolis (On), the great religious centre. The island of Rawdah, identified with Heliopolis, provided the only natural stepping stone between the two, as well as a means of controlling traffic on the river.

Watermarks: In ancient times the channel of the Nile eastward of the island was far wider than it is now. There is foundation evidence of a number of early fortifications and in the Roman period a stronghold stood here that was twin to the one rebuilt by Trajan across the river in Babylon (Misr al-Qadimah, "Old Cairo"). As the river receded westward the space between Rawdah and Babylon was gradually narrowed, and by the 15th century only the present channel was left. Before the building of the High Dam, the southern tip of Rawdah could thus be connected to the

east bank for most of the year by a causeway. During the annual flood, between July and mid-September, a pontoon bridge was laid.

Since Pharaonic times Rawdah has been the site of a **Nilometer**, used by every government down to the British Occupation to determine the height of the flood, upon which would depend the richness of the harvest and consequently the level of land-tax to be paid. It is from the Nilometer, in fact, that the residential district now covering most of the island takes it name – Al-Manyal, which means "measure of the Nile" – and the official name of the island as a whole is actually "Al-Manyal ar-Rawdah".

A flood of less than 16 cubits (one cubit = just over 24 inches, approximately 54 cm) meant that no tax would be exacted. The announcement that this level had been reached was made by a crier; the next day the ceremony of opening the entrance of the city's main canal – the Khaliig al-Misri, now covered by Shari Port Said – took place, in the presence of the governor and other officials, with a huge crowd of spectators both on foot and in boats.

Known in modern Arabic as *al-miqyaas*, the Rawdah Nilometer is the oldest Muslim structure now extant in Cairo: it was built by order of the Abbasid caliph al-Mutawakkil in 861 to replace one installed by order of an Umayyad caliph 150 years earlier, which had been carried away by the flood. In 872 Ahmad ibn Tulun declared his independence by having the caliph's dedicatory inscription removed. (There is a modest fee for entrance into the enclosure around it and the guardian who opens the building that shelters the Nilometer will expect a tip in addition.)

The building's conical dome is not part of the original Nilometer: completed in 1895, it is a replica of the Ottoman-style dome that covered the Nilometer in the 17th and 18th centuries – as known from a traveller's measured drawing – which was apparently burnt by the French. The tiles that line it, **Pleasure boats have plied the Ni for centurie:**

though modern, are good imitations of the 17th-century Isnik tiles that lined the old dome. A wooden model shows how the Nilometer worked.

In the middle of a square stone-lined shaft that descends below the level of the river is the Nilometer itself, an octagonal column divided into cubits, which stands on a millstone at the bottom of the shaft. A stairway around the walls of the shaft leads past inlets at three levels, which admitted water through three tunnels connected with the river. (Just after the Ottoman Conquest, six and half centuries after the Nilometer was built, one of these inlet tunnels was used by a Mamluk in an unsuccessful attempt on the life of Selim the Grim.) The level of the uppermost inlet is indicated by recesses in the walls that are outlined with what a Gothic architect would have recognised as "tiers-point" arches, but they were built three centuries earlier than the earliest European example.

Culture houses: Next to the Nilometer within the same enclosure is a charming relic of the more recent past: a pavilion belonging to the **Manastirli Palace** complex. Built in the 1830s by Hasan Fu'ad Manastirli Pasha, an official of Muhammad Ali's government, the pavilion was restored in 1989 and 1990 and is used for receptions by the Ministry of Culture. The palace gardens, which remained intact until 1945, had walks sheltered by breast-high walls, pergolas, and trellises, which shielded the harem ladies from wind, heat and the gaze of passing boatmen. The palace itself was demolished after the Revolution to make room for the waterworks that now occupy its site.

Under the fifth of the Fatimid caliphs a mosque was constructed here that survived at least down to the 15th century. The licentious, rose-loving seventh caliph had a pleasure house erected nearby called the Hawdaq, where he kept his favourite Badawi mistress: it was as he rode homeward one November night, still glowing from her caresses, that he

was stabbed to death by a 10-man hit-team of Assassins in 1130.

In 1241 the last effective Ayyubid sultan, As-Salih Ayyub (1240–49), built a fortress with 60 towers that covered most of the rest of the southern half of the island. The Turkish slave soldiers he purchased were known as the *Bahri* (riverine) Mamluks because of their island barracks. From their ranks came the sultans who ruled Egypt from 1250 to 1392. When power shifted to the Circassian Mamluks, however, the Bahri barracks fell into disuse and were quarried for stone, a thrifty move that typifies monumentalists throughout Egyptian history. Used as a gunpowder magazine by Muhammad Ali, the remains of these barracks blew up in 1830.

Until 1952 Rawdah remained quite verdant and largely horticultural. The northerly half was laid out by Ibrahim Pasha in the 1830s as a botanical garden, patches of which still survive. The zone south of Shari Rawdah gradually became a residential district in the four decades after the completion of the Abbas II Bridge in 1907 and it still exhibits vestiges of gentility. The centre, however, was built rather hastily during the 1950s and has a raw look that will probably never disappear.

The **Manyal Palace** complex on Shari as-Saray was the chief residence and private museum of Prince Muhammad Ali (1875–1955), younger brother of Abbas II Hilmi. The palace is identified by the rusticated limestone wall two storeys high that surrounds its garden and seals it off from the outside world. Recognised as Crown Prince and Heir Apparent from 1936 until 1952, Prince Muhammad Ali was widely regarded as having a claim to the Egyptian throne that was as legitimate as those of his uncle King Fu'ad or his first cousin King Faruq.

Prince Muhammad Ali played a graceful part in court, diplomatic, and social life and is always identifiable in old photographs from the jaunty angle at which he wore his tarboush. Childless

Manyal Palace Throne Room.

148

by his French wife – the prince was monogamous – he bequeathed his property to the nation on his death, which means that, uniquely among the properties of the Muhammad Ali family now administered by the state, it was not acquired after the Revolution through seizure or confiscation.

Laid out in the Ottoman manner, the palace complex has separate buildings for different functions. They were begun in 1903 and not completed until 30 years later, but contain elements from older structures. The western part of the estate has been transformed into the **Manyal Palace Hotel**, operated by the Club Méditerranée. Nothing is open to the public here except the gardens, where the government under the Revolution built the concrete bungalows that constitute the hotel. The number of plant species has been sadly reduced, though the surviving cacti, banyans and philodendron still testify to the prince having inherited his forebears' passionate concern with bringing diversity to Egypt's over-simplified ecosystem.

The eastern and far more interesting part of the grounds is entered by way of the huge **Salamlik** or reception palace on Shari as-Saray, which has two gorgeous reception halls upstairs. Other buildings are sign-posted at the guichet where entrance tickets are sold. The two-storey **Haramlik** displays the splendid domestic circumstances of a cultivated Middle-Eastern gentleman in the early 20th century.

The **Throne Room** – not a real audience hall, but a full-scale model of one, rather business-like despite the Ottoman-baroque décor – contains portraits of both the men and the prominent women of the Muhammad Ali dynasty. The 14-room **Museum**, well worth a visit on its own, displays the Prince's superb collections of furniture, calligraphy, glass, silver, textiles, costumes, and porcelain. The **Hunting Museum**, to the right of the main entrance, is filled with royal trophies of the chase, which cover its walls.

nting
seum in
Manyal
ace.

DARB AL-AHMAR

The old quarter skirting the Citadel, which is studded with hundreds of fine examples of Islamic architecture, is bounded on the west and south by elements of two former water systems – to the west by the Khalig al-Misri, an ancient canal that became so insalubrious that it was paved over in 1906 to make the wide thoroughfare called Shari Port Said, and to the south by the 14th-century aqueduct that supplied the Citadel with water for irrigation. To the north it ends by the walled enclosure of Al-Qahirah, and on the east by the Muqattam escarpment.

Masterpiece mosque: Most of the monuments in this district date from the era of the Mamluks (1250–1517). But 400 years earlier one of the world's great architectural masterpieces was built by **Ahmad Ibn Tulun**, a Turkish general from Mesopotamia who became ruler of Egypt. Ibn Tulun created his own royal city below the limestone spur where the Citadel now stands and held court in splendid luxury. His vast congregational mosque, big enough to contain a complete army for Friday prayers, was erected between AD 876 and 879 and is now all that remains to testify to the magnificence of Al-Qatai, his new capital.

Often repaired and embellished over its 1,100 years of life, the **Mosque of Ibn Tulun** has retained its original majestic simplicity unchanged. In style it echoes the architecture of Baghdad under the Abbasid caliphs, where Ibn Tulun grew up. The building consists of a square enclosed by a massive flat-roofed arcade of baked brick, which is covered with fine plaster and surmounted by anthropomorphic cresting. Flanked on two sides by outer courts or *ziyadahs* and thickly walled on the exterior, the arcade creates a courtyard covering more than 4 acres (nearly 2 hectares), with an ablution fountain in the middle. On the

eastern or Mecca-facing (*qiblah*) side are several *mihrabs*, ornamental recesses or wall-treatments indicating the direction of prayer, including one that dates from the Fatimid era. Here also is the wooden *minbar* – a structure like a staircase, which serves some of the same function that a pulpit fulfils in a church – the oldest in use in Cairo, the third oldest in Egypt, and one of the finest. It dates from 1296 and was made for the Mamluk sultan Lagin, who had taken refuge in the mosque in 1294 when he was still only an amir and the building was largely in ruins. Implicated in a political murder, Lagin vowed that if he survived he would restore the mosque that had sheltered him, a promise that was carried out when he became sultan two years later.

The decoration, carved in stucco, shows a wonderful inventiveness and richness of pattern. A band of sycamore wood carved with verses from the Qur'an runs under the eaves around the entire circumference of the building. More

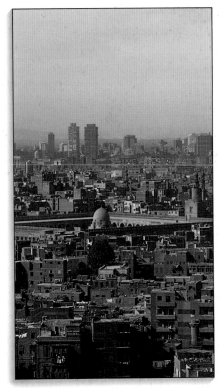

than 1¼ miles (2 km) long, it has never been studied. The minaret, a replacement built by order of Lagin, is certainly modelled on Ahmad ibn Tulun's original, which was modelled in turn on the ziggurat-like minaret of the Great Mosque at Samarra near Baghdad. Its stairway is outside and corkscrews to the lantern at the top.

Alleys and houses: After Al-Qahirah had been built to the north as their royal enclosure by the Fatimids in the 10th century and the Citadel had been begun to the east by the Ayyubids in the 13th, the area between them filled up with the estates of Mamluk amirs, who kept many dependents and retainers and sometimes small private armies. Around them gathered the merchants and craftsmen who served their households. Their hippodrome and stables, their armourers' and saddlemakers' bazaars, their baths, the shops of their butchers and bakers and candlestick-makers, grew up among a maze of narrow streets and alleys north of the mosque of Ibn Tulun, many of

which still present vistas full of incident and charm.

Two late Mamluk houses, one of the 16th, the other of the 17th century, are actually built against the northeast corner of the mosque. Connected together, they were restored and lived in between 1934 and 1942 by Major **Robert Gayer-Anderson** Pasha (1881–1945) and now function as a **museum** to display his collection of Byzantine, Syrian, Persian, Turkish, Indian, Chinese, and English furnishings and *objets d'art*. Built of sturdy stone, with plentiful *mashrabiyyah* screening the upstairs windows, these houses provide a good idea of old-fashioned Cairene living. The marble-floored *salamlik* (reception hall) with its cushioned divans would have been the scene of male gatherings, which the women could view from a screened balcony above.

Good authority holds that the well in the courtyard contains water from the Great Flood and leads to the magical realm of the Sultan of the Bats, whose

Left, ancient and modern shopping.

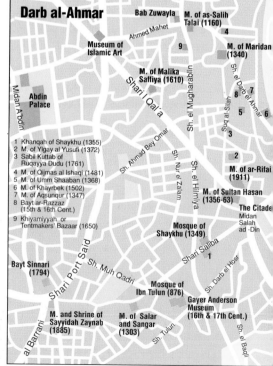

Darb al-Ahmar

Bab Zuwayla
Ahmed Mahet
M. of as-Salih Talai (1160)
Museum of Islamic Art
M. of Maridan (1340)
M. of Malika Saffiya (1610)
Sh. el Mugharabin
Sh. el Darb el Ahmar
Shari I Qal'a
Midan A'bdin
Abdin Palace
Suq al-Silah
Sug al-Silah

1 Khanqah of Shaykhu (1355)
2 M. of Ylgay al Yusufi (1372)
3 Sabil Kuttab of Ruqayya Dudu (1761)
4 M. of Qijmas al Ishaqi (1481)
5 M. of Umm Shaaban (1368)
6 M. of Khayrbek (1502)
7 M. of Aqsunqur (1347)
8 Bayt ar-Razzaz (15th & 16th Cent.)
9 Khiyamiyyah or Tentmakers' Bazaar (1650)

Sh. Ahmad Bey Omar
Sh. Nur el Zalam
Sh. el Hilmiya

M. of ar-Rifai (1911)
M. of Sultan Hasan (1356-63)
The Citadel
Midan Salah ad-Din

Mosque of Shaykhu (1349)
Shari Saliba

Bayt Sinnari (1794)
Shari Port Said
Sh. Muh Qadri

Mosque of Ibn Tulun (876)
Sh. Darb el Hosr

Gayer Anderson Museum (16th & 17th Cent.)

M. and Shrine of Sayyidah Zaynab (1885)
M. of Salar and Sangar (1303)
Sh. Tulun
Sh. el Baqli
al Barrani

seven daughters lie sleeping under spells, each in her golden bed. Also known as **Bayt al-Kiridliyyah** ("The House of the Cretans"), this museum is worth a leisurely visit.

The street that leads eastward up to the Citadel from the northern corner of Ibn Tulun is called **Shari Salibah**, meaning "Cross Street", because its east-west passage cuts directly across the city's medieval high street, the Qasabah, at right angles. To the west it turns a few corners and eventually emerges in Shari Port Said.

In the middle of the Muslim month of Ragab every year, the whole area is bedecked with tented booths and streamers for the saint's *mawlid* (festival), which attracts hundreds of thousands of male participants, among whom lurk a few professional thieves, especially pickpockets. The *mawlid* is colourful, but a little rough, and sensible women avoid the area during this celebration.

Framed by the solemn opposing facades of the **Mosque and *Khanqah* of Amir Shaykhu,** commander-in-chief of the 'Mamluk armies under Sultan Hasan, the eastern arm of Shari Salibah still evokes the 14th century, despite hurtling buses, 7-Up stands and blaring radios. It makes its way up to the *maydan* below the Citadel, which offers a wonderful panorama of variously striped and crenellated mosques and minarets. On the left loom the soaring walls of the **Tomb and Madrasah of Sultan Hasan**, universally acknowledged to be the noblest example of Cairene Mamluk architecture, remarkable for its size, the harmony of its proportions, and its gorgeous decoration.

Plague money: The seventh son of Sultan An-Nasir Muhammad, Sultan Hasan acceded to the sultanate in 1347 at the age of 12, after five of his brothers, all mere puppets in the hands of powerful and rapacious amirs, had come to sticky ends. That same year the country was ravaged by the Black Death: as many as 10,000 people died each day and the wealth of most of the richest

mluk narets.

victims found its way by default into the royal coffers.

With the cash that had come to him as a beneficiary, Sultan Hasan initiated construction of this mosque, which began in 1356 and lasted seven years. Hasan himself disappeared in 1361, presumably murdered, after an interrupted reign lasting only 11 years in all, and therefore never saw the tremendous building completed, though it brought him enduring fame.

In contrast with the congregational mosque of Ibn Tulun, Sultan Hasan's mosque is combined with four residential colleges (*madrasahs*) and a mausoleum. Originally attached to it at the northern end were more apartments, a well, and a market, all of which have disappeared. Over the towering main entrance, 121 ft (37 metres) high, is an elaborate canopy of stalactites, repeated within the vestibule.

The original magnificent bronze-ornamented doors were later appropriated for the mosque of al-Muayyad

Shaykh, where they may still be seen. A bent passageway leads to a cruciform central court, where four great arched recesses or *iwans* create sheltered spaces for instruction in the four schools of Islamic jurisprudence, the Hanafi, the Shafii, the Maliki and the Hanbali. Multistoreyed collegiate living quarters for teachers and students are built into the corners of the court.

At the back of the eastern *iwan* is a particularly handsome *mihrab*, a jigsaw puzzle of coloured marble flanked by pairs of Crusader Gothic columns. Around the three walls of this *iwan* runs a band of Naskhi script. From the domed tomb chamber behind it, six ground-level windows offer a view across the *maydan* up to the Citadel that is splendid and unobstructed.

Across the street is the **Rifa'i Mosque**. Because it was planned as a complement to its Mamluk neighbour in scale, fabric, and architectural style, many tourists mistake it for an ancient monument. It was begun in 1869, however, six centuries later than the Sultan Hasan mosque, at the order of Hoshyar Kadineffendi (the Princess Dowager Khushyar), the mother of the Khedive Ismail, and was clearly conceived as a dynastic mosque. Designed by Husayn Fakhri Pasha, with construction overseen by the Princess Dowager's chief eunuch, it incorporates the tombs of a Sufi saint and a Companion of the Prophet. The mosque was not completed until 1912, but was used for burials from 1885 onwards. In it are interred the Khedive Ismail, his mother and various of his children and relations. The roofed and carpeted interior is magnificently adorned with Mamluk-inspired motifs designed by Max Herz Bey, the architect of the official Comité de Conservation des Monuments de l'Art Arabe, founded in 1881. Herz had already built the Museum of Islamic Art.

Streets for processions: The traffic that used to roar up the thoroughfare between these two great mosques, Shari Muhammad Ali (also known as Shari

Rifa'i and Sultan Hasan Mosques.

Qalaa), has mercifully been diverted.

Laid out by order of Khedive Ismail in 1873, Shari Muhammad Ali required the demolition of 700 old houses, bakeries, baths, and mosques. Until 1970 the street still conveyed some delusions at least of grandeur, but now it is more dismally dilapidated and devoid of charm than any of its humbler and far more ancient neighbours. Nineteenth-century bourgeois houses filled in the area to the south of the street, called Hilmiyyah, a suburb for officials built on the site of an ancient pond, while the area to the north has retained much of its medieval character.

Three medieval streets – the Darb al-Ahmar, the Suq as-Silah, and the Qasabah – ramble northward from below the Citadel or from Shari Muhammad Ali to meet before the Fatimid gate of Bab Zuwayla. Leaving his residence in the Citadel, the sultan would ride on ceremonial occasions – such as departures on pilgrimage, the opening of a military campaign, or the convening of a court – down either the Suq as-Silah or the Darb al-Ahmar. At the head of such a procession, says one 13th-century eye-witness, came an amir carrying the emblem of state, the Royal Saddle-Cloth, covered in gold and precious stones, followed by two pages in yellow silk and gold brocade, mounted on white horses. Then came the sultan's standard bearer, a flute-player and a singer chanting the heroic deeds of former kings, and finally Sultan Baybars himself, dramatically clothed in black, surrounded by halberdiers uniformed in yellow silk. Over his head a page held the State Parasol of yellow silk, crowned with a golden bird. On either side an amir held a Poniard of State and a third amir followed carrying the Mace of State, with drummers and chanting poets. A guard of jingling Mamluks presumably brought up the rear. No doubt the ladies behind their *mashrabiyyahs* were delighted with the spectacle.

Today the **Darb al-Ahmar** is still lined with interesting old buildings,

some in good condition, others in a state of imminent collapse. As the road leads down from the Citadel, one of the first monuments on the right is the picturesque **mausoleum** of the very last of the independent amirs, Khayrbek, who betrayed his fellow Mamluks to the Ottomans in 1516 and was rewarded by being made governor. The siting of the angular but harmonious building illustrates to perfection the ingenious use of irregular spaces, forced upon architects by the density of settlement in the city, while the intricately carved stone dome marks the apex of Mamluk imperial craftsmanship.

Almost next door is the **Mosque of amir Aqsunqur**, older by 180 years (1347), which contains the tomb of six-year-old Kuchuk, the brother of Sultan Hasan, who was murdered in 1341. Three hundred years later (1652) the mosque was renovated and embellished by an Ottoman officer, who had the walls half-heartedly covered with Damascene tiles, in conformity with the taste favoured in the Ottoman capital. Tourist guides consequently call the building the **Blue Mosque**, but anyone expecting it to resemble the famous Blue Mosque in Istanbul will be disappointed.

Upstairs, downstairs: Further along on the left, projecting over the street just beyond the splendid stalactite doorway of the *madrasah* and mausoleum of Khwand Baraka, the mother of Sultan Shaaban (1368), are the *mashrabiyyah* casements of a huge old house: **Bayt ar-Razzaz**, largely 18th-century, but constructed around a 15th-century core. Though it is dilapidated within, luxurious traditional features survive: two courtyards, a lofty *salamlik* with a lantern in the roof, a loggia (*maqad*), and three or four salons in the *haramlik*, where the women and girls of the household were theoretically cloistered. Goings-on in the street below, over which the *mashrabiyyah* provided excellent vantage, were lively, however, and there were other diversions. Lowering a basket on a rope allowed small purchases to be made, undoubtedly accompanied by plenty of chatter. Female reciters, fortune-tellers, and merchants were always allowed in, and eunuchs and servant-girls could come and go as they pleased.

Bayt ar-Razzaz has its own bathroom, but the women probably also made weekly expeditions to public baths, which provided opportunities not only to meet women from other households, but also to engage in extramural intrigue and even exchange billets-doux.

In the lanes feeding into the Darb al-Ahmar today, furniture-makers and upholsterers ply their trade, assembling gilt chairs and settees in the ever-popular Franco-Italian pseudo-Louis XV/XVI style that is referred to locally as *Luigi Khamastasher*.

A little further on, the tall portal of the **Altunbugha Maridani Mosque** invites the visitor to step into its hushed and shadowed courtyard, a favourite subject for Orientalist painters. It was built in 1339 by a son-in-law of the prolific

Craftsmen in the Darb al-Ahmar: a brass worker

Sultan an-Nasir Muhammad. A superb 14th-century wooden *mashrabiyyah* screens off the sanctuary area, the roof of which is supported by a splendid collection of columns borrowed from Ptolemaic, Christian, and earlier Islamic buildings.

The marble dado, badly damaged by rising damp, is exceptionally beautiful, as is the *mihrab*, which is decorated with mother of pearl and blue faience, as well as with coloured marbles. Here the Darb al-Ahmar is joined by Suq as-Silah, the Armourers' Bazaar, the second of the three streets leading north from Shari Muhammad Ali.

As the Darb al-Ahmar curves left from this point towards the Fatimid gate of Bab Zuwayla, the **Mosque of amir Qijmas al-Ishaqi** (1481) appears on the right. Restored in the early 1980s, it has particularly fine carved stucco windows and varicoloured marble panelling. It is joined to its *kuttab* or school by a little bridge over a side-street.

Medieval high street: The third old north-south street, running parallel to Suq as-Silah and Darb al-Ahmar, is the **Qasabah,** the high street of medieval Cairo, which runs all the way from Fustat northward past the mosque of Ibn Tulun. Crossing Shari Salibah and Shari Muhammad Ali, it continues northwards, changing its name and its character several times before arriving at Bab Zuwayla. In the part of it called the **Saddlemakers' Bazaar** not a saddle is to be seen, but there are plenty of friendly fruit and vegetable vendors.

There is not much sign of a sieve either, where it metamorphoses into the **Street of the Sievers**. Only just outside Bab Zuwayla, as it becomes the covered 14th-century **Suq al-Khiyamiyyah** or **the Tentmakers' Bazaar** does it live up to its name.

In tiny shops on either side of the street, tentmakers still sit cross-legged on raised platforms, stitching away at the bright appliqué from which the walls and ceilings of tents, marquees, and temporary pavilions are traditionally

broidering Qu'ran gold ead.

fabricated. To suit the tastes of modern interior decorators, however, elegant colour-schemes have been introduced that are much less baldly primary than traditional ones. Rag rugs, canvas bags, and knapsacks of every stripe, popular with locals as well as with tourists, are found on the left as one emerges from the Khiyamiyyah opposite the great gate of Bab Zuwayla, the southern entrance to Al-Qahirah.

Here the Qasabah meets the Darb al-Ahmar, which has already absorbed the Suq as-Silah. A continuation of the Darb al-Ahmar, which now changes its name to **Shari Ahmad Mahir**, heads west along the wall of the Fatimid enclosure to Shari Port Said. This rackety, ramshackle and usually rather crowded lane is one of dozens in Cairo that are rewarding to walk down. The ingenious and often beautiful contrivances manufactured here make a wonderful assortment, ranging from wire rat-traps and birdcages to butchers' blocks, mallets, barbecue grills, chains, sunshades, deckchairs, blankets, harnesses, tack and adornments for donkeys, marble table-tops, balusters, and tinned buckets. Tucked into one unpromising corner is a traditional apothecary, who sells the ingredients needed for potions to remedy infertility, warm an indifferent heart, or restore lost potency. Important to many recipes, it would seem, are dried hedgehogs.

Across Shari Port Said from the point where Shari Ahmad Mahir runs into it stands the **Museum of Islamic Art**, erected by Herz Bey in 1903 to house not only Muslim antiquities, but also the Khedivial Library. The library – now *Dar al-Kuttub,* the National Library – moved to new quarters on the Corniche in Bulaq in 1980, and the collection of Islamic art, increased by material from excavations, purchases and donations, now includes over 75,000 objects, filling the entire building. The superb craftsmanship displayed in marble, wood, metal, ceramics, and glass is further evidence of princely tastes.

In the Tentmakers Bazaar.

THE RAG-PICKERS

One man's rubbish may be another man's riches. In Cairo last year's fashions and fashion magazines are both sold as *rubabikya* ("old clothes", from the Italian *roba vecchia*). The *rubabikya* man, who travels the city with his donkey and cart, sells them in turn – like the old bottles he also buys, which are eventually recycled to hold new wine – and they will find second, third, and fourth lives elsewhere in the city. Residents have sometimes been surprised to find their own discarded correspondence wrapping peanuts or melon seeds purchased miles way from home.

More miscellaneous rubbish – scraps of food, paper, metal or plastic – has a different fate. Though there have been attempts at organising a rubbish collection system within the public sector, as is usual in the West, they have all foundered. Capital costs have proven too large, maintenance has proven impossible, and no-one, after all, has been able to come up with a practical solution to the problem of what to do with the rubbish once it has been collected.

In contrast with this failure, a large and profitable recycling business is run by Cairo's private-sector rubbish collectors, the *zabbalin*, who live in "informal-sector" settlements of up to 17,000 people on the eastern outskirts of the city below the Muqattam. The *zabbalin* use donkey carts to collect their rubbish, moving from house to house and building to building throughout the city. In the case of large buildings they pay a fee to the landlord for the right to collect tenants' rubbish, while householders pay, in turn, to have their rubbish removed.

Dividing rubbish into its constituent parts, the *zabbalin* reprocess 80 percent of what they collect. One ton of dirty Cairene plastic fetches them as much as LE 450; a ton of pressed and baled paper is worth between LE 150 and LE 200; a kilo of aluminium sells for LE 1, a kilo of copper for LE 3. Clothes are either resold whole to a *rubabikya* man or torn into strips for rag rugs; bones are hauled to rendering plants to be made into glue; lightbulb filaments are sent back to the factories where they originated. Being Christian, the *zabbalin* keep pigs, which eat all the organic material in the rubbish and are eventually sold to Christian butchers in the city. Waste from the pigs goes to a fertiliser factory.

The efficiency of the system rests on the fact that the *zabbalin* in the most part live miserably, doing most of the sorting in their own squalid homes, which they share with their donkeys, pigs and buffalo. Their children play amongst swarms of flies on rat-infested mounds of rotting refuse, which are strewn with evil surprises: broken bottles, shards of rusty metal, old nails, used razor blades, discarded syringes. Two toddlers were blown to bits in 1989 by a hand-grenade some unthinking collector had carelessly thrown away. Infant mortality for the *zabbalin* is far higher than anywhere else in the city.

Despite a great deal of talk about "modernising" rubbish collection and thus phasing the *zabbalin* out, they have proven more efficient than any competitors and the city depends upon them. In 1990 the Cairo Governorate banned their donkey carts, but such bans had been pronounced many times before.

Some *zabbalin* were able to borrow enough to purchase Toyota pick-up trucks, which cost LE 28,000 new and LE 8,000 secondhand; others rented trucks from the rich. Most, however, went on as usual until the ban died a natural death, as Cairo's bureaucratic decrees do tend to do.

Anyone can collect rubbish, but not everyone can dispose of it as efficiently as the *zabbalin*. Cairo produces some 7,000 tons of rubbish daily. Burning it in furnaces, the solution proposed by American experts in 1980, when the latest technology was promised by their government, is not only expensive, but environmentally unsound. Dumping sites within the environs of the city have already been filled to capacity. The nearest such site today is at Kilometre 14 on the road to Suez, which means that the cost of transport can only be justified if loads are extremely large. Faced with such uneconomic alternatives, the exasperated would-be big-business competitors have taken to selling the rubbish they collect to the *zabbalin*. Their methods may be primitive, but the world may yet be forced to learn from their example.

AL-QAHIRAH

The walled royal enclosure founded by the Fatimids in AD 969 was named **Al-Qahirah**, "The Subduer". Three quarters of a mile long by half a mile wide – thus enclosing slightly more than a square kilometre – its oblong outlines are clearly discernible today. They are indicated by streets that still follow the lines of the original mud-brick enclosure walls, which were rebuilt in stone in 1085–92 and 1171–76. Stretches of these stone walls still stand, pierced by three massive fortified gates: **Bab al-Futuh** (1087), in the centre of the northern wall, **Bab an-Nasr** (1087), in the same stretch of wall nearby to the east, and **Bab Zuwayla** (1092), in the centre of the southern wall. Linking Bab al-Futuh at the north and Bab Zuwayla at the south is a street that has been a vital artery since medieval times.

Bisecting Al-Qahirah, this street continues beyond both Bab al-Futuh and Bab Zuwayla to link up the entire city. Named at this point after the first Fatimid caliph, Mu'izz li-Din Allah, it has various names in short stretches further north and south, but is otherwise conveniently known as the **Qasabah** or High Street. Running parallel to the Qasabah from Bab an-Nasr southward is another important street, called **Shari al-Gamaliyyah**. Crossing the Qasabah at right angles and thus dividing the oblong of Al-Qahirah artificially into two zones is **Shari Al-Azhar**, which was cut through in 1927 in order to bring tram service to the Mosque of Al-Azhar.

Fatimid splendour: Sections of the Qasabah are bazaars and therefore have names derived from the particular trades or occupations carried on in them. The widest and most monumental part of the central section within Al-Qahirah is still called **Bayn al-Qasrayn**, meaning "Between the Two Palaces": the name refers to the two enormous palaces that housed the caliph and his retinue during Fatimid rule (969–1171). They were destroyed eight centuries ago. In the **Eastern Palace**, which contained some 4,000 rooms, the caliph lived with his wives and children, slaves, eunuchs and personal servants, numbering between 18,000 and 30,000 people. Opposite stood the **Western Palace**, housing visitors of state and more retainers. Between these two palaces was a parade ground on which 10,000 troops could assemble; and around them were orchards and pleasure gardens, stables, and barracks.

Free to gratify their exquisite taste in the fine arts, scholarship, and music, in clothing and personal adornment, the Fatimids lived in almost unbelievable luxury. Historians have recorded the wealth left by two daughters of Mu'izz, for example, the founder of Fatimid rule in Egypt: five sacks of emeralds, 3,000 chased and inlaid silver vessels, 30,000 pieces of Sicilian embroidery, 90 crystal basins and ewers, 12,000 dresses, and nearly 3 million gold dinars, worth

a sum that in modern terms is literally incalculable.

More than once, however, they were reduced almost to penury by low Niles, bad harvests, plagues and rebellions; and after the accession of the Ayyubids, their material wealth – including 120,000 manuscripts, the greatest library of the medieval world – was dispersed for the last time. Except for the objects preserved in the Museum of Islamic Art, the old palaces and their treasures have disappeared. Three important mosques from the golden age of the Fatimids survive, however, within what was the royal enclosure – Al-Azhar, Al-Hakim and Al-Aqmar – and a fourth – As-Salih Tala'i – still stands just outside Bab Zuwayla.

Oldest university: Shari Al-Azhar, now carrying a flyover in addition to its normal traffic, slashes across the Qasabah and brings heavy traffic right past the main entrance of the **Mosque of Al Azhar**, "The Resplendent", the most famous seat of learning in the Muslim world. Founded in AD 970, this mosque has undergone restoration at least six times and many of its original features have been lost. Its essential configuration, however, has remained unchanged. It is a congregational "Friday" mosque – it is large enough, that is, to hold the crowds that assemble to hear the Friday sermon – with a courtyard surrounded by keel-arched arcading. Like marvellous barnacles, later *madrasahs*, mausoleums and minarets of the most intricate kind have become attached to this simple nucleus.

For 1,000 years scholars and pilgrims, the pious and the merely curious, have beaten a path to Al-Azhar's doors. In the shade of its arcades knots of students from many lands gathered to sit at the feet – literally – of scholars lecturing on exegesis of the Qur'an or the Hadith, on points of Muslim law, or on Arabic grammar. In its heyday Al-Azhar also offered lectures in medicine, astronomy and mathematics. Students would have learned the Qur'an from dictation by

The Mosque of Al-Azhar.

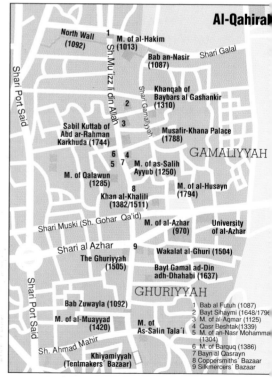

Al-Qahira

North Wall 1
(1092)   M. of al-Hakim
                (1013)
Sh. Mu'izz li din Allah
                Bab an-Nasir   Shari Galal
                (1087)

Shari Port Said

Shari Gamaliyyah

                Khanqah of
              2 Baybars al Gashankir
                (1310)

Sabil Kuttab of   3
Abd ar-Rahman   Musafir-Khana Palace
Karkhuda (1744)   (1788)

              6 4   GAMALIYYAH
              5 7 M. of as-Salih
M. of Qalawun   Ayyub (1250)
(1285)
              8   M. of al-Husayn
              Khan al-Khalili   (1794)
              (1382/1511)

Shari Muski (Sh. Gohar Qa'id)
                M. of al-Azhar   University
                (970)   of al-Azhar

Shari al Azhar   9
The Ghuriyyah   Wakalat al-Ghuri (1504)
(1505)
                Bayt Gamal ad-Din
                adh-Dhahabi (1637)

Shari Port Said

                           GHURIYYAH

Bab Zuwayla (1092)

M. of al-Muayyad   M. of
(1420)   As-Salin Tala'i

Sh. Ahmad Mahir

Khiyamiyyah
(Tentmakers' Bazaar)

1 Bab al Futuh (1087)
2 Bayt Sihaymi (1648/1796)
3 M. of al-Aqmar (1125)
4 Qasr Beshtak(1339)
5 M. of an-Nasr Mohammad
  (1304)
6 M. of Barquq (1386)
7 Bayn al Qasrayn
8 Coppersmiths' Bazaar
9 Silkmercers' Bazaar

heart in village schools as children. Other learning was also by rote, which meant that neither printed texts nor even sight itself was overwhelmingly important; many of the students were therefore blind. Later they would return home to hand on the wisdom they had acquired by this traditional method.

The shaykhs of Al-Azhar can still be distinguished in crowds by their sober grey robes and distinctive red *birette* wrapped in white muslin turbans – the same costume that is worn by "Arab philosophers" as depicted by Renaissance painters like Giorgione and Raphael. Since the Revolution Al-Azhar has evolved into a modern university, with faculties of commerce, medicine, engineering, agriculture, dentistry, pharmacy, modern languages, humanities, and science supplementing traditional Islamic studies. Some of its nondescript new buildings stretch along Shari Al-Azhar to the east.

On the other side of Shari al-Azhar and across the square is the **shrine of Sayyidna** (Our Lord) **Husayn**, grandson of the Prophet, murdered in AD 680. To save his head from desecration by the Crusaders, it was brought to Cairo from Askalon in Palestine in 1153. A beautiful 12th century wooden cenotaph was discovered in 1903 under the floor of the tomb chamber. Exposed in 1939 when the floor was retiled, it is now in the Museum of Islamic Art. The present tomb chamber is 18th-century and around it stands the great mosque built between 1864 and 1873 by Khedive Ismail. A popular shrine, the mosque is officially used by the President of the Republic and members of the government on ceremonial state occasions and at special feasts.

Traditional Cairo: Between them, Al-Azhar and Sayyidna Husayn form the living heart of traditional Cairo. At Ramadan, on the birthday of the Prophet, and particularly during the ten-day *mawlid* of Husayn, as many as two million pilgrims flock in from the provinces and the countryside to join native

heart of ditional ro.

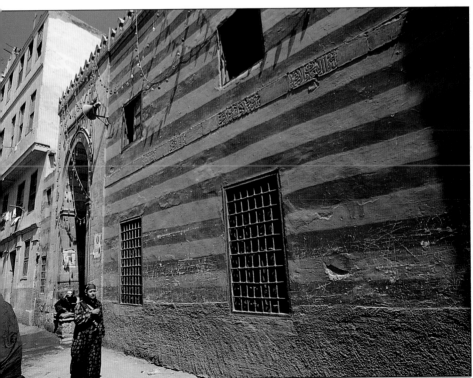

Cairenes in celebration. For these country folk, as for Chaucer's pilgrims, such feasts are a holiday. They camp anywhere they can, in parks, verges and waste spaces and – alas – in many of the medieval monuments, where official guardians make unofficial fortunes during the 10-day celebrations.

Bright tenting is erected and festoons of lights are strung up around booths offering goods, amusement or entertainment. A traditional feature for children are sugar dolls. There are rifle ranges, tests of strength, roundabouts and swings, storytellers, singers, and reciters of devotional texts. At night there is *dhikr*, rhythmic repetition of the name of God to the beat of drums, which leads to trance. Mountains of street food – *ful* and *taamiya*, *kusheri* and kebabs, peanuts, pancakes (*fatir*) and sunflower seeds – are devoured.

Profitable trade: The old Fatimid enclosure was opened up for ordinary folk by Salah ad-Din in 1169. Inheriting the commercial role of Fustat, Al-Qahirah

soon became the centre of a mercantile network stretching from Spain and Morocco to India and even China, with which Egypt had traded directly by sea since Roman times. The sea route from Europe around Africa to the Indies remained undiscovered until the end of the 15th century and the old overland Silk Road through Central Asia was unsuitable for fragile or perishable goods. Cairo thus became a highly organised entrepôt specialising in Eastern luxuries – pepper, spices, incense, silks, and porcelain – which were resold to Italian merchants for the European market. These merchants in turn brought furs, amber, musk and mother of pearl to Egypt. Black slaves, ivory and gold came from the South, wood, ores and metal from Asia Minor.

Profits were enormous. The sultans, who meanwhile exacted a duty of 10 percent on all goods in transit, went into business themselves, building their own *khans* or *wakalat*, warehouses with long-term residential accommodation, which were not intended, like the caravanserais of Persia, merely for overnight stays. *Wakalat* sprang up throughout Al-Qahirah and in the Nile port of Bulaq and some of them are still in use as commercial premises.

A restored example open to the public is the **Wakalah of Al-Ghuri**, established by the next-to-last Mamluk sultan at the beginning of the 15th century in a lane next to Al-Azhar. Ground-floor rooms now display examples of traditional crafts such as copper-engraving, stucco-carving, ivory and mother-of-pearl inlaying, marquetry, mosaics and leatherwork.

Some travellers sought lodging among their fellow countrymen or co-religionists, distinguished from the 14th-century onward by the colour and headdress or cut of clothes and frequently living in enclaves. Names of streets and alleys in this part of Cairo still refer to pockets of Greeks, Armenians, Jews, Ethiopians and a dozen other ethnic or religious groups. Between the mosque

Eating *al fresco* durir Ramadan.

of Sayyidna Husayn and the Qasabah is a labyrinth of tiny streets that have grown up within what were actually two or three old *wakalat*.

Khan al-Khalili: The city's most famous tourist bazaar takes its name from the fact that it is situated in the ruins of one of them, a 14th-century *wakalah* called the Khan al-Khalili. The **Khan al-Khalili bazaar** is on every tourist's itinerary and most people enjoy browsing through its welter of "Oriental" wares – gold and silver, real and artificial gemstones, brassware, copperware, leather and ivory, perfumes, carpets and *gallabiyyas* – for a morning or an evening. The workmanship of new items and the quality and variety of old ones have deteriorated mightily, however, since the days when Cairo was the marketplace of the world.

Merchants beckon from the doorways of cupboard-sized shops and invite the visitor in for a glass of mint tea or a cup of Turkish coffee. The hospitality is genuine and it is unheard of in this bazaar actually to be swindled. The age-old game of bargaining, however, is played over every purchase, whether or not the customer knows it. He will therefore be courteously treated, but also acutely observed; and should he show foolish ignorance of the value of what he wants, he may pay a little extra for his folly. Somewhere between outrageous asking prices and niggardly offers, a rational bargain can usually be struck that will preserve each party's self-respect. If this operation proves impossible, the would-be buyer can flounce off without causing offence. Arrangements may be made for larger purchases to be sent abroad. Shipped by merchants with a reputation to uphold, they always arrive at their destination.

Many tourists never penetrate further than the Khan al-Khalili into the traditional fabric of the city. They are missing a great deal, for within a few steps are fascinating – if sometimes rather insalubrious – nooks and crannies: authentic popular bazaars teeming with

ourist addresses, han al-halili.

life, a wealth of medieval architecture in mosques, *madrasahs*, palaces, *sabil-kuttabs*, streets full of people, things and activities that are instructive and diverting.

This is Naguib Mahfouz territory, the setting for the Nobel-prizewinner's *Trilogy* and *Midaq Alley*. For the most part, though, the middle class he describes moved out to the suburbs two or three decades ago, following in the footsteps of earlier ex-residents, the aristocrats who built the mosques and lived in the palaces down to the middle of the 19th century and the black and white slaves they bought and sold here.

The stretch of the Qasabah right beside Khan al-Khalili is the **Goldsmiths' Bazaar (Suq as-Sagha)** where both Cairene ladies and their country cousins come to buy earrings, bracelets and necklaces. Gold and silver are sold by weight and every shopkeeper has a set of scales, so there is no bargaining here. Next comes the **Coppersmiths' Bazaar (Suq an-Nahhasiin)**, which has been in this place since the 14th century. Here brassware and copperware are also sold by weight, which means that a better bargain may be had than in Khan al-Khalili.

Between the palaces: Northward the street widens out into the **Bayn al-Qasrayn**, which for centuries was the most important space in the city. On the left (western) side of the street is one of the finest architectural ensembles in Egypt, a splendid assemblage of walls, monumental portals, and minarets. The first structure in this ensemble is the massive complex built in 1284 for the Mamluk sultan **Qalawun**.

Qalawun, whose name means "Rich Present" in Turkish, had been a relatively expensive slave. Beating off Crusaders and Mongols as well as local rivals, he battled his way to the top and stayed there, founding a dynasty that was to last for almost 100 years. His complex includes a *madrasah*, a mausoleum, a mosque, and the remains of a hospital (*maristan*) that was famous throughout the medieval Muslim world,

Merchants and merchandise in Khan al-Khalili.

attracting the best physicians and medical researchers. A clinic still operates on the site. Qalawun died while conducting a successful siege of Acre at the age of 70 and is buried here, with his son An-Nasir Muhammad, in a tomb chamber adorned with granite columns, marble panelling and majestic calligraphy, dimly lit by stained glass windows far up under a lofty dome.

Of all the Mamluk sultans, **An-Nasir** had the longest and most splendid reign. Though he later put up great buildings elsewhere in the city and preferred in the end to be buried with his father, part of the *madrasah*-mausoleum complex next door was at one time intended to be his own mausoleum. The eclecticism of its elements demonstrates the outreach of Mamluk power: the Gothic-looking doorway is truly Gothic, having been brought from a Crusader church at Acre, while the Spanish-looking filigree stucco-work on the minaret is truly Spanish, having been carved by Andalusian craftsmen, Muslim refugees from Christian persecution. What is left of the interior was restored in the late 1980s by the German Archaeological Institute and the Egyptian Antiquities Organisation.

The third building in the ensemble is the **Mausoleum and Madrasah of Barquq**, the first of the Circassian Mamluk sultans, which was built in 1384. His son Farag built another and far grander mausoleum in the Northern Cemetery where Barquq is actually buried, but this one is grand enough. Nobly proportioned, it is a classic example of the cruciform *madrasah*, with four tremendous arcades. The stone panelling has porphyry insets. The wooden *minbar*, the stairway used as a sort of pulpit for the Friday sermon, was presented to the mosque by a subsequent sultan in 1440 and is a fine example of marquetry and inlay.

As the street proceeds northward a five-storey palace appears on the right, built over ruins of the great Eastern Palace of the Fatimids by the amir **Beshtak**, one of an-Nasir's many sons-in-law. The German Archaeological Institute has carried out concentrated restoration in this area of Al-Qahirah and has put plans and drawings on display here in a superb reception room with a coffered ceiling. In its day (1339) the palace had running water on every floor and the remains of an old water-raising system are still in evidence. At a fork in the street a few yards further on stands the *sabil-kuttab* (fountain-school) of **Abd ar-Rahman Katkhuda,** a charming little 18th-century building, which has also been well restored with German help.

Moonlit and eccentric: Noteworthy along this northern stretch of the Qasabah are the two other Fatimid mosques contemporary with Al-Azhar. **Al-Aqmar,** "the Moonlit", stands on the right-hand side of the street, well below the street level. Its ribbed facade with keel-shaped recesses has much in common with other contemporary Fatimid buildings, such as Al-Azhar and some of the saints' tombs in the Southern Cemetery.

●ffee-shop
sting place.

Another hundred yards up the street, past a market where the fine produce from what were the Muhammad Ali family's experimental farms is sold in season, stands the great congregational mosque built by **Al-Hakim**, the second Fatimid caliph. His 25-year reign is infamous for his acts of malevolent eccentricity, which only came to an end when he disappeared one night in February 1021. His mosque, too, has had a long and odd career. In the 12th century it was used as a prison for Crusader captives. In 1303 it was destroyed by the great earthquake of that year, but was later restored and used once more as a mosque, before falling again into ruin. Napoleon kept horses and gunpowder in it; subsequently it served as a government depot, then as a playground. In 1979 schoolboys were using it as a football field.

That year, however, in exchange for payments totalling $2 million, the Egyptian Antiquities Organisation gave *carte blanche* to a Shi'ite sect from western

India called the Bohra, who claim descent from the Fatimids, to carry out a "restoration". With Bohra students from India working as volunteer labourers, a practice which is unheard of in Egypt, they rebuilt the mosque, introducing new structures, marble floors, chandeliers, and many Indian touches. Sometimes visible in the neighbourhood of the mosque, they may be distinguished by their immaculate white caps, tunics and trousers.

The mosque now stands against the surviving section of the **North Wall** that connects the round-towered **Bab al Futuh** with the square-towered **Bab an-Nasr**. It is possible to climb these Fatimid towers, walk along the battlements between them, and admire the fine stonework of their Armenian architect, John the Monk, who was commissioned for the work by the Fatimids' Armenian general, Badr al-Gamali.

Splendid views southwards take in the mosque of Al-Hakim and a thousand domes and minarets. North is the Husayniyyah quarter, already a thriving settlement in the 14th century, famous for its patriotism, its butchers and glassblowers, and its saint, Shaykh Bayumi. Northeast and east are areas that were used for centuries as cemeteries, but where nowadays the living far outnumber the dead. Two great historians, Ibn Khaldun (1332–1406) and Maqrizi (1364–1442) are buried here not far from Bab an-Nasr, but the precise location of their graves has been lost under modern municipal development.

Shari al-Gamaliyyah leads south towards Al-Azhar from the Bab an-Nasr. It is lined with the ramshackle remains of several old *wakalat*: great doorways, courtyards adapted to new purposes, and skeletons of buildings, which have usually been stripped of their *mashrabiyyah* and turned into Dickensian slums. Two fine examples of domestic architecture are to be found in side streets.

Merchants' houses: **Bayt as-Sihaymi** is number 19 in the Darb al-Asfar, a lane

In the courtyard of Bayt as-Sihaymi.

that connects Shari al-Gamaliyyah with the Qasabah. Privately owned until 1961, this wonderful old residence is actually two houses joined into one, with a wealth of balconies, loggias and *mashrabiyyah*-screened windows surrounding a leafy courtyard, with a garden behind. The special province of the master of the house was the ground floor, where he conducted business, entertaining more important friends in a great reception room. The women of the household lived upstairs, secluded in a series of charmingly appointed chambers. Their main sitting room, overhanging the northern end of the courtyard, is decorated with Damascus tiles, rows of little cupboards, and a collection of blue-and-white export china. Sunlight filtered by *mashrabiyyah* moves across deep-cushioned window seats, beneath which is a secret cavity where valuables were hidden.

Further down Shari al-Gamaliyyah, past a picturesque corner where a mosque, a school, two *wakalat* and one or two other *mashrabiyyah*-clad old buildings congregate to form a fine ensemble, another lane leads off to the east. At the end of it is the **Musafir-Khanah** (1779–88), a great house also built round a courtyard, containing many finely decorated rooms. Bought by the Muhammad Ali family, it became the birthplace of the future Khedive Ismail in 1830. For the pedestrian walking back westwards from here towards the Qasabah, through a *suq* selling weights and weighing machines to Maydan Bayt al-Qadi, there is a fine view of the Qalawun complex and the Bayn al-Qasrayn.

Fringing the Qasabah southward from the Coppersmiths' Bazaar is a network of tiny alleys. In them and on the street itself are popular bazaars geared to the Cairene shopper, not to the tourist. Part of the **Suq al-Attariin** (**Herbalists' Bazaar**) is to the right, announced by the fragrances of cinnamon and cumin, saffron, coriander, cloves, cardamom and many mysterious roots, pods and

shrabiyyah tiling in as-aymi.

seeds neatly displayed in open sacks. In a shadowy court around the corner people may be pounding and sifting, throwing up clouds of golden dust.

Essences in rows of sticky bottles exude a heady mixture of smells: attar (the word is Arabic) of roses, jasmine, and lotus, the oils of sandalwood and myrrh with which the Mamluks were wont to anoint their fastidious persons. These days such heavenly odours are just as likely to have come in a plastic container from France, where they can be bought cheaply and in bulk, as from some field in the Fayyum, much less a romantic hillside in Andalusia or Khorassan.

Next comes a warren of shops selling fabric (*qumaash*), a subject in every household second in importance only to food. Cotton goods, tablecloths, sheets, curtains, winding sheets, crocheted buttons, bindings, edgings and laces, are stacked to the roofs. Dominating business here is a famous shop called **Ouf's**, which sells cloth in every form and is a Cairene institution.

Both the Herbalists' Bazaar and the cloth market extend south of Shari Al-Azhar, which cuts through Al-Qahirah at this point and can only be crossed by using a green-painted iron bridge. The section of the Qasabah immediately on the other side of Shari Al-Azhar was the subject of one of David Roberts' most famous lithographs, which shows it as it was in 1839. Traditionally designated as the **Silk-Mercers' Bazaar**, it still offers bales of rayon, nylon, cotton and muslin for sale.

The Ghuriyyah: The area that contains this bazaar is called the **Ghuriyyah,** thanks to its having been mostly owned by one of the last Mamluk sultans, Qansuh al-Ghuri, In 1504 he built the mausoleum and *madrasah* that stand here on opposite sides of the Qasabah: Roberts' lithograph shows the space between them roofed to create a covered bazaar. Al-Ghuri also built the Wakalat al-Ghuri that is described above, as well as a palace – its remains

are still visible behind the mausoleum – and a superb *hammam* (bath), which was restored in 1990 by Egyptian Antiquities Organisation. The *hammam* can be reached by plunging into the tunnel at the right corner of the mosque and bearing on past shops and crumbling walls for about 100 metres. Al-Ghuri's buildings together constitute the last great Mamluk architectural complex.

Rugs, handwoven white blankets, and the woollen shawls and scarves that are worn with such panache by men from Upper Egypt and the Sudan are sold in the dimly-lit Tunisian Bazaar (Suq al-Ifriqiyyah), a passage parallel to the Qasabah to the right. Southwards on the Qasabah shops display all manner of household goods: brass bedsteads, tarboushes (the only such shops left in Cairo), feather dusters, and mountains of flimsy shoes.

Beyond another mosque and another *sabil* the street jogs right, then passes between the Wakalah of Nafisa Bayda (As-Sukkariyyah, "The Sugarhouse") **In the Herbalists' Bazaar.**

174

and the great **Mosque of Muayyad Shaykh** before arriving at the Bab Zuwayla. Muayyad had been gaoled on this site for drunkenness by his master Barquq and swore that if he survived he would demolish the prison and build a mosque on the spot. When he became sultan himself in 1412, he spared no expense to fulfil the vow.

For this last great courtyard mosque, Muayyad erected two imposing minarets on the top of the adjacent Fatimid gate and built an adjoining bath complex that is palatial in scale. The interior of the mosque is decorated most lavishly, in marble and stucco, ebony, mother of pearl and blue faience. As a crowning touch he bought the bronze and silver doors from the mosque of Sultan Hasan and had the portal of his own new structure, completed in 1420, redesigned to fit them.

The massive **Bab Zuwayla**, finished in 1092, marks the southern boundary of Al-Qahirah. It is built in the same formidable style as the two northern gates; and through it, before the Ottoman Conquest, no fewer than six caliphs and 56 sultans passed in victory or defeat. Only the élite would have been admitted in the days of the Fatimid caliphs, when its great iron-studded doors would have been heavily guarded, ready to be heaved shut at any threat of civil unrest. By Circassian Mamluk times, however, they had obviously ceased to have any military significance.

From the Mosque of al-Muayyad Shaykh there is access to the top of the gate, where echoes of 10 centuries drift up from the street below. Here executions were traditionally carried out, the most famous being that of the last Mamluk sultan, the handsome and heroic Ashraf Tumanbey, hanged here by Selim the Grim in 1517. As the noose tightened round his neck a vast crowd of Cairenes assembled to witness roared out the opening words of the Holy Qur'an – "Bismillah ar-Rahman ar-Rahim!" – "In the name of God, the Merciful, the Compassionate!" – three times.

tside the timid walls
Bab
wayla.

THE CITADEL

The Citadel, the most prominent landmark on Cairo's eastern skyline, was originally built by Salah ad-Din (1171–93). Sited on a steep limestone spur that rises 245 ft (75 metres) above the city, it functioned as both a fortress and a miniature royal city. It thus continued what was already a tradition among Cairo's rulers, who had tended for centuries to build enclosures for themselves, their families, and their retainers at a watchful distance from their ordinary subjects. Within its walls they could isolate themselves from the common people, yet keep an eye fixed on the country's daily affairs. Here, unobserved by their subjects below, sultans and pashas acted out their miniature dramas of power for nearly 800 years.

Salah ad-Din: According to legend, Salah ad-Din chose this outcropping of the Muqattam hills as the site of his Citadel because of its healthy air. He is said to have tested the atmosphere at various places in Cairo by hanging up pieces of raw meat in each site. Everywhere the meat rotted after only a day and a night – except on the Muqattam range overlooking the city, where it remained fresh for more than two days.

The spur of the Muqattam escarpment where the Citadel now stands had long been famous in any case for its cool breeze. In AD 810 the Abbasid governor Hatim ibn Harthama had built a pleasure pavilion, known as "The Dome of the Winds", on the site, far from his troublesome subjects, where he could enjoy his summer evenings with handpicked singing girls and his drinking companions.

The devout Salah ad-Din had little time for such frivolities. Despite the legend of the meat, his main concern was not the healthy climate of the elevation, but its military advantages. He had been reared in Syria, where every town had its own citadel serving as the local stronghold for the ruling prince; and the Muqattam spur was the only natural site for such a Syrian-style fortress. Its central position enabled Salah ad-Din to dominate Cairo, while posing a major obstacle to any invader.

The Citadel's original **Ayyubid walls and towers** were erected between 1176 and 1183, using the most up-to-date of the castle-building technology developed out of 100 years of resistance to the Crusaders. The stone walls are 30 ft (10 metres) high and 10 ft (3 metres) thick, with upper ramparts and interior corridors. Round towers project from their outer face, allowing the defending garrison to direct flanking fire at enemy soldiers trying to scale the walls.

Within the Citadel, the **Bir Yusuf (Salah ad-Din's Well)** supplied the fortress with its own sacrosanct source of drinking water. Cut 285 ft (87 metres) through solid rock down to the level of the Nile, its shaft is wide enough to contain a ramp for the animals that supplied the power for the machinery that

lifted the water. A masterpiece of medieval engineering, the well was one of the Citadel's most frequently-visited tourist attractions in the 19th century, but is unfortunately closed to the 20th-century public.

The reign of the second Ayyubid, Sultan al-Adil (1200–18), was spent consolidating the empire founded by his brother, Salah ad-Din. Throughout Syria and Egypt, all the citadels in his domain were either rebuilt or enlarged. In 1207 he personally supervised the reconstruction of the Citadel of Damascus, while his son Al-Kamil, governor of Egypt, strengthened the fortifications of Cairo. Some of the towers built by Salah ad-Din – the **Burg al-Haddad (Blacksmith's Tower),** for example, and the **Burg ar-Ramlah (Sand Tower),** which controlled the narrow pass between the Citadel and the Muqattam hills – were now felt to be too small for adequate defence and were more than tripled in size by being encased in gigantic new constructions.

Around the perimeter of the walls Al-Kamil planted multi-storeyed and well fortified square keeps up to 80 ft (25 metres) high and nearly 100 ft (30 metres) wide. Three of these massive square towers can still be seen overlooking the Citadel car parking area, just off Shari Salah Saalem.

On the death of his father, Al-Kamil (1218–38) became the first Ayyubid sultan to live in the Citadel. He built a palace complex in what is today the Southern Enclosure and established the royal stables beneath the western slope of the Citadel hill on Maydan ar-Rumaylah, which is currently known as Maydan Salah ad-Din. Although nothing of Al-Kamil's palace survives, its site remained the centre of the Egyptian government until the second half of the 19th century.

Mamluks move in: After the Mamluks overthrew the Ayyubids in 1250, their first great sultan, Baybars al-Bunduqdari (1260–77), isolated the palace compound of Al-Kamil from the rest of the

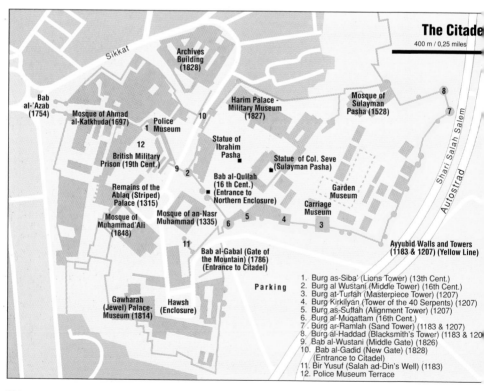

Citadel by constructing an interior wall that divided the fortress into two enclosures linked by an inner gate, the **Bab al-Qullah**. The **Northern Enclosure** contained the barracks of the sultan's army and the offices of his secretariat, responsible for keeping the fiscal and administrative records of the Mamluk state. All public entrances led into this part of the fortress, where visitors were carefully screened before being allowed to pass through the Bab al-Qullah into the more restricted palace grounds of the **Southern Enclosure.**

During the various reigns of An-Nasir Muhammad (1294–95, 1299–1309, 1310–41), most of the earlier buildings in the Southern Enclosure were torn down and replaced by much grander structures, which would better reflect the majesty of the Mamluk Sultanate. The only building of this new Mamluk complex still standing, however, is the **Mosque of an-Nasir Muhammad**, begun in 1318, finally finished in 1335, next to the Bab al-Qullah. One of the

finest arcaded-style mosques in Cairo, it is in fact the only Mamluk building in the Citadel to survive more or less intact down to our own time. Its inner court is surrounded by a series of elegantly proportioned double arches, supported by a virtual museum of reused Pharaonic and Roman-period columns.

The interior marble decoration, originally 16 ft (5 metres) high, was stripped from the walls in 1517 in the aftermath of the Ottoman conquest of Egypt. The two minarets have upper pavilions covered in ceramic tiles, a Persian decorative technique that had a brief vogue in Cairo after An-Nasir Muhammad established peace with the Mongols of Iran and a master mason came from Tabriz to work in his service.

West of the mosque was the great **Hall of Justice**, where the sultan held public audience twice a week. It was surmounted by a huge green dome, which towered above the other structures in the Southern Enclosure. Beside the Hall of Justice was the **Qasr al-**

Ablaq (Striped Palace), constructed of alternating courses of black and yellow marble. The Striped Palace was used for official ceremonies and for conducting affairs of state. Erected in part on a platform artificially built up against the western side of the Citadel hill and thus overlooking Maydan ar-Rumaylah, it had a private staircase leading down to the **Royal Stables** in the **Lower Enclosure**, where An-Nasir Muhammad kept his 4,800 horses.

Women's quarters: The **Royal Harem** was on the site now occupied by the Mosque of Muhammad Ali. It was surrounded by a wall and contained numerous pavilions, separated by small gardens and arcaded walkways. Each of the sultan's four acknowledged wives had her own building within the compound and controlled her own household staff. The harem had additional accommodation for over 1,200 people, including concubines, slave girls, and other palace servants. The barracks of the eunuchs guarded the main entrance to the

harem, the Bab as-Sitara (Veil Gate), which led to the Citadel kitchens and Salah ad-Din's Well.

A passageway running beside the Royal Harem connected An-Nasir Muhammad's mosque with the **Hawsh (Enclosure)** at the southernmost tip of the palace complex, added to the Citadel in 1335, when an Ayyubid quarry was filled with earth, levelled, and enclosed with walls. In the Hawsh the sultan received his male friends and held informal court ceremonies on such occasions as the Prophet's birthday, when hundreds of Sufi mystics were brought to the Citadel to chant the Qur'an throughout festivities that lasted all night long. Apart from reception rooms and meeting halls, the Hawsh also contained a private garden, a polo field, and the royal stockade, where 2,000 head of cattle were kept ready at hand beneath the Citadel kitchens.

Ottoman rule: Under the **Ottoman governors** (1517–1798), the Citadel remained the administrative headquarters of Cairo, but the authority of the provincial government was carefully divided to ensure that no one challenged the sovereignty of the sultan in Istanbul. The governor thus had no jurisdiction over the *defterdar* (treasurer) or over the commanders of the Ottoman Janissary and Azab regiments stationed in the fortress. These troops, in turn, were forbidden all contact with the Egyptian population and were not allowed to marry until after they had retired: the name *Azab*, in fact, means "bachelor". The Citadel was thus divided among these different Ottoman factions. The governor lived in the Hawsh, the Azab troops occupied the lower stables and the Janissaries controlled the Northern Enclosure.

Squeezed among these rival centres of power, the palace complex of the former Mamluk sultans was claimed by no one and gradually fell into ruin. During the 16th century, however, the Ottomans rebuilt the Bab al-Qullah and the interior wall separating the Northern

Prison cell i the Citadel.

and Southern Enclosures. They also erected the massive **Burg al-Muqattam,** which today rises above the entrance of the Citadel off Salah Saalem Highway. The tallest tower in the fortress, it is 80 ft (25 metres) high and has a diameter of 79 ft (24 metres).

Three of the four surviving mosques in the Citadel date from the four centuries between 1517 and 1914, when Egypt was an Ottoman province. To provide his regiment with their own place of prayer, a commander of the Azab troops, Ahmad al-Katkhuda, built a mosque in 1697 within the lower stables. Its pencil-shaped Ottoman minaret is still visible from the square directly beneath the Citadel, but the interior is unfortunately in ruins and it is currently closed to the public. In 1754, another Azab commander rebuilt the outer walls of the Lower Enclosure and added the fortified gate called the **Bab al-Azab.** A prominent landmark, the gate is defended by two towers, which project into Maydan ar-Rumaylah and have been

strikingly restored by the industrious Egyptian Antiquities Organisation.

The strictures governing the lives of the janissaries and the Azab troops began to break down in the late 16th century, when a sequence of incompetent sultans lost control of the Ottoman Empire. Soldiers were allowed not only to marry, but also to build houses for their families within the Citadel. By the mid-17th century it had become an enclosed residential district complete with private domiciles, shops, markets, coffee houses and public baths, all interconnected by a maze-like network of streets. As regimental discipline declined still further, soldiers drifted off into civilian careers and eventually became little more than armed artisans and shopkeepers who were living within the Citadel walls.

The Janissaries and Azab troops were finally evicted from the Citadel during the brief French occupation of Egypt (1798–1801), when Napoleon Bonaparte garrisoned the fortress with his

a-stall ner and liceman, e Citadel.

own troops. The *savants* accompanying his army were impressed by the Mamluk ruins in the Southern Enclosure, of which they fortunately made a record. Despite the derelict condition of the Mamluk palaces and government buildings, they were regarded by the French as among the most awe-inspiring Islamic monuments in Cairo.

Renovations: Muhammad Ali Pasha (1805–48), however, was no antiquarian. Establishing himself in power after the withdrawal of the French, he set about reorganising the Citadel with the same ruthless determination he brought to all his modernising programmes. The outer walls were rebuilt to suit the needs of a modern army and the decaying medieval buildings in the interior were replaced by the latest Ottoman-style palaces, the most up-to-date European-style barracks, military schools, and armament factories.

It is because Muhammad Ali's renovation of the Citadel was so thorough that visitors now find little in the fortress that dates from before the 19th century. The only Mamluk building he preserved was the **Mosque of an-Nasir Muhammad**, which he found it convenient to convert into a warehouse. What can be seen today is in fact the result of changes made when Muhammad Ali reversed the roles of the two main areas of the Citadel, making the Southern Enclosure public and the Northern Enclosure private, to enclose his own harem palace and the headquarters of his army.

The Southern Enclosure is today dominated by the colossal **Mosque of Muhammad Ali** (1830–48). This building is quite alien in spirit to the characteristic architecture of the rest of the city, which is essentially Mamluk, as later members of the ruling family recognised. Built in the style sometimes called Ottoman Baroque, it imitates the great religious mosques of Istanbul, but lacks the solidity, power, and soaring grace that mark the best Ottoman architecture; and its decoration, a hybrid of

The Military Museum.

184

European, Pharaonic and Islamic designs, strikes some tastes as overwrought, florid, and even gaudy. Whatever its flaws, the mosque's imposing size, spectacular hightly visible setting, apparent importance, and ease of access make it one of the most popular tourist sites in Cairo. Its most impressive feature is the inner prayer hall, where the arrangement of domes and semi-domes, lifted 172 ft (52 metres) above the floor by four gigantic piers, successfully achieves the Ottoman ideal of a vast covered interior space.

The Pasha himself is buried here under a three-tiered white marble cenotaph. The ornate clock tower in the outer court was given to him in 1846 by Louis Philippe, in belated exchange for the obelisk – one of a pair – that the French had removed from in front of the Luxor Temple and set up in the Place de la Concorde in Paris in 1833.

South of the mosque in the Hawsh are the remains of the **Gawharah ("Jewel") Palace**, a rambling, two-storey structure in the Ottoman style favoured by Muhammad Ali. Built between 1811 and 1814, the Gawharah was the centre of the Egyptian government until 1874, when the Khedive Ismail (1863–79), Muhammad Ali's grandson, moved his family and his administration to the vast new Abdiin Palace. A museum for many decades, the Gawharah was gutted by fire in 1972 and partially restored 10 years later. The administrative wing has however not been rebuilt, but a refurbished audience hall and private apartments now display furniture and curios that once belonged to the Muhammad Ali dynasty.

The **National Police Museum**, opposite the Mosque of an-Nasir Muhammad, includes a number of display halls and archaeological remains, which are arranged on and around the terrace that Muhammad Ali built over the site of the Mamluk Striped Palace, using the debris of the demolished Mamluk buildings of the Southern Enclosure as his building material. In 1983 a hall from the Striped Palace was discovered, buried deep beneath the rubble. It can now be seen at the southern end of the terrace. Between 1882 and 1946 various British regiments were quartered in the Citadel to sustain the Occupation (1882–1954/56); one relic of that time is a small military prison. Also visible are a collection of antique fire engines and a museum displaying dioramas of the history of Egyptian law enforcement since Pharaonic times.

This museum is housed in Muhammad Ali's **School of Artillery**, which is perched on top of the 13th-century **Burg as-Siba (Lions' Tower)**. Built by Sultan Baybars al-Bunduqdari, the tower was decorated with a frieze of carved stone lions, which may still be seen. They were the sultan's heraldic emblem, derived from his name, which means "Lord Lion" in Turkish. The main attraction of the Police Museum's terrace, however, is its spectacular view, for it was originally intended as an artillery platform from which the city could be bombarded. From here is the full panorama of medieval Cairo's minarets and domes. On a clear day it is possible to see across the Nile as far as the Pyramids of Gizah.

Mamluk massacre: Beneath the terrace is the Lower Enclosure, once the site of the sultan's stables, now occupied by disused 19th- and 20th-century military factories and warehouses. Running between the buildings directly below the Lions' Tower is a passageway down to Bab al Azab where a famous incident took place in March 1811, when Muhammad Ali invited 470 members of the most powerful Mamluk *bayt* to attend a ceremony at the Citadel. At their departure the Mamluks found the Bab al-Azab locked against them from the outside, trapping them in this narrow passageway with high walls, at the top of which the Pasha's Albanian sharpshooters stood waiting. Those who had not received invitations to these grim festivities were undoubtedly grateful for the snub: legend has it that one Mamluk escaped the slaughter, but that seems unlikely.

Passing through the Bab al-Qullah into the Northern Enclosure brings the visitor to Muhammad Ali's **Harem Palace**, constructed in 1827 in the same Ottoman style as the Gawharah. The statue in front of the entrance is a copy of the equestrian **statue of Ibrahim Pasha** by Charles Cordier that has stood in Maydan Opera since 1882. This palace was a major residence of the viceregal family until 1874, when Khedive Ismail moved his government to Abdiin. Briefly abandoned, it was converted into a military hospital during the British Occupation and returned to Egyptian possession only after World War II.

In 1949 the palace became the permanent home of the **Egyptian Military Museum**, founded by King Faruq (1936–52) to glorify the achievements of the Muhammad Ali dynasty. Since the 1952 Revolution new sections have been added which deal with Egypt's various 20th-century wars, including a whole wing devoted to the October War of 1973.

There are some displays of great interest, though many of the events commemorated are apt to strike most foreigners as somewhat obscure. The palace itself, however, is a fascinating example of 19th-century Ottoman architecture; and the landscape murals, the slim columns with gilt capitals, and the extravagant mouldings on the cornices and ceilings of its great halls are still regarded as the height of good taste by much of Cairene society.

Especially attractive is the Summer Room, which contains an elaborate and beautiful cooling system of marble fountains, basins, and channels, probably the last intact example of such a system in Cairo. Standing in the livery court behind the carriage gate at the southern end of the museum is a **statue of Sulayman Pasha**, which originally stood in Maydan Sulayman Pasha in the centre of the city and was brought here in 1963.

Copy of the statue of Ibrahim Pasha by Charles Cordier.

Beyond the Harem Palace is a small **Carriage Museum**, housed in what was the officers' mess for the British units stationed in the Citadel until 1946. It contains eight carriages formerly used by the Muhammad Ali family, which have been borrowed from the larger Carriage Museum in Bulaq. Behind the museum is the **Burg at-Turfah (Masterpiece Tower)**, the largest and most accessible of the square keeps al-Kamil built in 1207. The wooden floors and white-washed walls of the interior date from the British Occupation, when the tower was used as a warehouse.

At the far end of the Northern Enclosure is the **Mosque of Sulayman Pasha**, erected in 1528 to serve the Janissary regiment quartered in the Northern Enclosure. The first Ottoman-style mosque constructed in Egypt, it reflects the taste of the Turkish armies of occupation rather than the building tradition of Cairo and is a charming example of Ottoman provincial architecture, tiny by the monumental standards of Istanbul, but well kept and welcoming, with a garden that catches cooling breezes. Among the dependencies of the mosque is the shrine of a Muslim saint, Sidi Sarya, which served as a mausoleum for prominent janissary officers. Their graves are marked by tombstones carved with representations of their official headdress.

The Citadel is currently the most popular non-Pharaonic tourist site in Cairo: it is not too far from the Khan al-Khalili bazaar, has parking accommodation for scores of buses, is much less crowded than the city below it, and offers cooler and fresher air. Whether or not modern visitors realise it, these attractions of location, space, privacy, and a better atmosphere are what originally earmarked the Citadel as the favoured residence of Egypt's rulers for nearly eight centuries. The fortress may have changed substantially since the days of the Ayyubids and Mamluks, but in its own strange way it continues to fulfil many of its original functions.

*layman
*sha, the
*st Ottoman-
*le mosque
Egypt.

CITIES OF THE DEAD

Cairo's two greatest Muslim cemeteries – the Northern (or Eastern) Cemetery and the much older Southern Cemetery – fringe the eastern edge of the city below the Muqattam hills. Western journalists refer to them sensationally and collectively as "The City of the Dead", as if they were a single unit, though they actually grew up at different times, are topographically separated by the limestone spur of the Citadel, and have quite different atmospheres. People live in both of them, a situation that the journalists explain by quoting from official statistics showing a housing shortage. Foreigners – even Arabs – made the same observation and offered the same rationale as long ago as the mid-14th century, however, and as far as anyone knows Cairene cemeteries, despite their name, have always housed not only the dead, but also the living.

Traditional rites: Here it is Egyptian tradition, not Muslim law, that prevails. A body is interred on its side facing Mecca, shrouded but uncoffined, in accord with orthodox Muslim stricture. Contrary to the further prescriptions of Islam, however, typical Cairene burial places are not mere unmarked grave sites, but consist of permanent structures, two or three rooms entered through a walled court. The body is placed in a cavity under the courtyard or beneath the floor of one of the rooms and a cenotaph is used to mark the spot. Such permanent structures demand caretakers and guardian, who soon gather communities around them, the more rapidly if the buildings are used for purposes other than occasional interments. Squatters have occupied some rarely used tombs or those whose ownership is obscure, but in others the inhabitants are there perfectly legally, as guardians of their ancestors.

The tombs of popular Cairene saints are always thronged, but on Thursday evenings, Fridays, and major holidays, living Cairenes frequently visit their own family tombs – as ancient Greeks and Romans did and as modern Europeans used to do – to have picnics among the graves. Planned to accommodate visiting family and friends or when necessary to provide a place for staying overnight, modern Cairene tombs are clean, light and airy.

The Mamluk sultans and amirs used their tomb complexes in the cemeteries for parties. Piety provided the excuse, but was otherwise purely incidental. Every guest wore his most extravagant clothes: silk from China – where the host's porcelain cups, bowls, and serving dishes also came from – embroidered by the ladies of his harem, or brocade manufactured in the Mamluks' own workshops. The inlaid metalwork basins, trays, ewers, and cauldrons, or the exquisite fine-knotted carpets and cushion covers against which each princely guest reclined were also of local manufacture.

Amidst an abundance of flowers, perfume and incense, eating, drinking and music probably received most attention, but there were also archery contests or horse-races. The Northern Cemetery actually began as a hippodrome, evolving quite naturally into a royal necropolis only later.

Celebrity shrines: The Fatimids encouraged the cult of saints; tombs built under their rule to serve as saints' shrines include those of a number of relatives of the Prophet. The tombs of Muhammad Gafari (1120) and Sayyidah Atikah (1125), for example, a great-great-great-grandson and an aunt of the Prophet, lie a little south of the mosque of Ibn Tulun near the *Mashhad* (**Shrine**) **of Sayyidah Ruqayya** (1133), a daughter of Ali, nephew and son-in-law of the Prophet. Clustered together in a compound on Shari Khalifa, the continuation of the Qasabah that links the Fatimid enclosure with the Southern Cemetery and Fustat, these three tombs still function as shrines. Muslims visit them to pray for intercession and receive *baraka* (blessing). A visit to Sayyidah Ruqayya, one of the patron saints of Egypt, is considered no less effective for her actually being buried in Damascus. Opposite, in the shadow of an ugly, unfinished-looking mosque, is the **Tomb of Sheger ad-Durr,** wife and widow of the last Ayyubid and, for a few months in 1250, queen of Egypt.

Further down the street is the **Mosque of Sayyidah Nafisah** (died 824), another of the patron saints of Egypt. A popular place, because of its special *baraka*, for couples to go to have their nuptials blessed – Islam prescribes no specific wedding ceremony – the modern mosque (1897) stands on the site of her 9th-century tomb and is particularly beloved by the local populace.

Behind it is the **Tomb of the Abbasid Khalifs** who were reinstated in Cairo after Baghdad was overrun by the Mongols. Their status as successors of the Prophet was used to give legitimacy to Mamluk rule and they served as puppets

until the time of the Ottoman Empire.

The Southern Cemetery: The traveller Ibn Battutah writes in the 14th century that **the Southern Cemetery** is "a place of peculiar sanctity and contains the graves of innumerable scholars and pious believers." By this time it had also become a thriving urban quarter, as today, with its own streets, houses and shops. Its most venerated local shrine is the **Mausoleum of Imam ash-Shafii**, the founder of the Shafiite school of Islamic law, who accompanied Sayyidah Nafisah to Egypt.

The mosque adjoining his tomb dates from 1891, but the tomb itself was first built by order of Salah ad-Din in 1180. Salah ad-Din's carved teakwood cenotaph for the saint still stands in the tomb chamber, which has been partially rebuilt several times and is now surmounted by a lead-covered wooden dome erected in the 18th century. The dome is topped by a small copper boat, weathered green, which was traditionally filled with grain for birds.

A tomb of th Muhamma Ali family.

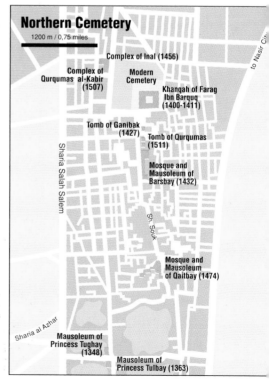

Northern Cemetery

1200 m / 0,75 miles

Complex of Inal (1456)

Complex of Qurqumas al-Kabir (1507)

Modern Cemetery

Khanqah of Farag Ibn Barquq (1400-1411)

Tomb of Ganibak (1427)

Tomb of Qurqumas (1511)

Sharia Salah Salem

Mosque and Mausoleum of Barsbay (1432)

Sh. Souk

Mosque and Mausoleum of Qaitbay (1474)

to Nasir Cit.

Sharia al Azhar

Mausoleum of Princess Tughay (1348)

Mausoleum of Princess Tulbay (1363)

This shrine attracts pilgrims from all over the Muslim world. Supplicants circumnambulate the cenotaph or sit before it, meditating, quietly praying, chanting aloud, or perhaps imploring through tears. The infirm come seeking health; the dying sometimes come to die. They speak to the cenotaph as if it were the saint in person and murmur a tender "*Ma-salaama, ma-salaama!*" – "Goodbye, goodbye!" – in parting.

Near the shrine of Imam ash-Shafii is the **Hawsh al-Basha,** constructed by Muhammad Ali in 1820 as his family tomb, though he himself is buried at the Citadel. The exterior of the Hawsh is unpromising, but the interior is maintained by the family in all its splendour, with Ottoman baroque cenotaphs jostling for space under a circus-awning ceiling. In one small chamber some of the Pasha's own guard of Mamluks are buried. They are not, as one guidebook claims, victims of the famous massacre of Mamluks that he perpetrated at the Citadel in 1811, but Circassian body-guards and servants he purchased for himself and his family.

The tombs of many Bahri Mamluk amirs stand in the Southern Cemetery, distinguished by their domes and minarets. A freestanding minaret and a pair of ribbed domes on either side of an arch mark the **Sultaniyyah** (c.1360), for example, a tomb complex that originally included a *khanqah*, a retreat for Sufis. The neighbouring **Tomb of Amir Qawsun** (1335) is similar, but little remains of the original building save the dome and another freestanding minaret, this one topped by a ribbed cap. Older tombs, including that of Egypt's only famous medieval poet, the mystic Ibn al-Faarid (1182–1235), lie close to the foot of the Muqattam Hills.

The Northern Cemetery: Where a fortified wall used to divide the **Northern Cemetery** from the city a six-lane highway now serves, preserving the cemetery as a haven from Cairo's crowds, noise, exhaust fumes, and grey concrete. The cemetery's sandy streets wind

wlid **in the thern etery.**

between buildings and are mostly too narrow for cars, which are therefore replaced here by donkey carts. In addition to its large human population, of which not many are usually in view, the Northern Cemetery also offers sheep, goats, cats and chickens.

The first tombs in the Northern Cemetery were those of Sufis who had retreated to the desert in search of seclusion. By the 14th century the city had already spread 8 miles (13 km) north and south and land was at a premium. In this desert area northeast of Salah ad-Din's walls, however, there was still open space; and it was here that Sultan An-Nasir Muhammad (1294–1341) indulged the Mamluk passion for horsemanship by building a hippodrome, which has since disappeared.

Still extant in part, however, are the mausolea of the Uzbek **Princess Tulbay** (1363), his principal wife, and of the Qipchaq **Princess Tughay** (1348), a freed slave-girl, his favourite, the sultan's preference being clearly reflected

in the relative size of the two tombs.

The **Khanqah of Farag ibn Barquq** (1410), one of five great complexes in the cemetery, is also one of the most impressive buildings in Cairo. It took 11 years to build. Sultan Barquq's son, Sultan Farag, who ordered the construction, could work in the desert on a scale and with a freedom that constrictions in the city would not have allowed. Almost square in plan, it has symmetrical twin domes and minarets. The fortress-like initial effect belies the serenity of the interior. The splendidly decorated tomb chambers, restored in the 1980s and a bit raw-looking for modern tastes, may well have been retouched by Ottoman painters.

North of this complex are two others: the five-part **complex of Sultan Inal** (1456) and the enormous **complex of Amir Qurqumas al-Kabir** (1507), both part of long-term projects undertaken by the Polish-Egyptian Group for Restoration of Islamic Monuments. A hundred yards (91 metres) south of the Khanqah of Farag ibn Barquq, beyond two small domed tombs – one of them is the Tomb of Qurqumas, brutally transplanted here in 1980 from its original site at the entrance of the mosque of Al-Hakim in Al-Qahirah – is the **complex of Sultan Ashraf Barsbay**. The main building, constructed in 1432 for the sultan and his family, is a mosque with a tomb, under a carved stone dome that exhibits the first use of the star motif. Next to the mosque are the remains of a *khanqah*, but the buildings have long since disappeared.

Mamluk jewel: The **Mosque of Qaytbay** (1472) is further down the same road. Depicted on the Egyptian one-pound note, it is an architectural jewel and was likewise part of a large complex: the drinking trough and partially restored apartment house (*rab'*) to the north, the gateway to the south, and the group of buildings immediately west are all contemporary and were part of the same foundation. The mosque, however, was undoubtedly the focus.

Tomb resident.

The dusty square in front of it is the best place to admire its elegance. The appeal of the interior may depend upon whether or not the windows in the prayer hall are opened, to show the manipulation of light and space. Elsewhere in the building an ingenious arrangement of vents, apertures and shafts suffuses everything with lambency. The artfulness of its design and construction can be appreciated further by ascending the minaret. Apart from the view it provides a good vantage point for a look at the dome: with its intricate intertwining of star and floral motifs, stone carving in Cairo reached its apex.

Around the corner to the left is a glassblower's establishment, where so-called "Muski" glass is offered in designs that never otherwise reach the market. Immediately to the west of the mosque stands Qaytbay's reception hall, which is now used as a school, while the schoolyard doubles as a sheepfold. Here, to the accompaniment of children reciting, chattering, and screaming, the local flock is born, reared, sheared and slaughtered. Nineteenth-century photographs show the Northern Cemetery sparsely settled, with many open spaces. The 1967 war led the government to build low-cost housing for refugees nearby and row upon row of concrete blocks stretch northward.

In both cemeteries municipal services have begun to be provided, including gas, water, electricity, post offices, bus stops, and even police stations. For the Northern Cemetery's inhabitants the monuments are another service: Sufis use the Mosque of Barquq, children receive Qur'anic tuition in the Mosque of Barsbay, and the Mosque of Qaytbay makes a convenient anchor for one end of a washing line. Figures from 1937 give the tomb-dwelling population as 10,000; and by 1980 it had grown only to 25,000, showing a rate of increase far lower than elsewhere in the city. Since 1980, however, the Northern Cemetery has been increasingly invaded by neighbouring quarters.

main street tombs.

AZBAKIYYAH

The **Azbakiyyah** was originally a seasonal pond that covered about 45 acres (18 hectares) between the walled enclosure of Al-Qahirah and the Nile and was filled every July and August by the annual Nile flood, which entered the lake through a canal. North of the pond was the predominantly Coptic quarter of Al-Maqs, which was identified among Muslims with the manufacture of alcoholic drinks and therefore had a somewhat louche reputation.

In 1484 the Circassian Mamluk amir Azbak min Tutuh cleared the canal, deepened the pond, and built a palace on its southern shore, overlooking a street known as **al-Atabah al-Zarqa** (The Blue Threshold). The palace was named the Azbakiyyah, after its owner, and gave its name in turn to the elegant entertainment district that soon grew up around the pond, a popular retreat for Mamluk grandees, who would sail on the lake on late-summer evenings, listening to music or indulging in less licit pleasures.

Fashionable suburb: Under the Ottoman governors (1517–1798) the Azbakiyyah developed into a genteel suburb inhabited by rich merchants and government officials. By the 18th century the southern shore of the Azbakiyyah had become the stronghold of the Mamluk beys. Around the lake, which had already begun to replace the Citadel as the real centre of the Egyptian government, they constructed mosques and palaces.

The most magnificent **Mamluk palace** on the Azbakiyyah was built on the western bank of the lake in 1798 by Muhammad Bey al-Alfi (Alfi Bey). The year it was completed, however, the French invaded, the Mamluks were expelled, and Napoleon Bonaparte commandeered the palace as his personal residence. He ordered the lake to be drained, dyked and turned into a large

square. It then served as a parade ground, where pageants were staged for the benefit of Egyptian notables, whom Bonaparte hoped to win to his side. But the doctrines of *liberté, égalité,* and *fraternité* fell on deaf ears. Within three months of Bonaparte's arrival the city rose in the first of many revolts, to be bombarded into submission by French artillery. Most palaces around what had been the southern shore were destroyed.

Muhammad Ali: After the French withdrawal in 1801 the Azbakiyyah once again became a lake. In the ensuing struggle between the Mamluks and the Ottoman army the area suffered further damage, though the Christian quarter of Al-Maqs, just to the north, had some luck: a wealthy Coptic official was of such service to the Ottoman sultan's sister during her visit to Egypt that she secured permission for him to build a new church there. Constructed in 1800 on what is now Shari Kanisat al-Marqusiyyah, between Shari Clot Bey and Shari Gumhuriyyah, it became the seat of the Coptic Patriarchate. A new building in the Greek style, the present **Church of St Mark at Azbakkiyah**, replaced it on the same site in the 1860s and remained the seat of the Patriarchate until the modern Cathedral of St Mark was consecrated in Abbasiyyah a century later.

Muhammad Ali Pasha (1805–48) redeveloped the Azbakiyyah. Along its southern shore, which was renamed **al-Atabah al-Khadra** (The Green Threshold), he constructed his family's own palaces and gardens, as well as public buildings in the latest Istanbul style. In 1837 the depression that held the seasonal lake was permanently filled and a park was laid out on the site, while Shari al-Muski, the focus of the foreign diplomatic and mercantile community, was widened and extended.

More modernisation: Two theatres and several taverns left behind by the French still did business and were soon joined by Cairo's first European-style hotels: the Hôtel Giardino, where Gérard de

Nerval stayed in the spring of 1843; the Hôtel Coulomb, founded by the Pasha's own cook; the Hôtel du Nil, where Gustave Flaubert resided during December 1849 and January 1850; and the New British Hotel, founded a few months earlier by an Englishman named Samuel Shepheard, an establishment that was to become the most famous of all Cairo's hostelries under its later name – **Shepheard's British Hotel**. It occupied what had once been the grounds of the palace of Muhammad Bey al-Alfi, where Napoleon had made his headquarters.

Inspired in part by the renovation of Paris carried out under Napoleon III, Khedive Ismail (1863–79) began in 1867 to build a modern, carefully planned, European-style Cairo, with the Azbakiyyah as its heart. He reduced the size of Muhammad Ali's park and transformed it into a formal garden, containing a central pond, fountains and exotic trees. Shari al-Muski had already become a Western-style commercial district, with shops, restaurants, theatres, and hotels catering to an increasingly cosmopolitan local taste. Old palaces were torn down to make way for roads and public buildings, including a new **Khedivial Opera House**, which was inaugurated with a gala performance of *Rigoletto* on 29 November 1869, one of the highlights connected with the opening of the Suez Canal.

Around his new garden Ismail laid out large squares, from which radiated broad straight streets lit by gas and lined with arcaded pavements. These streets connected Azbakiyyah and Shari al-Muski with the main railway station (first opened in 1854), the Abdiin Palace (completed in 1874), and the rest of the Khedive's new capital. Shari al-Muski was extended beyond the Khalig al-Misri to the Mosque of al-Husayn and other streets – Shari Muhammad Ali, for example – were likewise cut into medieval Cairo, linking it to the modern city.

During the reigns of Tewfiq, Abbas II Hilmi, Husayn Kamil, Fu'ad, and Faruq, which included 70 years of the British Occupation (1882–1952), the Azbakiyyah enjoyed a continuing heyday as the fashionable centre of modern Cairo. New luxury apartments and office buildings were constructed throughout the district for the city's expanding population of Europeans and wealthy Egyptians. Around the Azbakiyyah garden were to be found the largest department stores in Cairo, such as the extravagantly baroque Umar Effendi on Shari Abd al-Aziz and the Art-Nouveau Sednaoui's on Maydan al-Khazindar.

Edwardian elegance: Elegant new hotels replaced comparatively modest establishments: Shepheard's, rebuilt on more sumptuous lines in 1891, with its famous terrace overlooking the thoroughfare connecting the city's main railway station with Abdiin Palace; the Continental, a sumptuously decorated rival, opposite the Opera House; the Eden Palace on Maydan al-Khazindar; and at least half a dozen other establish-

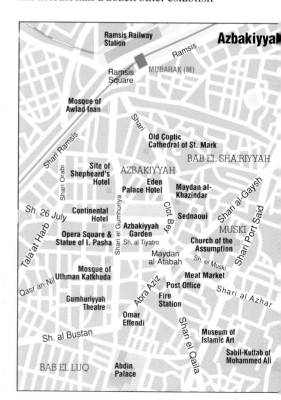

198

ments that combined the conveniences of Europe with the luxury of the Orient. These grand hotels made the Azbakiyyah the focus of Cairo's social season, when Western tourists and foreign residents spent the winter in a round of sightseeing, sport, tea-dances, fancy-dress balls, concerts, and formal dinners.

Maydan al-Atabah, where the palace of Amir Azbak once stood, became the site of Cairo's post office and fire station, as well as the main terminus for the newly introduced electric tramways, which by 1905 had been extended throughout the city. As the Azbakiyyah continued to grow in importance, new streets, wide enough for automobiles, were added to Ismail's original plan. In 1927 Shari al-Azhar was pushed through the heart of the medieval city to run parallel to Shari al-Muski, which had proven too narrow for the motorised vehicles of the 20th century.

Azbakiyyah and the streets to the north also provided more profane entertainment: this was a red-light zone referred to as the Wasaa, with European, Egyptian, Nubian and Sudanese prostitutes.

The district today: It is hard to imagine that the Azbakiyyah was ever fashionable. This once-prosperous heart of Ismail's new capital is now a shabby border zone, where modern Cairo gradually blends into the medieval city. Its most famous landmarks have either been destroyed or become dilapidated relics of an extremely bygone era. The exquisite wooden Opera House, for example, with its entire historic collection of manuscripts, costumes, and sets, was burned to the ground in October 1971 and on its site the government has planted a multi-level car park. Cordier's equestrian statue of Ibrahim Pasha, Ismail's father, moved here from the other side of Azbakiyyah in 1882, still holds pride of place in the centre of the square, however, which will probably always be known in Cairo as **Maydan Opera** (al-Ubira).

Across the street, the Hotel Continental has been nationalised. Stripped of

dnaoui's
ce world-
nous
partment
re was
tored in
89.

claims to either comfort or charm, it has only its imposing size to suggest that it was once the rival of Shepheard's. But what of Shepheard's itself? North of Opera Square, on the corner of Shari al-Gumhuriyyah and Shari Muhammad Bey al-Alfi, a vacant lot enclosed by a wall of billboards marks its site. Burned to the ground in the Black Saturday arson attacks presaging the 1952 Revolution, it survives only as luxurious legend, a myth of elegance and prestige that has no relation at all to its current namesake on the Nile Corniche or, indeed, to any of Cairo's new hotels.

Perhaps the most telling symbol of the district's decline is the Azbakiyyah garden itself. After the 1952 Revolution, Shari 26 July was extended eastward, cutting the garden in half and making nonsense of its design. Its central pond was buried under asphalt and concrete. The construction of a bus depot, a traffic authority building, and other public-sector structures reduced what was left of its green space by

another third. It is now surrounded by a metal barricade and barbed wire, which further disfigure it, but do nothing to prevent people from walking on its withered grass.

The Azbakiyyah was built for Cairo in the late 19th century, when it was inhabited by 600,000 people. Today the area's crumbling pavements with their broken arcades are jammed with people, its share of the city's over-population, while the broad streets that were built with such pride by Ismail are choked with creeping cars, crammed buses, and creaking trams. Wonderful old buildings throughout the area, the few reminders of former splendour, are abused, neglected, ignored or simply obscured by exhaust fumes.

Lively market: And yet, for all its decline, the Azbakiyyah remains lively and even vibrant, filled with thriving shops, stalls and open-air markets. They offer their merchandise not to the rich and fashionable, but to the city's poor and middle-class. Establishments selling goods of the same kind tend to group themselves together, in the manner of a bazaar, where zones are defined by what is sold in them. In Maydan al-Atabah, for example, are second-hand watches, used sunglasses, kitchenware, clothes, and cassette players, not to mention some of the seediest bars in town.

In areas between such main thoroughfares, along side streets that have often remained unchanged since before Ismail built his modern city, are still more markets of other kinds: the distribution centre for recycled glass and paper, the sweetmakers' quarter (identified as such since Ottoman times), a wholesale meat market (not recommended for the squeamish), and shops supplying all the paraphernalia for Egyptian funerals or weddings. And rising above this teeming commercial activity, which clearly follows an urban logic that is more medieval than modern, are the decaying buildings of Azbakiyyah's *belle époque*. Such topsy-turvy juxtapositions are part of the city's charm.

Left, provocative pose in Maydan Opera. Righ one of **Donington's illustrations** for *The Arabian Nights.*

CITY OF ARABIAN NIGHTS

The cycle of tales that Westerners call *The Arabian Nights' Entertainment* – or just *The Arabian Nights* – is always known in the Middle East as *The Thousand and One Nights*. and is based upon a much smaller earlier collection, called *The Thousand Nights*, which is not Arab in origin at all, but Persian. Nor is it a secret that the great city at the heart of *The Arabian Nights* as we now read them is not really Baghdad in the reign of the Abbasid caliph Harun ar-Rashid (AD 786–809), but Cairo as it was under the Burgi Mamluks (AD 1382–1517). Edward William Lane (1801–76), the great Arabist and ethnographer who made the classic English translation, believed that most of the tales in *The Arabian Nights* were in fact written by a late-medieval Cairene.

Near the beginning of "The Tale of the Jewish Physician" occurs a famous encomium on the city: "He who hath not seen Cairo hath not seen the world: her soil is gold, her Nile is a marvel; her women are like the black-eyed houris of Paradise; her houses are palaces; and her air is soft, more odorous than aloes-wood, rejoicing the heart. And how can Cairo be otherwise when she is the Mother of the World?"

The Mother of the World is an old lady now and somewhat longer in the tooth than when that description was penned. Her palaces are rapidly being demolished to make way for jerry-built concrete high-rises and her air, though still temperate, has achieved one of the world's highest pollution indexes. She has become, in other words, a thoroughly modern Third-World metropolis. There is nevertheless something to be said for her wondrous Nile and for Cairene women. And gold not only still surfaces occasionally from her soil, but does so in ways that might been excerpted from the stories of Sindbad or Ali Baba.

In 1990, for example, *Saidi* workmen employed by the Egyptian Antiquities Organisation were repairing the house of Zaynab Khatun in the neighbourhood of Al-Azhar. Most of the house dates from the early 18th century, but one portion was built in 1482. Unknown to the bureaucrats supervising them, the workmen found a secret chamber, a stone-lined pit under a layer of tiles, that had been installed in the older part of the house by its original owner. And in the pit they found several clay pots filled with gold coins, nearly 3,000 of them in all, dating from the reigns of the Burgi Mamluk sultans, which were worth millions in London or Geneva. The coins were legally the property of the Egyptian state, but the *Saidi* workmen, being human, divided the cache among themselves. They were eventually apprehended: when a handful of the coins were sold for a pittance to a fence, one of them thought the others had cheated him out of a few pounds, lost his temper, and revealed everything to the police.

Every old house in Cairo contains such hiding places, ranging from cubicles the size of a strongbox to spaces big enough to hold several people standing upright; and larger buildings are apt to sit over one or more underground passages or tunnels. A long-forgotten tunnel to the river was found, for example, when a hospital was demolished in Garden City in 1986: though less than 50 years old, it had been built on the site of a 15th-century palace, whose owners had provided themselves with a secret escape passage to the Nile.

At Bayt ar-Razzaz in Darb al-Ahmar, there are similar tunnels leading to an unknown destination somewhere in the middle of the city. Since the tunnels are infested with vipers, which undoubtedly contribute to the salubrity of the neighbourhood by keeping down the vermin, this destination is likely to remain a mystery. At the complex of Qurqumas al-Kabir, on the other hand, in the Northern Cemetery, a magnificent system of underground chambers and passageways has been cleared by a Polish restoration team and thoroughly investigated.

Edward William Lane is most famous for his *Manners and Customs of the Modern Egyptians,* an account of Cairo life as he saw it between 1825 and 1849. Though the city was being transformed by Muhammad Ali, enough of medieval tradition remained for Lane to be able to use his own experience to help him understand the colourful ways described in *The Arabian Nights*. Even now those ways have not totally disappeared.

BULAQ AND ZAMALEK

Far off the usual tourist track and still linked to the rest of the city by just two main roads, the Corniche and Shari 26 July, **Bulaq** is an interesting place to visit. Its southernmost zone, just north of the Nile Hilton and the Egyptian Museum, has been rechristened Maspero, to honour the Museum's first director. It is dominated by the **Ramses Hilton** hotel, the **Ministry of Information**'s huge circular Radio and Television Building, and the elegant white high-rise belonging to the **Foreign Ministry**, which took 20 years to build. Further north the Corniche crosses Shari 26 July, which goes over a bridge to Gazirah. The bridge is named for Bulaq's most famous Circassian Mamluk monument, the **Mosque of Abu'l-Ila** (1495), which is up Shari 26 July to the right, not far from the bridgehead. Next to the mosque is a building with horses' heads on its gables, the Royal Stables, and in its second courtyard is the **Carriage Museum**, from which vehicles have been taken to furnish the small museums in the Northern Enclosure at the Citadel and the People's Assembly.

Beyond Shari 26 July on the Corniche is the **General Egyptian Book Organisation (GEBO)**, which now contains the **National Library (Dar al-Kutub)**, notable for the extraordinary manuscript collections assembled by the Muhammad Ali family, second only to those in Istanbul. Formerly in the Museum of Islamic Art – where the coins that also used to be part of the collection have remained – the manuscripts have deteriorated sadly, there have been sensational thefts, and consequently very few are now put on display. Further along the Corniche a kind of urban renewal has been half-heartedly attempted with erection of luxury office blocks, one of them a gift from the Chinese government.

Further north again is the sub-district of Sebtiyyah, which specialises in fabrication from sheet metal. One area here is referred to as *Wakalat al-Belah* ("Date Warehouse"), a name that has become associated more with old clothes than dates and is sometimes loosely applied to all the old-clothes markets in Bulaq.

Ramshackle port: Behind the businessmen's and bureaucrats' pomp and circumstance of the Corniche remains the reality of the ramshackle one-storeyed old Nile port. Below the grimly pretentious Cairo Plaza stands the Ottoman **Mosque of Sinan Pasha** (1571), built by a Grand Wazir, the viceroy of Sulayman the Magnificent, and the 16th-century *hammam* that was part of the original complex still functions nearby. There are over 60 architectural monuments dating from the 14th to the 18th centuries in Bulaq, most of them as yet unlisted by the Ministry of Culture, including mosques, private houses, and some 19 *wakalat*.

What Bulaq is better known for, however, is its machine shops and its market

Preceding pages: the new Foreign Ministry building and the TV and Radio building in Bulaq. **Left,** where the Nile begins to work.

204

for usable junk: not only old clothes, but also elements removed from demolished buildings, second-hand ironmongery, discarded machinery, spools of wire unwound from dynamos, and miscellaneous slightly used spare parts for internal combustion engines.

Among the carefully sorted piles of greased or rusting metal and through the glare of the blowtorches, the outlines of Ottoman *wakalat* and Muhammad Ali's factories can sometimes still be made out. The junk itself is sometimes surprising and can be fascinating – millstones, carved pediments, early 20th-century engines from Sheffield or Frankfurt-am-Oder, wheels from long-abandoned carts. Shops selling ships' shackles, brasswork, tackle and cordage recall the old port' s past. South and east of the Sinan Pasha mosque are narrow streets with old dresses and overcoats displayed on racks stretched over them from side to side, especially near the Mamluk-style **Mosque of Mustafa Shorbagi Mirza** (1698).

The area closest to the Abu'l-Ila Bridge is Cairo's motor-car graveyard. Here wrecks are dismantled, the pieces being distributed to dealers specialising in particular items, such as headlamps, handles, shock-absorbers and springs, hubcaps or even entire engines, which are all carefully classified according to make, model, and year. On Shari Abu'l-Ila is a motor-car showroom that indicates the profits to be made in the junk business: a second-hand Mercedes goes for LE 120,000, a new BMW for LE 170,000, and samples of either, parked by their owners, may be seen nearby.

Gazirah: While Bulaq was becoming prosperous, the islands offshore slowly merged to form one big island between Bulaq to the east and Duqqi and Aguza on the Gizah shore to the west. Called *Gazirat al-Bulaq*, then simply *Gazirah* – which means "island" – this island now has an area of less than a square mile (about 2 sq. km). It was left to farmers and their mud huts until well into the second half of the 19th century.

As Bulaq entered its second decline, however, Gazirah began to be developed. Its southern third, where it has been allowed to remain green, is occupied by several parks and sporting clubs. The tree-shaded streets of the northern two-thirds constitute **Zamalek**, Cairo's most fashionable residential suburb, which was made popular first by the British occupiers and now shelters an enormous amount of local and foreign wealth and chic.

Development on the island dates from 1863, when the Khedive Ismail began construction of a palace on the eastern shore opposite Bulaq. One legend has it that it was built for the Empress Eugénie, who was expected to be a guest at the opening of the Suez Canal. Another has it that it was conceived as a harem to accommodate three of his 14 wives. It was already in use by 1868 and certainly accommodated European guests, including Eugénie, who had been invited to the celebrations marking the opening of the Canal in November 1869.

The most famous of the many architects who worked on the palace were Julius Franz Pasha and Karl von Diebitsch. A German trained in Vienna, von Diebitsch designed a modular system for cast-iron architectural elements and used it to create the new building's porticoes, as well as an exquisite small palace, the Gazirah Kiosk (famous later as the "Casino") at one end of the garden. The most up-to-date fittings were imported from Europe, including furniture, oil paintings and chandeliers purchased at the 1867 Exposition Universelle in Paris. The interiors alone cost nearly LE 900,000.

The grounds were laid out by the Parisian landscape-designer Barillet-Deschamps, who also designed the Gizah Zoo and Ismail's final version of the Azbakiyyah Garden. They covered most of the island and incorporated an aquarium, a zoological garden full of wild animals and exotic birds, walkways which were lit by gas lamps and lawns adorned by statues from Europe's

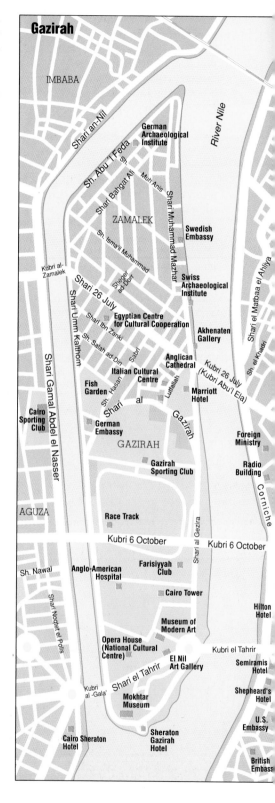

most prestigious *ateliers* of the time.

Before his deposition in 1879, the Khedive was stripped of all his properties, including the Gazirah Palace, by his European creditors. Mortgaged by the Rothschilds, it became a hotel in 1880 and by 1893 it was under the same management as Shepheard's. Between World War I and 1952 it returned to private hands, but the Revolutionary regime sequestrated it and converted it once again into a hotel. The gardens were wrecked to install concrete bungalows and a fire lit by workmen destroyed the Kiosk.

Transformed again between 1977 and 1982, the **Gazirah Palace** now forms the central section of the **Marriott Hotel**. Much of the building has been furnished with original pieces, and there's a chance that the chair you sit on may once have supported some royal or imperial bottom. The cast-iron porticoes created by von Diebitsch, originally installed by German craftsmen, have been beautifully restored. Within the grounds

of the hotel there is still statuary and a beautiful fountain, but the only other feature remaining of Barillet-Deschamps' grand design is a **Fish Garden** with a grotto-aquarium on the other side of the island, between **Shari Hasan Sabri** and **Shari Gabalayyah**. The fish are Nile species, dull and grey compared with the ones to be seen in the Red Sea, but the grotto itself is still good for a game of hide and seek.

In 1872 the **Qasr an-Nil Bridge** was opened, with lions imported from Paris keeping guard at each end – the lions have survived, though the bridge was replaced in 1933 – to link the island with the mainland permanently for the first time. The island was still undisturbed by the hubbub of the city centre, however, which then lay around Azbakiyyah. The Gizah shore was still mostly farms and gardens.

The Club: British officials administering the Occupation found the island's green spaces perfect for creating a tropical version of what they had been used

e Marriott el, once Gazirah ace.

to back home. The first British institution created in Cairo was the Khedivial Sporting Club, established in 1882 on land given by the Khedive Tewfiq within the first few days of the Occupation as a recreation ground for British officers. Modelled on the Hurlingham Club in London, the Club covered most of the centre of the island and was lavishly equipped with polo fields and cricket pitches, lawns for croquet, tennis, and bowls and an 18-hole golf course. Sir Ronald Storrs, who served under four successive British proconsuls, describes it as "the other British headquarters. It was difficult for foreigners to be elected," he adds, "and not easy for Egyptians even to make use of."

The 1907 Rulebook specifies that membership should be kept to 1,000; and by the time the British left, 50 years later, this limitation had risen only to 3,000. Except for descendants of Muhammad Ali, their dependants and a handful of rich Westernised families, the exclusive club had almost no Egyptian members.

Though half as big as it was before the Revolution, it carries eight times as many members; and the Shooting Club in Duqqi is far harder to get into. The **Gazirah Sporting Club** is nevertheless still regarded as "exclusive". Nouveaux riches parade its precincts during the evenings, displaying chunky gold and designer-label clothes. The cricket pavilion has been transformed into a mosque. Nationalisations took the polo fields, removed half the golf course and made the starting gate at the race-track, surrounded by an Arab Socialist Union recreation ground, invisible from the grandstand. The greens, the croquet and bowls lawns, and the flowering trees still exist, however, tea is still served at the clubhouse, and there is still a well-maintained cemetery for pets.

A small agricultural village stood south of the Khedivial Sporting Club until the late 1890s – when Lord Cromer, wishing to improve the view from his windows in the new British Residency,

just opposite on the mainland, persuaded the peasants to move to Imbabah. On this old site the Royal Society of Agriculture established what later became the **Gazirah Exhibition Grounds**, running right across the island. Housed in the **Planetarium** building here is a curious **Museum of Egyptian Civilisation**; one floor up is the **Gazirah Museum**, a display of miscellaneous paintings and *objets d'art* confiscated from the Muhammad Ali family, much of it interesting, all of it in need of lighting, cataloguing, dusting, cleaning, and redisposing in an intelligible order.

Intended for international events, the Gazirah Exhibition Grounds soon proved too small to hold even local crowds. In 1982 new International Exhibition Grounds (*Ard al-Ma'aarid*) were opened at Madinat Nasr (Nasr City), which made room at the Gazirah Exhibition Grounds for construction of a new **National Cultural Centre**. Known as the **New Cairo Opera House**, it was given to the Egyptian people by

Tea at the Gazirah Sporting Club.

the Japanese government as a replacement for the old Khedivial Opera House in Maydan Opera, burnt to the ground in 1971. Completed in 1988, it contains three stages, as well as exhibition halls and practice rooms, and has hosted troupes from Japan, the US, the UK, Germany, France, Austria, the Soviet Union, Spain and Bulgaria. Ballet is particularly popular.

Many of the old fairground pavilions were meanwhile refurbished and are used to house permanent or temporary exhibitions. Among them are the **Nile Hall** (Saray an-Nil) and **Al-Mustadira** (Artists' Syndicate Building) close to the main entrance, which show works by contemporary artists, and Saray an-Nasr, the new quarters of the **Museum of Modern Egyptian Art,** moved here from Duqqi in 1991.

Zamalek: While the southern end of the island remained green, the northern end was becoming Zamalek. Many villas were built between 1890 and 1940, including several for British adminis-

trators, a few of which – highly prized – are still owned by the British government and used by the Foreign Office. Until 1954 Zamalek remained, in fact, not so much a part of Egypt as a little Europe, even a little England, though the largest houses were actually more likely to be owned by Egyptians than by Englishmen.

The names written above the doors of apartment blocks on Shari Saray al-Gazirah, which runs beside the Nile in front of the Marriott Hotel – Nile View, Pyramids' House, Dorchester House, and Park Lane – suggest a population whose years in Egypt revolved around the office, the Turf Club, the Gazirah Sporting Club, annual bookings on P&O, and perennial thoughts of Home.

On the other side of the island, connecting it near its southern end with the Gizah shore, was the English Bridge, constructed in 1914, officially known as the Pont des Anglais and therefore soon nicknamed the "Pongly Zongly" by British children living in Zamalek.

Gazirah
b's
gest
mming
l.

Further north was the Zamalek Bridge which carried the tram from Bulaq to Gizah and the Pyramids, which has now been superseded by the 15 May Bridge: nothing remains but its supports. Upstream, towards the 6 October Bridge, a sailboat still serves as a ferry between the island and the west bank.

The opulence of the 1920s is embodied in the **Amr Ibrahim House**, opposite the main exit gate of the Gazirah Sporting Club on Shari Gazirah, a Khedivial-style *salamlik* constructed in 1927 for a great-great-grandson of Ibrahim Pasha. Art lovers are served by the Ministry of Culture's **Akhenaten Gallery**, housed in another villa on Shari Maahad as-Swissri or by the **Italian Cultural Centre**, which stands behind the Amr Ibrahim House under a huge old tree that formerly belonged to the grounds of the Gazirah Palace. A museum of the sculpture of Egypt's only internationally known artist, **Mahmud Mukhtar** (1891–1934), glorying in everything Egyptian, is in the gardens south of the National Cultural Centre on Shari Tahrir. One of Mukhtar's two statues of Saad Zaghlul, the founder of the Wafd, whose exile by the British gave rise to the 1919 Revolution, stands in the *maydan* at the Gazirah end of the Qasr an-Nil Bridge.

Revolutionary change: As the Revolution became more socialist, it could not ignore élitist Zamalek. Many villa-owners went quietly abroad, hoping things would blow over. Others had their property sequestrated out from under them. The Revolution's most visible monument on Gazirah is the **Cairo Tower**, 613 ft (187 metres) tall, opened on 11 April 1961.

In 1957, after refusing to help build the Aswan High Dam, the Americans presented Nasser with $3 million in cash, ostensibly to pay for a new armour-plated car and uniforms and training for his bodyguard. The gift was made through Kermit Roosevelt, the CIA's major man in Cairo. Correctly interpreting it as a blatant attempt at **The new Opera Hou:**

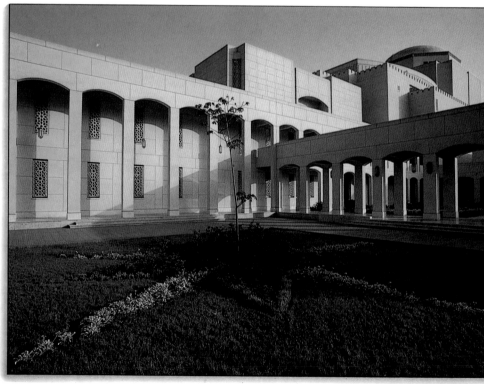

bribery, Nasser resolved to use the money for something that would be extremely conspicuous and would be of no practical benefit to anyone at all. The result was the Cairo Tower.

After the Aswan High Dam put an end to annual flooding in 1964, the west bank of the Nile was rapidly developed. By 1975 the inhabitants of Zamalek no longer had their celebrated uninterrupted view of the Pyramids, 12 miles (20 km) away to the southwest. As the populations of the west bank increased, more bridges were needed. The **15 May Bridge**, joining Imbabah with Bulaq, and the **6 October Bridge**, designed to link Duqqi with a highway system running all the way to Abbasiyyah, were constructed during the 1970s and 1980s.

Zamalek today: Peace and quite often dramatic views up and down the river enable landlords to charge the highest rents in town. Many Egyptian residents are rich – their summers are spent travelling in Europe or at holiday villas in Agami on the north coast, they keep poodles or Rottweilers as pets, they have Audis, BMWs or Mercedes sitting in their garages. Many flats are rented out to foreign managers, consultants and diplomats. There are more embassies in Zamalek than in any other district in Cairo.

Shops cater to the tastes of the local residents: supermarkets sell *sushi* and imported cocoa, as well as sliced turkey breast, spiced beef, and smoked salmon; the Marriott bakery offers blueberry pie and brownies. Restaurants employ Western chefs. Within the past 20 years, however, the Zamalek has actually become less Western, not more. Its nighttime population density has more than tripled, its daytime density more than quadrupled.

Most of the newcomers are Egyptian; not all of them by any means are identifiable as middle- or upper-class. During the day, apart from hordes of students of all ages, the streets are crowded with providers of services, ranging from maids and *bawabs* (doorkeepers) to the clerks in multitudes of commercial enterprises. There are embassy employees, secretaries in public and private-sector firms, and hundreds of bureaucrats working for organisations like the enormous Ministry of Culture, which maintains offices that occupy several buildings. The rich may shop at boutiques and supermarkets, but to satisfy this different kind of purchaser, the main streets now offer a colourful variety of locally-made cheap goods that would have been found a decade or ago only in a *baladi* ("indigenous") district. Even in front of supermarkets local meat, vegetables and fish are now displayed openly on the pavement, rather than being hidden away, as they used to be.

Shari 26 July in Zamalek has become, in fact, the best street in Cairo for seeing the wonderfully Middle-Eastern contrasts – of wealth and poverty, vulgarity and breeding, youth and age, deprivation and luxury, nature and artifice, glitz and chic, trendiness and tradition – that enliven the city as a whole.

RESIDENTIAL DISTRICTS

Visitors to **Abbasiyyah** will be hard put to imagine that this amorphous traffic-choked sprawl ever contained the tree-lined avenues and elegant villas that made the district famous earlier this century. For the pre-1939 generations Naguib Mahfouz describes in *Qasr ash-Shawq*, however, the second novel of his Cairo Trilogy, Abbasiyyah was the home of rich families, beys and pashas who lived in grand style among flowering lawns and trees.

Now the gardens have disappeared and the few remaining villas, squeezed between apartment blocks, have been converted into schools. Even the Urabi Café in Maydan al-Gaysh, where Mahfouz once sat drinking coffee with his friends, has disappeared: there is a butcher's shop in its place. Under pressure of demographic, economic and political change Abbasiyyah, like the rest of Cairo, has more or less imploded.

Named after Muhammad Ali's successor, Abbas I, who founded it in 1849, the district was originally isolated from the rest of the city by strips of desert, which made it ideal for quartering mercenary soldiers. Abbas built barracks and then a palace in his new viceregal suburb, which was laid out in European fashion around pleasant squares and intersecting avenues. His death, however, put paid to further development: the mercenaries were sent home and Abbasiyyah was more or less abandoned for nearly 30 years. In 1882 British troops occupied the barracks, which brought the district back to life; and during the decade of boom between 1897 and 1907 it became home to the class of foreign and Egyptian businessmen who were commercialising the district of Ismailiyyah.

It was thus also home to a sizeable portion of the city's Jews, whose red-brick community centre off Maydan al-Gaysh is a reminder of their confidence

Preceding pages: riverside construction at Maadi. Below, Abbasiyyah Sakakini Palace.

214

and economic power. Most of them have long since left and the few who remain have the mournful task of watching the Abbasiyyah's five synagogues fall into yet further decay. The largest of them, the **Maabad al-Yehudi** (the Jewish Temple), stands ignored in Maydan Mustashfa al-Qawat al-Gawiyyah (Air Force Hospital Square). The Air Force Hospital was formerly the French hospital, one of many such establishments in the district. More explicit reminders of Abbasiyyah's past are the Greek and Italian hospitals, which still have a few foreign nuns on their staffs.

South of the hospitals the florid **Palace of Habib Pasha as-Sakakini** stands in the centre of its own square, striking an aristocratic note among the adjoining middle-class apartment buildings. Built in 1897 it has recently been "restored", after years of service as an improvised replacement for the Royal Museum of Hygiene, a much larger building near Abdiin Palace, built for the purpose in 1927 by King Fu'ad. And further south

there is the great 13th-century congregational **Mosque of Sultan Baybars al-Bunduqdari** (1260–77), victor over the Mongols and creator of the Mamluk Empire, which dominates **Maydan ad-Dahir**. It is locally referred to as the *Madbah al-Ingliizi*, meaning "the English abbatoir", because the British used it as a slaughterhouse during the Occupation. It had already served the French as "Fort Sulkowski" and had then been used as a soap factory, a bakehouse, and a quarry for building materials. Restored in 1989, it may slowly return to its original function.

Linking the old traditional districts of Husayniyyah and Azbakiyyah with the 20th-century suburb of Heliopolis, Abbasiyyah takes in a mass of densely populated housing, the **Coptic Cathedral of St Mark** (begun in 1967 and still under construction) and, further to the east, the 1950s campus of Ayn Shams University. Behind Ayn Shams is Cairo's major state mental hospital: in popular parlance a "trip to Abbasiyyah"

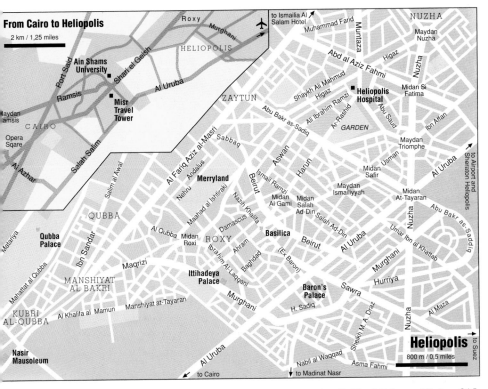

means a fit of madness. Past Ayn Shams on the road linking Abbasiyyah to Heliopolis is the **Gamal Abd an-Nasir Mausoleum and Mosque**, where the Republic's second president is buried.

Heliopolis: One measure of the direction of the country's development since Nasser is the fact that his house in **Heliopolis** now faces a Kentucky Fried Chicken franchise. This prosperous suburb, built between 1905 and 1922, has nothing whatever to do with ancient Heliopolis (On): the name "Heliopolis" was simply chosen as a marketing gimmick, to be used in English and French advertising, by the extraordinary man who built it, the Belgian entrepreneur Baron Edouard Empain.

Known to Cairenes themselves as **Misr al-Gadidah** ("New Cairo"), it is better preserved along its original lines than Abbasiyyah, however, and is now home to many members of the city's professional classes and many of its simply rich. The earliest inhabitants were nearly all Egyptians, but 80 percent were Christian or Jewish, not Muslim; and even now Heliopolis has a very large Christian minority. A villa-owning Heliopolitan these days probably drives a Mercedes, is the agent of a foreign company or two, and sends his children to the American University.

Empain is buried in the **Basilica** he built at the heart of his new city. It is a building which sets the tone for the surrounding area; a quarter-size version of the Hagia Sophia in Istanbul, designed by Alexandre Marcel, architect of the Muhammad Ali Club and one of the planners of the Petit Palais in Paris, who specialised in the exotic: for Leopold II of Belgium Marcel had built the Japanese pagoda and Chinese temple at Laeken, for the Maharajah of Kapurtala, a Renaissance palace.

In contrast with much of the rest of the city, Heliopolis still gives a visitor some sense of space. Like Garden City it was planned – less exclusively for the rich and without the curving streets – along lines suggested by contemporary ex-

periments in England. A fundamental influence was Port Sunlight, the model town near Liverpool in the UK which was built by Lever Brothers Ltd, the soap manufacturers, in 1888. Four types of residence were created – workers' flats, bungalows, apartment buildings, and villas – by teams of architects and builders that included Europeans, Syrians and Egyptians.

The entire area was carefully zoned. Each villa or apartment building was to conform with the neo-Islamic style of the whole settlement. None was to exceed a specified height for the zone it stood in or to occupy more than a specified percentage of its plot, the rest being taken up by plants or trees. Interiors were to be comfortable in ways familiar to European experience. The most luxurious have high ceilings, tall windows, and a plan of interconnecting rooms around a central hall. There is nothing like them in Port Sunlight.

This approach to city planning tempered 19th-century rationalism with Orientalist fantasy. The vast facade of the **Heliopolis Palace Hotel**, for example, is a collage of elements from Islamic architecture as practised in many Muslim countries. The largest hotel in the world when it was built in 1910, it was taken over by the Egyptian government and turned into the **Urubah Presidential Palace**. Opposite, on the other side of Shari Ibrahim al-Laqany, the lobby of what was once the offices of the Heliopolis Company features a complicated arrangement of arcaded balconies and a profusion of bright stained glass. Empain planned a complete aesthetic environment for his new city, providing exactly the new and sanitised sense of the "Orient" that "Orientals" themselves had come to long for.

Members of the Muhammad Ali family built enormous villas in Heliopolis. For himself Empain had Marcel design the **Indian Palace**, which now stands derelict on the road to Cairo Airport. Modelled directly on a temple Marcel had seen in southern India, the palace

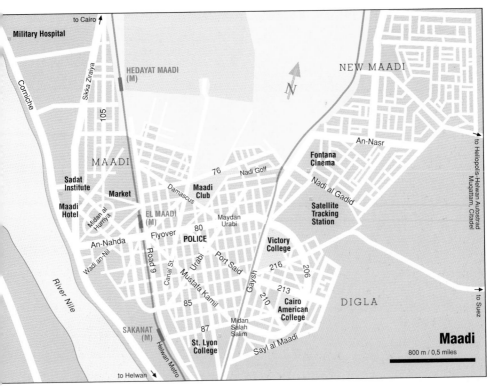

was a giant advertisement directed at the European tourists Empain hoped would choose Heliopolis as the starting point for a leisurely pavane up the Nile.

Maadi: While Empain was busy to the northeast of the city, the Delta Land and Investment Company bought land on the river to the south, laid it out in a grid of avenues and squares, and created the suburb of **Maadi**. The Company was responsible for planning, zoning, and common standards. The avenues were planted with flowering trees that bloomed at different seasons. Long-term residents remember when strictly enforced municipal regulations allowed no high-rises, no radios after 10 at night, and no walls between properties, only living hedges. There were severe fines for noise, rubbish-dumping, and failure to maintain verges as gardens. Streets were policed by constables on bicycles and Camel Corps patrols, resting after a week in the desert tracking smugglers, bivouacked under the trees.

Apart from the fact that none of these regulations is now observed, much else has changed. Families of the original Egyptian inhabitants remain, but British residents left in 1956 and the foreign presence now is liberally supplied by Asians and Africans, as well as Europeans and North and South Americans. Beyond Maadi to the east the districts of **New Maadi** and **Digla** have been built and the Camel Corps has had to move out – the desert is now too far away. Villas have been torn down and replaced with apartment blocks; and though a group of 50-storey towers on the Corniche has stood unfinished since 1981, those already completed have raised the population density beyond levels that would be acceptable in Europe or America. It is now higher than the density of Cairo as a whole was in 1973, when the city was already overcrowded. Even these changes have failed to destroy Maadi's original design, however, and many of the older streets still have green quietude and charm.

Helwan: Further down the Metro line

The Japane Garden in Helwan.

218

is **Helwan**. Now associated mainly with heavy industry, massive pollution, and labour unrest, Helwan is centred around the remains of a dilapidated spa town. In the 19th century the spa's curative waters brought a spate of building activity and a period of fame as Helwan-les-Bains. It was at this time that the **Japanese Gardens** were laid out, the hospital that overlooks was them built, and many of the area's villas were constructed. Helwan-les-Bains was popular with the rich and King Faruq had a house or two in the vicinity. Today it is only the most curious visitor who would bother to make the trip from Cairo.

Shubra: One way to approach **Shubra**, at the opposite end of Cairo from Helwan, is by Metro. From the Mubarak stop (Maydan Ramses) an exit leads over the railway bridge into Shari Shubra, the district's arterial main road, which began life as an elegant promenade leading to the **Shubra Palace**, built between 1809 and 1812, the summer residence of Muhammad Ali.

Shubra has left such pretentious origins behind, however, and so large a percentage of the city's population now live here that – according to the Egyptian government itself – parts of Shubra have the highest population density in the world. The over-population has given it a secure place in popular humour: a character in a play who has returned to his home district after several years in America refers to it as "the State of Shubra"; and it is often called – in reference to the fact that more than half the people in the world are Chinese – "the People's Republic".

Shubra is not one district, but five: in addition to Shubra proper there are Shubra al-Balad, Shubra al-Mazalaat, Shubra al-Khayma, and Shubra as-Sahil. Its history is bound up with the 1897-1907 boom and with the consequent influx of foreigners. The city's large Greek and Italian communities – both dispersed by the Revolution – were centred here. Some areas still have ornamentally stuccoed buildings along straight streets laid out in logical fashion, showing their bourgeois past; others are a chaos of muddy alleys crowded with dwellings jerry-built of mud-brick.

The district has always had a strong Coptic population, and today Shubra is an area of scattered churches and strong religious feeling. Starting in 1986, visions of the Virgin have been reported in the Shubra church of St Demiana and people flood in from all over Egypt on these occasions in the hope of seeing her. The excitement reaches such peaks that the police are obliged to throw up a cordon around the area until the Lady vanishes. In September 1990 a miracle was reported when a lame boy was made to walk.

Shubra's agricultural connections are maintained in **Rod al-Farrag market**, which supplies the city with fruit and vegetables. A commonly-used venue for film-making, this was once an entertainment district catering to the rich village headmen who came to market on business, but lingered for pleasure.

Fruit vendor, Rod al-Farrag market.

GIZAH AND THE WESTERN SUBURBS

Gizah, Aguza, Duqqi, Mohandisiin and Imbabah, the new suburbs lining the west bank of the Nile opposite Cairo, possess little of the architectural variety or charm that can still be claimed by their neighbours to the east. Their appearance, factory-like and dull, marks surrender to 20th-century Middle-Eastern perceptions and values and to the pressures of time, money, and population. Their wide streets are intended to cope with fast-flowing traffic, not the Egyptian climate. Their grey glass-fronted blocks of air-conditioned flats create an atmosphere no different in any major respect from that of hundreds of other cities around the world.

Gizah: When Napoleon marched on Cairo 200 years ago the scene was very different. Green fields were interspersed with the small villages of Imbabah, Mit Okba, Hutya and Duqqi. To the south lay the town of **Gizah**, established by the conqueror Amr Ibn al-As in 642 as a garrison encampment to defend Fustat and Rawdah against Byzantine attack from across the river. It had hardly grown since. With only a few thousand inhabitants, Gizah's sole distinction was a palace belonging to Murad Bey, a Mamluk grandee.

The first permanent bridge across the main channel of the Nile was completed under the Khedive Ismail in 1872. It had little effect on the west bank, however, other than to make it practical for Ismail to build a palace in Gizah. The grounds of the building included botanical and zoological gardens designed by Barillet-Deschamps, the landscape designer he had brought back from Paris. After Ismail's deposition the palace became the second home of the viceregal collection of Pharaonic antiquities, which stayed there until 1902.

The gardens meanwhile went public in 1891, becoming the **Zoological Garden (***Hadiiqat al-Hayawaan***)**. With a collection including representatives of many of the species of the African continent, the Cairo Zoo was once one of the largest and best managed in the world. Now, however, the insignificant entrance fee means that it serves as a playground for many of the city's poor. Games of football and hopscotch, picnics and courtship along the walkways are just as popular as the polar bears, lions, elephants, and tigers. A disused bandstand and a small iron suspension bridge, beautiful, but sadly derelict, suggest a better era.

Cairo University nearby, which dominates the district, was founded in 1908 as the Egyptian University. It first convened in the former palace of Khairy Pasha in Ismailiyyah, now owned by the American University. Settled in Gizah in the 1920s, it was renamed Fu'ad I University and may be identified by the stately dome of its main building, designed by King Fu'ad's Court Architect, Ernesto Verucci, in 1926.

From the university's main gate a

Left, Gizah from above the Zoo. Right, art gallery proprietor, Gizah.

wide boulevard leads between the Zoo and the **Urman Gardens** westward to the statue by Mahmud Mukhtar called *Nahdet Misr*, "Egyptian Renaissance", erected in 1928. Representing a peasant girl and an awakening sphinx, it is a powerful symbol of political and cultural rebirth. The boulevard, likewise called Nahdet Misr, crosses the Kubri al-Gaamah (University Bridge) to the island of Rawdah.

Southward is a much older bridge, the Kubri Abbas (Abbas II Bridge), opened in 1907. Between these two bridges is a pleasant stretch of river where houseboats are moored and a handful of handsome villas still stand, easily accessible because of the Gizah Corniche (Shari Gamal Abd an-Nasir), which runs along the bank. Two great villas here are occupied by the French and Turkish embassies. A third was demolished in the 1970s to make way for a new American embassy, which was actually built, but in the event proved to be so badly constructed and full of design faults that it was sold as scrap before even being inaugurated.

The **Shawqi Museum** at 6 Shari Ahmad Shawqi, between the Gizah Corniche and Shari Gizah (Murad), was the residence of Ahmad Shawqi (1868–1932), court poet to Khedive Abbas II Hilmi, exiled by the British between 1915 and 1919. It gives a good idea of the elegant lifestyle of a literary gentleman at the end of the Khedivial era.

North of the University Bridge is the villa belonging to Muhammad Mahmud and Emilienne Luce Khalil, which was left to the nation with their collection of 19th-century French paintings and *objets d'art*, in 1962. The next villa to the north belongs to Mme. Jihan Sadat. Further north, not far from the Sheraton hotel, is the **Papyrus Institute**, created by Dr Hasan Ragab, former Egyptian ambassador to the People's Republic of China. Dr Ragab reintroduced the plant from which papyrus is made, *Cyperus papyrus*, which had been virtually extinct in Egypt for over a

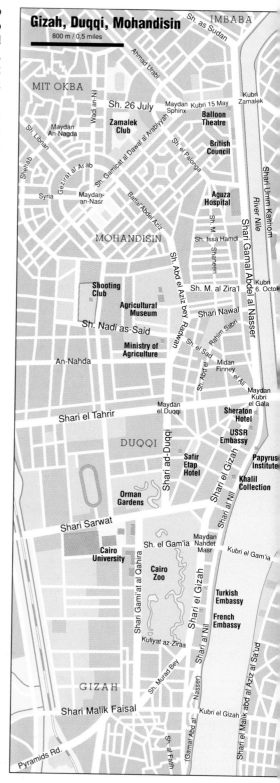

millennium, and rediscovered techniques of making papyrus. The Institute includes an art gallery.

Aguza: North of Gizah on the river, the sole surviving Nileside villa in Aguza is occupied by the **British Council**. The major landmark of the area otherwise is the **Balloon Theatre**, which took the place in part of the old Opera House during the bleak years 1971–88 and is still occasionally used for performances. Before the rise in oil prices in the mid-1970s allowed them to shop successfully elsewhere, Aguza was a summertime magnet for visiting Arabs: they customarily took furnished premises in the district and filled them with "maids", who earned enough in six weeks to live on for a year.

Duqqi: West of Aguza inland is **Duqqi**, whose major attraction for visitors is the **Agricultural Museum**, opened to the public in 1938. Up to the late 1960s residential property on the west bank was confined to the villages and a narrow strip of villas and gardens along the Nile. Mass residential development began after 1964, when the Aswan High Dam eliminated the annual flood. Until that time there was an unobstructed view of the Pyramids 12 miles (20 km) away across flat irrigated fields from virtually any point on the west bank.

In Gizah the land on either side of Shari al-Haram (Pyramids Road) was still almost exclusively agricultural. North of Gizah the Ministry of Awqaf (Mortmain Endowments) had already distributed land under its control among various syndicates representing doctors, engineers, agricultural engineers, journalists, university professors and army officers.

Neighbourhoods had been given the names of the professions that were supposed to be housed in them: Madinat Al-Mohandisiin means "Engineers' City", Madinat As-Sahafiyiin, the name of a small district based around Shari Ahmad Urabi, means "Journalists' City". Rather than providing shelter for socialists, however, Duqqi, Mohandisiin

ury living
Pyramids
ad.

and Aguza became the object of frenzied speculation.

Mohandisiin: Menus and shop windows in **Mohandisiin** suggest that the taste of the current population has been formed since they arrived – that is, within the past 10 or 20 years – by watching American movies and TV serials. The main drag is Shari Gamiat ad-Dawal al-Arabiyyah (Arab League Street), where the young rich drive fast cars loudly, California-style, late into the night. The modest three- or four-storey structures built by the syndicates have been knocked down and replaced by much taller apartment and office blocks; and Mohandisiin's wide streets and lower rents have made it attractive to private industry in search of office space. This is the local mecca for anyone in search of westernised living in Cairo.

Billboards advertise multinationals. Benetton, Stefanel and Naf-Naf and numerous local imitators maintain busy shops. Soft drinks and fast food are everywhere, not only *kofta* and *shawirma*, but pizzas and hamburgers. Wimpy's busy Mohandisiin branch, on what is now the most important *maydan*, has been the chief landmark of the area ever since it was opened in the late 1970s. Like Los Angeles, it is no place to be a pedestrian.

Imbabah: North of Mohandisiin lies the suburb of **Imbabah**, famous once as the location of King Faruq's favourite nightclub, the Kitkat, but now better known for its **Camel Market**. It is heavily built up with working-class apartment blocks and streets of motor-car repair shops. King Faruq, who had a penchant for nightlife, used to visit the **Swiss Club**, a villa in a large garden with an alley for bowls and a small shooting range, 200 metres up Shari Sudan from Maydan Kitkat and down a sidestreet to the right. On the Nile at Imbabah a row of houseboats offered the pre-Revolutionary rich a gamut of pleasures that ranged from drugs and gambling to bizarre varieties of sex.

As recently as the early 1980s there were green fields in Duqqi and Mohandisiin and herds of sheep were common. Both have now virtually disappeared, though it is still possible to visit the villages that used to stand among the fields and see where the sheep were raised. The actual little village of Duqqi for which the district around it is named lies behind the Ministry of Agriculture not far from Maydan Duqqi; Hutya is behind the An-Nabila Hotel on Shari Gamiat ad-Dawal al-Arabiyyah in Mohandisiin; and Mit Okba, boasting large brick extensions to its original mud huts, stands at the end of Shari 26 July in Mohandisiin, halting that road on its way to the new satellite city of 6 October.

Wandering through the narrow streets of these engulfed villages, with their carpenters' workshops, metal foundries, and bakeries, one cannot but reflect that grandmothers and grandfathers still living in them have known ways of life utterly foreign in every respect to anything they see around them now.

The Imbab Camel Market.

224

THE CAMEL MARKET

Camels loom large in the export versions of Egyptian culture – they appear in tourist brochures and guidebooks, on T-shirts and, of course, on cigarette packets – but apart from the beasts that lumber up and down the Pyramids Plateau carrying tourists, short-term visitors are unlikely to see any in the city.

Camels do exist, in fact, in large quantities in Cairo, if only temporarily. Egypt has an agreement with the Sudan under which 250,000 of them are imported every year; and scores of thousands of the beasts make their way to Cairo to be sold, mostly for food. At the Camel Market (Suq al-Gimaal) in Imbabah several hundred can be seen every day, in milling groups or tied up in kneeling rows, croaking and groaning as they are prodded, whipped and beaten by Sudanese drovers, the dealers who own them, and potential buyers.

If the camels seem unhappy, they have good reason. Many of them have recently undergone a trek from the south of Sudan or Somalia, then the gruelling 40-day journey which was recorded by Louis Werner in his documentary film *The Voice of the Whip*.

Hundreds expire en route. A few of these are shot by Bedouin raiders, particularly on the Sudanese border with Chad, but the rest die of sheer exhaustion. At Daraw in the south of Egypt they cross the Nile to a secondary market where they are sold to dealers before being packed into trains to complete their journey north to Cairo, to be sold to butchers.

Camel meat is the central ingredient in Cairene versions of two Turkish dishes: *shawirma* (the Turkish *çevirme*, known in Europe by its other Turkish name, *döner kebap*) and *bastirma*, a classic item of Middle-Eastern delicatessen, cured meat heavily flavoured with fenugreek, served in wafer-thin slices. Camel-meat *shawirma* is not a great success – the better establishments in Cairo all use lamb, as the Turkish formula prescribes – but Egyptian *bastirma* may be an improvement upon the original Turkish *pastirma*.

Carried by the Ottoman armies as far west as Vienna, *pastirma* was made of beef; and in Hungary, an Ottoman province for centuries, it became pastrami, the mild-flavoured cured beef that is well-known in the West. In Egypt, however, where cows were rare, camel meat was substituted for beef. Close-textured and tough, it can be sliced to perfect thinness and was therefore found ideal. The popularity of *bastirma* may be gauged by the reek of fenugreek - after a single indulgence, the essence of the plant continues to be exuded throughout the eater's system for days, scenting everything he touches – everywhere in Cairo.

A good healthy camel will fetch between LE 1500 and LE 2000. The drovers who bring them up from the Sudan, generally in herds of about 100 at a time, will spend a few days in lodgings at the Camel Market, then return to the Sudan for another herd. Dressed in brilliant white *gallabiyyas* and turbans, they sit around on benches drinking tea, while their employers negotiate noisily with the butchers.

The market is one place where a tourist is not by any means the centre of attention, but outsiders may feel slightly uneasy nonetheless. Camels are whacked hard enough to alarm the least tender-hearted observer. They are obviously discontent and they frequently bolt. And although they are usually hobbled, they can move extremely fast and have no concern whatsoever for what or who is in their path, but cut a riotous ill-tempered three-legged swath through the market, scattering all before them.

Those who have the time and the composure to study the ungainly beast, however, will admire its adaptation to the rigours of the desert. Its eyelashes, for instance, long and rather alluring, protect its eyes from the glare. Its cavernous nostrils can be closed to keep out desert wind and sand. In its hump is accumulated a hulk of fat during times of plenty that allows it to endure long periods without sustenance. A non-working camel can go without water for as long as 10 months, but a thirsty one may drink as much as 30 gallons (136 litres) at one go.

In at least one Arab saying, the wilful beast is held up as a standard of pulchritude: "To be beautiful, the gait of a woman should be like that of camel picking its way through mud."

SATELLITE CITIES

In 1900, when its population stood at 600,000 and no motor-car had yet been mass-produced anywhere in the world, Cairo was slightly smaller than it had been 500 years earlier, during the era of the Circassian Mamluks. Now the population has passed 15 million and 1.2 million cars are registered as belonging to local owners. The city covers an area of some 175 square miles (450 sq. km), with an average density of over 88,000 people per square mile (340 per hectare). Some districts suffer from overcrowding that is more severe, by official assessment, than anywhere else in the world.

Arab nationalists, who saw it as part of another Western plot designed to suppress the Arab masses; and from amateur economists, who imagined that there was a relationship between population and productivity. But Cairene couples who wish to maintain a middle-class living standard nowadays rarely have more than two or three children. By the year 2000 the population will nevertheless be well over 20 million. City planners have been unable to keep up with such growth, which was not officially acknowledged until its effects had been brought home by the collapse of the city's infrastructure, which has also silenced opposition.

Under Nasser, industry and government became increasingly centred on Cairo, but the capital's infrastructure was presumed to take care of

The major population increase has taken place since the 1950s. The legend of massive migration allowed officials to blame a mythical influx of *fellahin* for the city's ills – with the implication that everything would be all right if only they could be sent back to where they had come from – but in fact only 30 percent of the population explosion has been due to migration from the countryside, which was actually far heavier in the 1930s and 1940s than it has been ever since. Seventy percent of Cairo's explosive population growth has been due to the excess of births over deaths among people already living in the city.

The government runs a permanent birth-control campaign. In the 1960s there was opposition from Muslim pietists, who saw birth control as postponing the ultimate triumph of Islam; from

itself magically, without any maintenance. The construction of the Corniche was thus a political gesture more than a practical one and no major revision of Cairo's road system was undertaken to accommodate more cars until the 1980s, when a master plan was finally put into operation. Dozens of new fly-overs have been opened and the Ring Road has been built, which will eventually take heavy traffic around the city. The new Metro, constructed by the French out of the old lines running to Al-Marg in the north and to Helwan in the south, has proven a great success and two further lines are planned that will join the eastern and western banks of the Nile.

The water system, however, untouched during two decades of the Revolution, still fails to serve one third of the population, while leaking one half its volume into the ground, thanks to decay of its fabric (some of which dates back to Ismail) and illegal tapping. Groundwater has thus risen throughout the city to the point where in some areas there are permanent puddles; and every building in central Cairo is in some degree damaged by rising damp. Medieval monuments, in particular, have frequently deteriorated to the point of collapse.

The sewerage system, completed in 1914 and designed to serve a city of one million inhabitants for a maximum of 40 years, was left untouched until it exploded in 1964, when it was patched by the army, then ignored again for another 15 years. Its reconstruction, by American and British engineers, is one of the biggest engineering projects ever undertaken anywhere in the world.

The telephone system, one of the earliest outside Europe and America and once one of the best, was abandoned to its fate after 1961, when the last directory was issued. It was replaced in the early 1980s and a Cairene may now not only have a new phone, but may also make the kinds of calls that are normal elsewhere in the world.

Exacerbating all other difficulties has been over-population. The drab public housing blocks built during the 1950s in Shubra and Helwan were intended as political symbols, not to satisfy demand. Since 1960, in fact, three-quarters of all new residential structures in Cairo have been built within the "informal" sector: i.e., they have been built by private owners or entrepreneurs, often on land designated for other purposes or where ownership is obscure, without concern for the formalities of licensing or regulation and without reference to building codes or to the presence or absence of infrastructural support.

It was thanks to informal housing, which consumes an estimated 1,500 acres (600 hectares) of arable land per year, that the urban area of Cairo doubled between 1968 and 1982 alone. The official alternative to informal building is to encourage as many Cairenes as possible to live in the desert, thereby reducing stress on the city's infrastructure and saving arable land for food production. Settlements fall into two main categories. New cities, called 10th Ramadan, Sadat, and 6th October, have been established some distance away from the capital and can offer inhabitants employment in their own industrial zones. Dormitory or satellite towns, connected with the centre by the new Cairo Ring Road east of the city, such as As-Salaam, Al-Obuur, and 15th May, will house those working in the capital.

The new cities have been relatively successful in attracting industry. Companies have responded well to the prospect of a 10-year respite from taxation. In 1990, after only 11 years, 400 companies were either planning or had already set up enterprises in 10th Ramadan, making carpets, pharmaceuticals, plastic pipes, T-shirts, bathroom appliances and cheese; and most foreign dignitaries are taken on tours of the industrial zones in either 10th Ramadan or 6th October, focal points of an ideal Egypt of the future.

Unfortunately the people of Cairo, who were supposed to flock to the new cities, have not responded in quite so enthusiastic a fashion. Young married couples have been reluctant to take up the challenge of living away from family and friends; and their absence creates a vicious cycle: as long as there is insufficient population to support entertainment or amusement for such people and their children, these cities will remain unattractive to any new population. The city of 10th Ramadan is 36 miles (60 km) outside Cairo on the Ismailiyyah road and Sadat City is even further away along the Alexandria road.

Many of the companies based in the industrial zones that were supposed to support these new cities therefore still import their labour from the capital and hundreds of blocks of flats remain empty. Although major irrigation projects have made all the new cities relatively green, the buildings themselves are unimaginative rectangular concrete blocks. Painted in a variety of cheerful but rapidly fading colours, many of them are already deteriorating. At 10th Ramadan drainage was inadequately installed and water seeps through the gaps in the concrete cladding. It is unlikely that any of the new towns will reach their goals of 500,000 inhabitants each by the year 2000. At present 10th Ramadan houses only about 40,000.

The dormitory towns face many of the same problems. They too consist of large numbers of unimaginative blocks set in featureless landscapes. Frequently the electricity or water supply is not as efficient as it is in the city; and although these satellite towns are closer to Cairo than the new cities, a move to one of them still represents an abandonment of normal ties with family and friends. There have nevertheless been some notable successes: 15th of May City, west of Helwan in the desert, has grown very quickly and is well on its way to reaching its target of 150,000 inhabitants. The new extensions to Madinat Nasr (Nasr City) and Madinat as-Salaam (Salam City) near the airport have likewise filled up very quickly.

While official planners publicly declare themselves determined that Egypt's future must lie in the desert, most people are not yet convinced. Offered the alternative of a new flat in a concrete high-rise in the desert, many Cairenes would still prefer to live among the packed streets of Darb al-Ahmar or Bulaq ad-Dakrur. The city's old quarters and its new unofficial informal communities answer far more to Egyptian needs: companionship and scope for residential improvisation or for setting up a small-scale business or industry. They also have the vibrancy that is found elsewhere up and down the Nile Valley and is still sadly lacking in the desert.

MEMPHIS, SAQQARAH AND GIZAH PYRAMIDS

The first Pharaonic capital, **Memphis**, lies about 15 miles (24 km) south of Cairo and can be reached either by driving south from Cairo and crossing the Nile at the so-called Hungarian Bridge, just beyond Helwan, or by driving to Gizah and following the Gizah-Saqqarah road. A visit (and there are plenty of bus companies offering convenient guided visits) to Memphis and its necropolis at Saqqarah takes the better part of a day, but can conveniently be combined with a tour of the pyramids at Gizah and two interesting stops for shopping.

Not much remains now above ground at Memphis. No traces of the earliest city are visible, though recent borings have brought up Early Dynastic pottery from a depth of 20 ft (6 metres), well below the present water table, which is compatible with the ancient tradition that the city was founded 5,000 years ago as the capital of a united Egypt. Two thousand years later Diodorus Siculus estimated that the city was about 24 miles (38 km) in circumference – probably one of the largest in the ancient world and certainly very spread out, reaching at different times from southern Gizah to Dahshur. Its antiquity and its association with kingship, especially the coronation rites, meant that even long after it had ceased to be the capital, it was still a spiritual centre and a cultural epitome of Egypt. The name of its great temple Hakuptah – "the house of the *ka* of Pta" – became *Aigyptos* to the Greeks, whence came the name Egypt.

Modern agriculture, housing, and cemeteries have eaten into its ruins, reducing them to undulating mounds of brown earth amid palm groves. Most of the buildings, even palaces and fortresses, were built of mud-brick, which reverts to its original formlessness without much encouragement. Stone monuments have been removed over the centuries for new buildings; and though the

temples must have rivalled any in Egypt in their heyday, only a few denuded buildings have survived.

Most visitors start at the colossal limestone **statue of Ramses II** (1290–1224 BC) uncovered in 1820, but never re-erected because of its height – over 30 ft (10 metres) without its lower legs. It originally stood at the south entrance of the Temple of Ptah, but had already fallen by the time Strabo saw it in 24 BC. The museum built over it allows visitors to gaze down on the handsome face of the king and admire his perfect proportions.

Another colossal statue of granite in the museum garden also bears the name and titles of Ramses II, but artistically it belongs to the Middle Kingdom and has been identified as Sesostris II.

These colossal statues are only two of many unearthed in Memphis: a granite one found near the eastern entrance to the temple of Ptah – and thus, despite what guides say, not the companion of the fallen one here – now gazes out

eceding
iges:
ising at the
ramids.
eft, the
ihinx.
ight, hotel
r the
rramids.

through the exhaust fumes of Maydan Ramses in central Cairo.

The upper floor of the museum is also an excellent place from which to view the remains of Memphis. To the north palm groves mark the site of the **Great Temple of Ptah**, which once rivalled Karnak in its splendours. Ramses II rebuilt this temple on reclaimed river land. Nothing now remains but the ruined west portal, five minutes' walk up the road, and traces of a mud-brick enclosure wall. Beyond it are the scanty remains of successive royal palaces of the New Kingdom.

To the south is a Sacred Way, unearthed by accident during the construction of a new cafeteria, and to the west are small chapels, which may once have connected with the Sacred Way – the **Hathor chapel**, founded by the army, and a **Ptah chapel** of Ramses II. Buried under centuries of debris, both are now in a very bad state, with salt efflorescence pushing off the relief decoration. Apart from the wonderful alabaster sphinx in the museum garden, in fact, so little has survived the stone robbers that it is hardly worth lingering, especially when the monuments at Saqqarah are so magnificent.

First necropolis: The road to Saqqarah goes west, passing a small **Temple of the Apis Bull** on the right, where a black bull, the herald of the god Ptah, lived and gave oracles and was much visited by Greek tourists during the last centuries of paganism. When the bull died he was buried with full honours in a vault at Saqqarah and a search began for his successor.

The desert plateau of Saqqarah was the domain of Sokar, one of the gods of the Underworld, and was used as the necropolis of Memphis for over 3,000 years. Here, the dead were buried in their "houses of eternity", where their spirits could find shelter and receive the food offerings, necessary for their survival in the Underworld, which their families provided. On the other side of the road from the ticket office at the foot

Workers at the restoration the colossu of Ramses Memphis.

232

of the plateau lies the **Valley Temple of Unas**, which once had its own quay on a canal connected with the Nile. The causeway visible running west up the cliff from the temple for nearly half a mile (800 metres) eventually reaches the **Pyramid of Unas**.

Although there are tombs of the 1st and 2nd Dynasties along the northern escarpment, the most spectacular monument is the 3rd-Dynasty **Step Pyramid of Zoser** (2630–2611 BC). This first of all pyramids was so revered by later generations that it gave special sanctity to the whole site and brought ancient pilgrims to pay their respects and write pious graffiti. The tomb was originally planned as a stone *mastabah*, and shows several changes of design before achieving its present six-stepped form. The man responsible for it, Imhotep, was later deified and worshipped at Saqqarah, but his own tomb has not yet been found. The idea of burying the king below a stepped or straight-sided pyramid seems to reflect belief in the cycle of birth, death and rebirth: the germ of all living things was believed to be contained within a Primeval Mound, which rose out of the waters of chaos at the time of creation. Burying the dead king in such a mound ensured his return to the creative matrix of the land, so that his magical and divine powers were continually present for the well-being of the country.

The Step Pyramid is surrounded by an enormous walled **Enclosure**, convincingly restored under the direction of the architect J-P Lauer. Past the original doorway with its imitation palm-log ceiling and eternally open door, a corridor of papyrus-bundle columns leads to a large court in front of the pyramid. To the north-east, a series of buildings are actually simulacra – facades in front of rubble cores – of the shrines and palaces needed for the king's jubilee ceremony, the *heb-sed*. They are adorned with stone renderings of more transient building materials – wood, reeds, and sedge. On the north side of the pyramid, Zoser's

The Step Pyramid of Zoser at Saqqarah.

statue – a replica of the original – looks out from a sort of sentry-box (*serdab*) on the circumpolar stars. Beside the *serdab* is the funerary temple, from where offerings were presented to the dead king.

A path over the southern enclosure wall leads past a deep pit, the "South Tomb", which is, unfortunately, like the galleries beneath the Pyramid, in too dangerous a state for visitors. The top of the enclosure wall offers a superb panorama over South Saqqarah. In the distance are the two stone pyramids of Snofru (Khufu's father) at **Dahshur**: the southernmost changes the angle of its slope halfway up and is consequently known as the "Bent Pyramid".

Close at hand is the 5th-Dynasty **Pyramid of Unas** (2356–2323 BC) which is open and easily accessible. It is the first pyramid to contain chambers inscribed with the religious formulae known as the Pyramid Texts, which were recited during the funeral of the king to release his spirit, so that it might travel with the stars or the sun or change its form. Other texts refer to the offerings presented each day to the king in his funerary temple on the east face of the pyramid. Nothing much remains of Unas's funerary temple, but the **Causeway** leading off the east side to the Valley Temple has been restored and is well worth a visit.

Like urban sites, this cemetery also has layers of occupation. North of the causeway are the tombs of Unas's family and courtiers, with later Middle Kingdom tombs squeezed between. South are two boat pits and beyond them, above some Old Kingdom rock-cut tombs, the escarpment rises steeply to a huge New Kingdom cemetery where the tombs of the General (later Pharaoh) Horemheb and of Tutankhamun's treasurer, Maya, have recently been excavated. These tombs were partly dismantled during the Coptic period, when a vast monastic settlement, **Apa Jeremiah**, covered the whole of this side of the desert. Further down the causeway

Tourist bus arriving at Saqqarah.

some of its original decorated blocks have been restored. The way is then interrupted by the excavation of an earlier *mastabah* tomb, that of Nyankh-Khnum and Khnumhotep (closed to the public). Here a path leads round, past Portakabin toilets, to the front of the Step Pyramid Enclosure.

Best tombs: The tomb chapels beside Unas's causeway are decorated, but none is as colourful or complete as three outstanding examples elsewhere, the **tombs of Ptah-hotep**, **Ti**, and **Mereruka**. Ptah-hotep's tomb lies on the north-west side of the Step Pyramid enclosure, past the 5th-Dynasty pyramid of Userkaf. Most of the chapel he shared with his father, Akhet-hotep, is unfinished, but a tiny chamber contains exquisite reliefs of wild animals, fishing and bird-catching in the marshes, and everyday life, still brilliantly coloured. Further to the west is the tomb of Ti, overseer of two of the 5th-Dynasty pyramids clearly visible to the north at Abusir. The decoration here is also of the highest quality. The scenes are more varied in subject than Ptah-hotep's but lack colour. Within the inner chamber, behind a slot in the wall, the statue of Ti still looks out from the darkness of the Underworld.

Not far from Ti's tomb and usually surrounded by camels, horses, donkeys and their noisy owners is another entrance to the Underworld – the galleries where the sacred Apis Bull was buried, known as the **Serapeum**. Part of the long, dusty maze of tunnels is open. On either side are the vaults, each filled with a massive stone sarcophagus.

In the Ptolemaic period a Sacred Way led from the Serapeum to the valley. At the point where the path to Ti's tomb now crosses, this Sacred Way was adorned with a semicircle of statues of Greek poets and philosophers, now in very poor shape. The Way continued east over the top of the fine 6th-Dynasty tomb of Mereruka, a vizier of King Teti, whose pyramid lies in front. One of the largest private tomb chapels in the ne-

*ft, painting
m the tomb
Ptah-
tep. Right,
emphis
igation.*

cropolis, Mereruka's monument contains lively and varied scenes, not always as beautifully executed as the earlier reliefs, but outdoing them in detail and range of subject matter.

Weaving workshops: From Saqqarah the road back to Gizah passes the village of **Harraniyyah**, famous for the **Wissa Wassef tapestry workshops,** now managed by the widow of founder Ramses Wissa Wassef. The tapestries produced here have won world-wide acclaim and the school is training the second generation of weavers. A museum holds a permanent exhibition showing how the work of individual craftsmen has developed. In a different building tapestries, batiks and ceramics are offered for sale. Several other artists and artisans, producing ceramics or carpets, have settled in the neighbourhood and usually welcome visitors.

North of the Pyramids Road (Shari al-Haram) about 3 miles (5 km) is the village of **Kirdassah**, once a trading post for caravans crossing the desert to and from Libya, but now concerned mainly with the tourist trade. The main street has become a bazaar offering every merchandise connected with cloth: *gallabiyyas*, rugs and carpets, embroidery, and imitations of the work done at Harraniyyah. The selection is enormous and haggling is in order.

At the end of Shari al-Haram is the venerable **Mena House Hotel**, which has been glamorously readapted by the Oberoi chain. On the escarpment above are the **Pyramids of Gizah**, the only one of the Seven Wonders of the Ancient World that is still intact and a landmark hard to miss.

The Pyramids: Khufu (2551–2528 BC), second king of the 4th Dynasty, known in Greek as *Kheops*, chose to build his funerary complex north of Saqqarah near ancient Rostau, which was perhaps the northernmost suburb of Memphis. Profiting by the experience gained from his father's two pyramids at Dahshur, he built the **Great Pyramid**, the largest in Egypt (but not, apparently, in the

Tapestry from the Wissa Wassef workshops.

236

world: the pyramid of Quetzalcoatl at Cholula, south of Mexico City, is much shorter, but covers three times as much ground) and the most accurately orientated to compass points. Its size – it was originally 480 ft (146 metres) high and contains an estimated 2.3 million stone blocks – renders it virtually indestructible, though later generations have had a good try.

Almost all the fine white limestone casing that once covered it has been removed and 30 ft (10 metres) of stone is missing from the top. Medieval Arabs, looking for treasure excavated a hole in the north side and found a complex of corridors and chambers. Today one enters by this robbers' tunnel, which joins the ancient corridor leading up to the **Grand Gallery**, an extraordinary spacious hall, 28 ft (8.5 metres) high, and the so-called "King's Chamber", which houses a large broken sarcophagus. Incidentally, clambering into the pyramid is not recommended for anyone who suffers from claustrophobia.

Outside on the east face are the remains of the **Mortuary Temple**, a black basalt pavement. The usual causeway leads from here and disappears into the encroaching village below, where blocks from the **Valley Temple** have recently been uncovered 15 ft (4.5 metres) below ground level. Beside the causeway is the unmarked shaft leading to the burial chamber of the king's mother, **Hetepheres,** where her wonderful furniture was found. Reconstructed, it is now in the Egyptian Museum.

Several empty boat pits can be seen beside the pyramid. On the south side an intact one was excavated in 1954 and a dismantled **cedarwood boat** was uncovered. The boat is now housed, reconstructed, in the museum on the site. Another intact pit lies next to it and a recent fisheye-lens camera probe revealed a second dismantled boat within, in an advanced state of decay. The boats were probably used in Khufu's funerary cortège, then buried for his use in the Underworld.

The question of how the pyramids were erected has vexed generations of Egyptologists and engineers. There was no slavery as such in the Old Kingdom. What seems most likely is that during the three months of annual inundation, when no other work was possible, gangs of peasants joined professional quarrymen at Gizah and hauled the 2½-ton blocks into place, using ramps or levers to lift them. Most of the blocks were quarried locally and came from the depression south of the pyramids. The granite of the internal chambers came from Aswan, the fine limestone for the casing from across the river at Tura, south of Maadi.

A cemetery for Khufu's family stretches out in neat rows below the east side of the Great Pyramid; tombs of courtiers lie on the west. The strict organisation visible here suggests a tightly-controlled central government focused very much on the king, and it is interesting that later Egyptian tradition made Khufu a despot. Several of these tombs

are now open. None of their decoration is as varied as in the tombs at Saqqarah, but worth visiting are those of **Queen Meryankh** in the eastern cemetery, **Yasen** and **Iymery** in the western cemetery. Keys are obtained from the inspector's office.

The **second pyramid** belongs to Khufu's son, **Khafra** (2520–2494 BC), known to the Greeks from Herodotus as *Khephren*. Built on higher ground, it is slightly smaller – originally 471 ft (143 metres) high – and slopes at a slightly sharper angle. The lower courses were cased with red granite, the upper with white limestone, some of which has survived at the top: it is likely that the tips of all pyramids were originally covered in gold. Inside there is only one chamber, connected to the outside by two corridors, one of which is still blocked. On the east side are the remains of **Khafra's Mortuary Temple**, where the fine casing stones have been stripped away to reveal a massive core. The same technical capability can be

Below and right, aerial views of the pyramids and the Sphinx.

seen in the well-preserved **Valley Temple** at the foot of the causeway, where the red granite casing has survived.

The Sphinx: It was in this little building that a marvellous diorite statue of Khafra was found, with several other damaged statues of the king. Next door is the Guardian of the Necropolis – **the Sphinx** – now suffering badly from rising groundwater, wind erosion, and air pollution. This remarkable statue with the body of a lion and the face of King Khafra was sculpted out of the living rock at a point where a softer layer of yellow limestone runs between harder, greyer stone. The head has survived well, considering the serious attempts in the Middle Ages to disfigure it, and is of harder stone, but the striated body, composed of soft rock, is weathering badly. At least three attempts were made to repair it in antiquity, the first in the time of Tuthmosis IV (1401–1391 BC), who had a prophetic dream here and cleared away the ever-encroaching sand. The last ancient repair work was done in Roman times and it is currently being worked on by the Egyptian Antiquities Organisation.

The third pyramid is the much smaller one built by the grandson of Khufu, **Menkaura** (2490–2472 BC), called *Mykerinos* by Herodotus. It was never finished. Much of its casing is still unsmoothed and its Valley Temple was constructed of mud-brick rather than stone. It was here that the schist pair of King Menkaura and Queen Khamenebty (now displayed in the Boston Museum) was found, as well as the wonderful greywacke triads of the King accompanied by pairs of goddesses with Khamenebty's face, now to be found in the Egyptian Museum.

It would appear that the enormous efforts at Gizah had exhausted the country. The last king of the 4th dynasty, **Shepseskaf**, was buried not in a pyramid, but in a *mastabah* tomb at South Saqqarah; and the pyramids of the 5th and 6th Dynasties are rather shabby affairs by comparison.

DAY TRIPS

Cairo holds out endless possibilities for enjoyable expeditions, but there are times when a Western visitor wants something quieter and less thoroughly populated. From most places in town, countryside or desert is less than an hour away. Until the 1950s it was usual to find peace and quiet simply by climbing the Muqattam east of the Citadel, to visit the convent of the Bektashi dervishes, the Spring of Moses (Ayn Musa), the Mosque and Watchtower of Badr al-Gamali (al-Guyushi), or a small petrified forest – all of which now are either in military areas prohibited to the public or have simply disappeared under the new suburb of Madinat al-Muqattam. Other popular objectives for excursions were Helwan-les-Bains, which only the insatiably curious would now want to visit, or the large petrified forest that still exists, much diminished, in the desert behind Maadi.

To the water: To spend a pleasant day away from the city one must go much further afield. A trip to the Gizah and Saqqarah pyramids, with the journey broken at the Mena House Hotel, can still occupy an entire day, as it did at the beginning of the century, when part of the journey was made by train or tram. An hour and a half away by car to the east is **Ismailia**, which offers swimming in the Suez Canal. **Fayed**, on the Bitter Lakes half an hour south of Ismailia, has become fashionable with rich Egyptians for water-skiing and windsurfing.

Ambitious day trippers could try **Port Said**, which is situated an hour beyond Ismailia to the north at the mouth of the canal, which offers vaudeville architecture and duty-free shopping. **Alexandria**, the great Mediterranean port city, is a similar distance away on the other side of the Delta, but to go there and back in a day takes some six hours and leaves no time for fun.

The beach that is most accessible in a day is at **Ayn Sukhna**, 25 miles (40 km) south of Suez on the Hurgadah (Ghardaqah) road. From Cairo the journey takes about two hours. Although the beauty of the place is marred by a tanker terminal, a minefield barricaded with barbed wire, and a half-built five-star hotel, the coral reef offshore and the mountains rising behind the beach make the trip well worthwhile. Dolphins can sometimes be seen patrolling up and down the coast and during the spring and autumn, bird migrations wheel in the thermals rising along the cliffs.

Just outside Cairo on the Ayn Sukhna road is **Wadi Digla**, a steep-sided valley with water-carved rock formations, popular with the city's joggers and picnickers. About a kilometre from the Ring Road, opposite a cemetery, a car-worn track to the right leads to the head of the wadi.

More than an oasis: The most popular day-trip, however, is to the **Fayyum**, about two hours away by car or bus to

the southwest: the main road to the Fayyum from Cairo leaves the Cairo-Alexandria Desert Road just beyond the Gizah Pyramids. The Fayyum is sometimes spoken of as an oasis, but it is in fact an area of over 1,700 sq. miles (4,500 sq. km), half of it desert, irrigated from the Nile by a canal, the Bahr Yusuf. The canal was originally constructed under Amenemhat I in about 2000 BC, when the whole region was a marsh. Amenemhat's canal created an enormous lake some 59 ft (18 metres) above sea-level. Nearly 2,000 years later the Ptolemies began draining the lake and reclaimed over 300,000 acres (1,200 sq. km) of superb arable land, made fertile by Nile silt, transforming the Fayyum into the "Garden of Egypt". Over 315,000 acres (130,000 hectares), 30 percent of the Fayyum's total area, is now cultivated land.

Lake Qarun, at the northern edge of the Fayyum, represents the remains of Amenemhat's lake, diminished by evaporation and saltier than the sea. Its

surface measures 24 miles long by 5 miles wide (40 by 9 km). There is shooting here throughout the weeks of the water-fowl migration; and in summertime, picnics on Lake Qarun's beaches featuring fish fresh from the lake, grilled by the Fayyumi fishermen who caught them, are popular with Cairenes. The noise of stereos and loud drumming do much to spoil the serenity and mystery of the lake itself, however, and for a quieter time escape can be made to a large, freshwater lake created south of the Fayyum in the 1970s at **Wadi Rayaan**, which is accessible only by four-wheel drive.

Land in the Fayyum holds as much attraction as water. The region's capital, **Madinat Fayyum** (Fayyum City), is crowded, dusty and, except for its obelisk, three old mosques, and seven waterwheels, it is not really very interesting. Elsewhere in the Fayyum there are plenty of Middle Kingdom and Ptolemaic sites worth visiting, however, and the countryside is pleasant to wander through, boasting a great variety of vegetation. Here is a rare landscape for Egypt, with shady orchards, Coptic monasteries, moaning waterwheels, and occasional deep ravines. Particularly notable among the ancient sites are the Ptolemaic city of **Karanis (Kom Awshiim)**, left at the entrance into the Fayyum along the road from Gizah, and the temples of **Dimayh (Soknopaiou Nesos)**, above the northern shore of Lake Qarun, **Qasr Qarun (Dionysias)**, west of the lake and **Madinat Madi (Narmouthis, Ibion)**, the most important site in the Fayyum.

Amenemhat III's pyramid at **Hawarah**, just off the road to Beni Sueif from Madinat Fayyum, marks the site of the Labyrinth, which Herodotus declared to surpass even the Pyramids in wonder. Strabo, likewise awed, described it in detail 400 years later: it contained some 3,000 chambers, half of them above ground, half below. The sense of history here is made more potent by desolation: having lost its lime-

Beads and bird for sal in the Fayyum.

stone casing, the pyramid is a pile of mud-brick; and the Labyrinth, which was its vast mortuary temple, excavated with great difficulty by Sir Flinders Petrie in 1888, has been levelled since and is now little more than a cratered plain dotted with potsherds. In a cemetery near here Petrie found the famous Fayyum portraits. It is possible to return to Cairo from the Fayyum via the Nile Valley. The road leading north from Hawarah eventually enters the Nile Valley near the collapsed **Pyramid of Mayduum**.

The Barrages: The Barrages (al-Qanaatir al-Khayriyyah) are best approached 12 miles (20 km) north of Cairo at Qanaatir al-Khayriyyah, a village on the east bank a few hundred yards north of the point where the Nile splits into its Rosetta and Damietta branches. Originally conceived in 1833 by Muhammad Ali and his hydraulic experts, the barrages were planned as a means of regulating the flow of water into the Delta. Work began in 1835 under the great French engineer Mougel Bey. Building bulwarks strong enough to stop the Nile proved more difficult than expected, however, and cost overruns were ferocious. Three huge canals were opened, but in 1867 the dams were abandoned as unsafe. The project was finally completed between 1883 and 1891, as part of a vast irrigation scheme, by a British engineer, Sir Colin Scott-Moncrieff, who gave full credit to Mougel for the ultimate feasibility of his plan.

On the land between the redbrick neo-Gothic barrages are public parks with lush grass and trees of huge girth. Bicycles, horses, carriages and boats are available for rent. On Fridays and during public holidays the park becomes very crowded; and for a place on the grass during the spring holiday of Sham an-Nessiim it is advisable to arrive early. The most pleasant way of getting to the Barrages is by boat. Round trips aboard large and noisy craft leave from outside the Television Building in Maspero on

ailia.

Friday, Saturday and Sunday mornings. The time of departure and the price are dictated by the whim of the captain: if there are not enough people interested, he won't leave at all.

Sacred valley: Travellers to **Wadi Natruun**, 60 miles (100 km) from Cairo west of the Cairo-Alexandria Desert Road, may be surprised to know that in the Christian era it supported a large population. This lonely valley, where sparse vegetation rises up from sandy soil, is surrounded by the Western Desert. What water there is in the local lakes evaporates in the summer to leave deposits of salt and hydrated sodium carbonate, better known in English as "natron", from the Arabic *natruun*, which also gives the valley its name.

Wadi Natruun had been a sacred place under the Pharaohs long before both Christianity and monasticism were introduced in the 4th century by St Macarius. After he retired to the valley to meditate, over 50 monasteries were established. Buildings were erected using the remains of Pharaonic temples, around which hermits contemplated in their own individual cells or caves. When the Arab conqueror Amr ibn al-As reached Wadi Natruun in 641, he was met by several thousand monks, who welcomed him as a saviour from Byzantine persecution.

Only four monasteries remain – **Diyr Abu Maqar** in the south, **Diyr Anba Bishay** and **Diyr as-Suryan** in the middle and **Diyr Baramuus** in the desert to the north. From outside, they closely resemble each other, with their high, imposing walls, built for defence against Bedouin attacks. Inside there are churches, fruit trees, well-tended vegetable plots. Black-cassocked monks sit in the shade between performances of their offices chatting with pilgrims. It is from among their number that the Coptic Patriarch is chosen.

The characters of the four monasteries are most clearly defined by the exploits of their founders and the relics they contain. Coptic monks and laity alike tell elaborate legends of the early Christians. At Diyr as-Suryan, where women are not allowed, Mary Magdelene's hair will be produced. At Diyr Anba Bishay is the body of Saint Bishay himself, which is reputed to have remained in the same condition as the day he died, in the late 4th century. Until a century ago the corpse was actually kept under a simple sheet, from which the saint would stretch out a hand to those visitors who were specially favoured, but when he failed to salute the Khedive Tewfiq, the Patriarch ordered him to be coffined.

Except Diyr as-Suryan, the monasteries are open to both male and female visitors, but women are not allowed to stay the night at the rest houses. Visitors should be warned that the monasteries are closed during times of fasting, which are: Sexagesima Monday to Orthodox Easter (61 days); Advent (25 November–6 January); the variable period between Pentecost and the Feast of the Apostles, on 12 July; and two weeks

Coptic monk at Wadi Natruun.

before Assumption (7–21 August).

The Delta: Population pressure in the Delta has reduced most ancient sites such as **Bubastis** and **Sais** to a few dislocated blocks engulfed by modern housing, but one or two have survived the worst depredations and are worth the effort of a day-trip from Cairo.

At the north-east corner of the Delta, at what was once an important harbour site, lies **Tanis** (modern San al-Hagar), capital and royal burial place of the 21st and 22nd Dynasties. An enormous mound, red from the profusion of broken pottery littering the surface, rises steeply from desolate salt-flats. The entrance to the site is marked by a small building that displays some of the objects found here. A path leads round to the entrance of what was once a vast temple of Amun-Ra, reduced to a picturesque jumble of obelisks, columns and colossal statues, some restored to the vertical, but most lying where they fell. Many fragments bear the name of Ramses II, but the French archaeologists who work here have shown conclusively that the temple is later, founded by King Psusennes I (1040–992 BC), who imported older architectural elements to grace his new city and to give it an air of antiquity. Most were plundered from Ramses II's capital, Per-Ramses (modern Qantir) 23 miles (38 km) south, hence the prominence of that king's name.

South of the temple, a group of six royal tombs of the 21st and 22nd Dynasties were found almost intact. Their gold and silver treasures – including a falcon-headed coffin – are now in the Cairo Museum. Three of the tombs (numbers 1, 3 and 5) are decorated with mythological scenes from the Underworld that are worth seeing: the key is with the local inspector.

The Delta has become the focus of major archaeological activity, as population pressure has meanwhile put many sites in danger of being built over permanantly and thus becoming lost forever to Egyptological research.

ta farmers
e a tea-
ak near a
ter-wheel.

TRAVEL TIPS

GETTING THERE

BY AIR

Most major airlines land regularly at Cairo International Airport, a link between Europe and destinations in Africa and Asia. Its three terminals handle over 45,000 flights annually and have a very good safety record. The flag carrier is EgyptAir, which flies to Luxor, Aswan, and Hurghada (Ghardaqah), as well as internationally. Two smaller airlines, Air Sinai and Zas, also offer domestic flights.

BY SEA

Passenger ships, cruisers, and freighters call at Alexandria, Port Said, and Suez; car-ferries ply between Alexandria and Piraeus, between Alexandria and Venice, and between Nuwaybah (in Sinai) and Aqaba (in Jordan). From Alexandria, Port Said, or Suez, Cairo is 2½ hours away by train, bus, or taxi. From Nuwaybah the trip is four or five hours by taxi, longer by bus. It is technically possible to sail up the Nile Delta to Cairo from the Mediterranean, but no passenger service does so and no foreign private yachtsman has been permitted to do so since 1981.

Motor vehicles are most commonly brought into the country by sea. The owner of a vehicle must have a *triptyque* or *carnet de passage en douane* from a recognised automobile club. The multiple-entry permit then issued is valid for 90 days. The choice otherwise is to pay customs duties that can amount to 250 percent of whatever is deemed to have been the full purchase price of the vehicle. An International Driver's Licence and International Motor Vehicle Licence are necessary, as is the purchase of insurance on arrival. Also required is a deposit against road tax and customs duty, but a portion of these sums is refundable.

BY RAIL

Rail connections between Egypt and North Africa or the Levant no longer exist. Egypt had an efficient internal rail system earlier than most European countries, however, and Cairo is the centre of service to all parts of the Nile Valley. Of the three classes of accommodation only First Class, which offers air-conditioning on certain routes, is recommended. Service between Alexandria and Cairo is excellent: the train to take is the non-stop air-conditioned express, called the *turbino*, which runs three times daily. In Alexandria tickets can be bought at the Cairo Station (*Muhattat Misr*), which is the main railway station, or at Sidi Gabr station. In Cairo tickets can be bought at the main railway station in Maydan Ramsis or at such designated places as the Telephone Central office in Bab al-Luq. For booking reservations, especially for rail travel to Upper Egypt, travel agents may be helpful.

BY ROAD

It is possible to drive into Egypt from Libya, Egypt's neighbour to the west, and Israel, its neighbour to the north. To enter Egypt from Israel by private vehicle, however, requires special permission, which is not always granted and may take time to obtain.

The road system within Egypt connects all major cities. Primary roads, which work more or less like European or North American highways, include the Desert Road between Cairo and Alexandria, the main road between Cairo and Ismailiyyah, the new Red Sea highway, and portions of the new main road between Cairo and Luxor. Secondary and tertiary roads, however, are apt to change suddenly from well-paved one- or two-lane stretches to dirt tracks. Major road-work, deep pot-holes, barriers or obstructions, official and otherwise, can appear without warning on any road, primary, secondary, or tertiary, at any time; and drivers' reactions, discipline and skills may leave much to be desired even during daylight hours. At night nearly all roads are badly lit and drivers of trucks and buses, steeped in die-hard *machismo*, customarily use what they mistakenly believe to be stimulants to give themselves the illusion that they are wide awake and functioning at full efficiency. Driving at night should therefore be avoided. If inescapable, it should be confined to well-lit urban areas alone.

Buses into Cairo are plentiful from all main towns, as are shared taxis, which can be very cheap indeed. Excellent bus services ply non-stop between Cairo and Alexandria and there is regular service from the border with Israel.

TRAVEL ESSENTIALS

VISAS & PASSPORTS

All visitors to Cairo need valid passports and visas, which are available upon entry into Egypt. Visas may be acquired in advance from Egyptian consulates, which are to be found in every major capital and in many other large cities. Applications in person will require 24 hours for processing; a self-addressed stamped envelope containing your passport, a passport photo and the required fee will save a personal appearance, but will mean a waiting period of two weeks. A single-entry visa allows one entry into the country for a stay of one month. If you plan to leave and re-enter, a multiple-entry visa is necessary. Tourist residence visas are available that allow prolonged stays. Student visas, which are granted only to students who can show that they are actually already registered in Egyptian universities, are usually valid for one year. Visas can be extended at the Passport Department of the Mugamaa, the ministerial complex on the southern end of Maydan at-Tahrir (Tahrir Square).

STUDENTS

An international student card is useful for occasional discounts.

MONEY MATTERS

The Egyptian pound (in Arabic *gineh*, both singular and plural, abbreviated as LE) is divided into 100 piastres and is printed in denominations of 1, 5, 10, 20 or 100 (rare) *gineh*. Piastre notes come in denominations of 5 (rare), 10, 25 or 50; and there are coins worth 1, 5, 10 and 20 piastres. Travellers' cheques can be changed in most Cairo banks, where the official rate of exchange is posted daily. Changing money on the black market is a punishable offence. Major credit cards are accepted in all larger hotels and in many restaurants and shops.

HEALTH

A tourist who has within the past five days been in an area associated with a cholera or yellow fever epidemic may be required to show a valid inoculation certificate. Otherwise there are no specific health requirements for entry into Egypt. It is wise to ensure that diphtheria (in infants), tetanus and polio immunizations are up to date. Protection against hepatitis, typhoid and meningitis may also be important, particularly if you are travelling with children. Malaria, known throughout Africa south of the Sahara, is so rare in Egypt that special precautions are never taken.

Many visitors experience some degree of "Gippy Tummy", due to the ingestion of strange fauna. Danger is chiefly from dehydration. Diarrhœa that lasts longer than two days should be treated: remedies are available at any pharmacy. Uncooked, unwashed, or unpeeled fruits and vegetables should be avoided. Buffets featuring mayonnaise or food that has been microwaved, should be treated with prudence. Visitors are advised to drink only water known to have been filtered and boiled or bottled water. The locally bottled brand is called *Báraka*. It comes in 1.5 litre plastic bottles and in half-litre plastic flasks and is available virtually everywhere.

WHAT TO WEAR

Most important is comfort. Cairo has a desert climate: typically, it is very hot during the day in summer, cool during the day in winter, cool at night during the summer, and chilly at night during the winter. Air-conditioning is not unusual, but central heating is rare; and winter visitors often regret not having brought heavier underwear, since interiors can be uncomfortably cold.

Pure cotton and wool, worn loosely in removable layers, are the answer for all seasons. For men, evening clothes are unnecessary – a dark suit is correct for even the most formal occasions – but many restaurants require jackets and ties. Women often find Cairo nightlife an excuse for chic, but daytime touring in the city requires clothes that are "modest" and unobtrusive, with the shoulders and upper arms covered and skirt lengths below the knee. Shorts continue to be regarded as out of place for both men or women except on the tennis court. Mini-skirts cannot be worn in the streets of Cairo without exciting – at the least – unwelcome comment; and toplessness is discouraged on the sundecks or in the pools of even the most sophisticated hotels or clubs. Comfortable walking shoes and sunglasses are important. A shawl or scarf is useful for evenings and hats are important for touring outdoor sites during the day, since sunstroke is possible even in winter.

ELECTRICITY

Appliances such as hairdriers and shavers should be adjusted for the current, which is normally 220 volts, 50 cycles. Blackouts occur, however, so a battery-powered lamp or torch may be useful and is certainly handy to have in some of the darker Pharaonic monuments. Batteries of all sizes are readily available, as is colour camera film up to ASA 400 (*see page 285*).

ANIMAL QUARANTINE

All animals or animal products must be declared at the point of entry from overseas. Pet dogs and cats must have a valid rabies vaccination certificate and a veterinary certificate from their country of origin. Special permission from the Ministry of Agriculture must be granted before certain livestock, including cattle, sheep and goats, can be imported.

CUSTOMS

Each visitor is permitted to enter Egypt with 250 grammes of tobacco or 50 cigars and one litre of alcohol. Beyond this limit, each visitor is entitled to purchase – within a month of entry twice a year – four bottles of liquor at a tax-free shop inside the country, an extra allowance of tobacco, and a litre of perfume. There are tax-free shops at Cairo airport. In Cairo the main tax-free shop is on Shari Gamiat ad-Dawal al-Arabiyyah in Mohandisin.

Motor vehicles (*see below*), videotape recorders, movie cameras and projectors are all dutiable unless re-exported; firearms and explosives are prohibited, as are any books or other printed matter that may be considered subversive or incompatible with public interest. In practice, such materials can include any publications containing depictions of the female nude. Tools and equipment that are to be used only in connection with and during the duration of a specific project are supposed to be admitted duty-free, if such limited use can be shown somehow to be guaranteed, but sufficiently convincing proofs may be difficult to obtain.

RESERVATIONS

It is advisable to make hotel or cruise reservations from outside Egypt through an agent before you travel. In larger hotels blocks of rooms are normally reserved by agencies, leaving very little for the traveller arriving on his own without reservations, who may be told that there are no vacancies even when a hotel seems half empty.

ON ARRIVAL

A notice stamped in passports at entry into Egypt says "Registration Within 7 Days" but arrivals in Cairo should in fact be registered within 48 hours, either at the nearest police station or the Mugamaa, with re-registration at each new city visited. Hotels perform this service routinely, but visitors staying in private houses must make other arrangements to be registered. Their hosts may be held responsible for their failure to do so.

ON DEPARTURE

Egyptian currency must not be taken out of the country. Departure taxes, payable on exit, are LE 5.00 at Cairo Airport (usually paid by airlines, who include the charge in the purchase price of tickets) and LE 10.50 when departure is by road.

BACKPACKING

Egyptians believe themselves to be a warm-hearted, welcoming people. They are, however, puzzled by those young travellers who seem to make a game of dirt and poverty. Backpackers should be warned, in any case, that the Egyptian government's official – if unwritten – policy is to discourage all low-budget travelling indiscriminately.

Young male travellers with beards and/or backpacks can therefore occasionally find themselves jailed on trumped-up charges – the failure of an Egyptian passport control official to affix the appropriate stamp becomes an offence the foreign passport-bearer must pay for. There is no *habeas corpus* in Egypt and uncharged prisoners are customarily not only kept *incommunicado*, but also frequently moved from place to place. Since it is difficult to discover where a prisoner has been taken after arrest, it is difficult to obtain his release, no matter how much influence he or his friends and family may be able to muster. Backpackers should never travel alone, should carefully compare the stamps placed by Egyptian officials in their passports on entry, and should be extremely wary of pimps, drug-pushers, or illegal money-changers, who can be informers.

GETTING ACQUAINTED

GEOGRAPHY & POPULATION

Occupying the northeastern corner of Africa and the southwestern edge of Asia, Egypt has an area of 626,000 sq. miles (1,002,000 sq. km) more than 90 percent of which is desert. It measures 600 miles (1,000 km) from north to south and 750 miles (1,250 km) from east to west at its widest point. Libya lies to the west, the Mediterranean Sea to the north, Israel to the northeast, the Red Sea and the Gulf of Aqaba to the east, Sudan to the south. Entering from Sudan, the Nile river runs the length of the country from south to north, spreading out into the Delta just north of Cairo and emptying through several branches into the Mediterranean.

Most of the population (55 million) is urban, concentrated in Cairo and Alexandria, in the cities of the Delta, and in large towns along the Nile. Approximately 90 percent are officially Sunni Muslim; most of the remainder are Christians belonging to the Coptic Orthodox Church.

Cairo is situated on the Nile, 80 miles (135 km) west of the Red Sea 100 miles (160 km) inland from the Mediterranean. The Delta has been impassable in an east-west direction until recent times and Cairo has therefore been the point furthest north giving access to it, as well as to Upper Egypt. Cairo is not only Egypt's capital, but also its largest city, with a population officially estimated at over 14 million, but unofficially believed to be more than 17 million. The government itself has acknowledged that some areas of the city have the highest population density in the world.

LANGUAGE & POLITICS

The language of Cairo is Arabic, which is the official language of Egypt. In Arabic the name "Egypt" is *Misr*, which also happens to be the traditional name of Cairo throughout the Middle East. A republic, Egypt is thus officially and formally styled *al-Gumhurriyyat al-Arabiyyat al-Misriyyah*, the Arab Republic of Egypt (ARE). Its government is headed by a president (Hosni Mubarak since 1981), who is also Commander in Chief of the Army. He appoints the Prime Minister and a Cabinet of Ministers. Representatives elected from all districts of the country sit in a legislative body, the National Assembly. Fifty percent must be "workers" or "peasants". Women and Copts are represented according to a quota, which is made up by presidential appointment if an insufficient number of either should be elected. The Shura Council, an advisory council of 140 elected members and 70 appointed members, acts as an upper chamber.

TIME ZONES

Egypt is two hours ahead of GMT and six hours ahead of Eastern Standard Time. At noon in Cairo it is 2 a.m. in San Francisco, 6 a.m. in New York, 10 a.m. in London, 11 a.m. in Rome, 3.30 p.m. in New Delhi, 4.30 p.m in Bangkok, 7 p.m. in Tokyo, 8 p.m. in Sydney.

CLIMATE

Though the Northern Coast and the Delta have a Mediterranean climate, with an annual rainfall of 7 inches (18 cm), rain is rare in Cairo and further south. Summer days can be torrid (100°F/40°C) and even winter days may be warm outdoors, but nights in either winter or summer – especially on the Pyramids Plateau, at the Citadel, or on the Muqattam hills – can have a desert chill. Cairo's mild winter makes it the best season for tourism: summers are not only hot, but have become increasingly humid. During April and May the famous *khamsin* sandstorms may occur, which can last anything from an hour to one or two days.

BUSINESS HOURS

Banks are usually open from 8.30 a.m. to 1.30 p.m. daily except Friday and Saturday. Bank branches in major hotels often stay open until 8 p.m. **Clinics** and **private-sector**

offices in general operate from 9 a.m. to 2 p.m. daily in winter and from 9 a.m. to 1.p.m. in summer; they usually re-open between 5 p.m. and 8 p.m. and many clinics are open only during these evening hours. Muslim-owned offices are likely to be closed on Thursday afternoons and on Fridays, Christian-owned offices on Saturday afternoons and Sundays. **Government offices** function between 9 a.m. and 2 p.m. except Fridays (and sometimes Saturdays) and holidays (*see below*). **Museums** are generally closed on Fridays during the Muslim noon prayer (approximately 11 a.m. to 1.30 p.m).

Many **private-sector shops** are open on Fridays and Saturdays, but in central Cairo and in Khan al-Khalili most shops, large or small, public-sector or private-sector, Muslim, Christian, and even Jewish-owned, are traditionally closed on Sundays. All hairdressing, dry-cleaning, and ironing establishments are closed on Mondays. Greengrocers and other shops selling food are permitted by law to open daily as early as 8 a.m. and may either remain open virtually all day or close at 3 and re-open at 5 p.m, staying open until 8 p.m. or later. Other shops usually open between 9 a.m. and 1 p.m. and 5 p.m. to 8 p.m.

No Egyptian feels governed by calendars or time-clocks. To be sure of achieving an objective, it is therefore best to settle for the hours between 10 a.m. and noon on a day when the establishment in question is likely to be open. During Ramadan, in fact, the Muslim month of fasting, these hours may be the only ones during which business can be successfully transacted, since all business hours are radically curtailed and even Christian establishments open late and close early.

ANNUAL EVENTS

A diary of cultural events that are supposed to take place regularly in Cairo would be quite misleading. Even events that are billed as "annual" may be staged at intervals of either more or less than year or be cancelled altogether at the last minute. The only observances that can be counted upon to occur at the appointed times are popular religious festivals,: the great *mawalid* of popular saints like Sayyidna Husayn, Sayyidah Zaynab, Sayyidah Nafisa, or Imam ash-Shafii.

Four calendars, used for different purposes, are current in Egypt.

The **Western (Gregorian) calendar** – that is, the solar calendar introduced in Catholic countries by Pope Gregory XIII in 1582, also known as the Gregorian calendar, with years designated as BC and AD and months bearing recognisable forms of the familiar Roman names (January, February, and so on) – is commonly employed for all practical purposes, though many people refer to the months by number rather than by name.

National secular holidays, during which all government offices are closed, include the following:
Union Day – 16 February
Liberation of Sinai Day – 25 April
Labour Day – 1 May
Evacuation Day – 18 June
The Anniversary of the 1952 Revolution – 23 July
Armed Forces Day – 6 October
Suez Day – 24 October
Victory Day – 23 December
Sham an-Nessim ("sniff the breeze"), celebrated the Monday after Orthodox Easter, is a holiday for all Egyptians, be they Muslim, Christian, and Jewish, and dates back to Pharaonic times. The entire population goes to the countryside or to the city's few remaining urban green spaces for a picnic that traditionally includes hard-boiled eggs and pickled fish.

Pope Gregory's calendar is merely a revised version of the Julian calendar, named for Julius Caesar, who took time off during his dalliance with Cleopatra to commission it from the Alexandrian mathematician Sosigenes. Inherited by Christendom, this pagan calendar was displaced in Catholic countries after 1582, but continued to be used in England and America until 1752 and remained official in Russia and other Orthodox countries as late as 1929. It survives in Egypt as the **Coptic ecclesiastical calendar**, consisting of 12 months of 30 days each, which still bear their ancient Egyptian names – not Roman names – almost unaltered, and an intercalary period of five days. Regulating the religious year of the Coptic Orthodox Church, it has been adapted or changed by the Church only to the extent that its years are reckoned as passing within an Era of Martyrs, the first day of which (1 Thoth of the first year) was originally equivalent to 29 August AD 284. Thanks to the disparity between the Julian and Gregorian years, however, the Coptic ecclesiastical year currently begins on a date which is equivalent to 11 September in the Western (Gregorian) calendar.

The **Coptic agricultural calendar**, a popular version of the ecclesiastical calendar, is often used as a kind of almanac for planning agricultural activities and predicting seasonal changes in weather.

Major Coptic feasts are: Coptic New Year, 1 Thut (11 September); Christmas, 29 Koiakh (7 January); Epiphany, (19 January); Annunciation, 29 Phamenoth (7 March); Easter and Pentecost, which are "moveable" (i.e, fixed by lunar calculation) and coincide with the same feasts in all the other Orthodox churches; the Feast of the Apostles Peter and Paul (12 July); and the Feast of the Assumption, 16 Mesori (22 August).

The **Muslim calendar** is not solar, but lunar and designates dates according to their distance in lunar years from the Hijrah (A.H.), the Prophet's withdrawal with his followers to Medina from Mecca in AD 622. Used for formal and official governmental and religious purposes, it regulates the Muslim religious year, which consists of 12 lunar months of 29 or 30 days. Containing only 354 days, the Muslim calendar is thus 11 days shorter than the solar year. In relation to the Western (Gregorian) solar calendar, it therefore moves forward 11 days each year, completing a full cycle (and thus "losing" a solar year) every 33 years.

The most important Muslim observance tied to the calendar is the annual fast during the hours of daylight throughout the lunar month of **Ramadan**. Special days for Muslims, some of which are also official holidays (marked with an asterisk) include:

Islamic New Year's Day *, 1 Moharram. The first day of the lunar month of Moharram begins the Muslim year.
Ashurah, 10 Moharram. The anniversary of the martyrdom of Sayyidna Husayn, the Prophet's grandson, is not an official holi-

day, but provides the occasion for a *mawlid* or celebration at the great mosque of Sayyidna Husayn in Cairo. It is otherwise a day of special significance to Shi'i Muslims, of whom there are very few in predominantly Sunni Egypt.

Mawlid en-Nabawi *, The Prophet's Birthday, 12 Rabi' al-Awal, is preceded by a colourful parade of all the Sufi orders in Egypt, which takes place during the two hours just before sunset the previous day.

Laylat al-Esraa wa al-Mi'rag, 27 Ragab, is the date of the Prophet's miraculous journey to Jerusalem.

Laylat al-Qadr, 26 Ramadan. Occurring near the end of Ramadan, the month of fasting – during which business hours are curtailed, while the hours of darkness are spent in social activities – this night commemorates the revelation of the first verse of the Qur'an.

Id al-Fitr * (Ramadan Bairam). 1–3 Shawwal. Marking the end of the Ramadan fast, this feast is celebrated during the first three days of Shawwal, the lunar month following Ramadan.

Id al-Adha *, (Qurban Bairam).10–14 Dhu'l-Higga. Commemorating Abraham's willingness to sacrifice his son, this feast takes place 40 days after the end of Ramadan and is traditionally begun with prayers and the slaughter of a sheep.

RELIGIOUS SERVICES

Cairo not only has hundreds of mosques, but also scores of churches, which serve virtually every Christian denomination, Eastern and Western. Most numerous are the Coptic Orthodox, who hold services in Arabic and are not confined to one quarter, but may be found throughout the city. Also represented are the following persuasions: Coptic Catholic, Coptic Evangelical (Presbyterian), Greek Orthodox, Melkite (Patriarchates of Jerusalem and Alexandria, Archbishopric of Sinai), Greek Catholic, Armenian Orthodox, Armenian Catholic, Syrian Orthodox (Jacobite), Syrian Catholic, Chaldean Orthodox, Chaldean Catholic, Maronite (Catholic), Roman Catholic, Anglican, Lutheran, Presbyterian, Baptist, Church of God, Quaker, and Mormon. Times of services conducted in various languages are published in Saturday's newspapers.

Three Jewish temples are active and hold Saturday services according to ritual requirements, i.e, when 10 male worshippers are present. The largest is Shaar Hashamaim on Sh. Adli, between Azbakiyyah and Sh. Talat Harb (Sulayman Pasha).

COMMUNICATIONS

RADIO

Broadcasting began in 1934 and Egypt has long had both AM and FM stations. The Radio Cairo European Station can be found on FM95 from 7 a.m. to midnight. News in English can be heard on this station at 7 a.m., 2.30 p.m., and 10 p.m. BBC broadcasts in English may be heard on medium-wave at 639 kHz during daylight hours (5.45–8.15 a.m. and 10.30–11.30 a.m. GMT daily, extended hours on weekends) and at 1323 kHz between sunset and sunrise.

TELEVISION

The Egyptian government offers three channels. Channel 1 is on the air from 1.30 p.m. to midnight and shows one foreign-language film, usually in English, one night a week. Channel 2, which broadcasts many French, British, American or Australian films, serials, or special programmes, is on the air from 2 p.m. to midnight and offers news in French at 7 p.m., news in English at 8 p.m. Foreign films are screened in censored versions but without interruptions in the afternoons, usually beginning at approximately 3.15, and at least four nights a week, beginning at around 10.30 p.m. Channel 3 broadcasts only in the early evening. Broadcasts from CNN, the American Cable News Network, are screened in many locations in the city.

JOURNALS

The city's most distinguished newspaper *Al-Ahram*, was founded in Alexandria in 1876, but the other three of Cairo's four current Arabic-language dailies date only from the revolutionary 1950s. Since 1956 all other daily newspapers in Egypt have disappeared – Alexandria, for example, is now the largest city in the world without any paper of its own – and the number of foreign-language publications has dropped to a handful. The only English-language daily newspaper is *The Egyptian Gazette*, begun in 1881, which publishes a Saturday edition called *The Egyptian Mail*. Its two French-language counterparts are *Le Progrès Egyptien* and *Le Journal d'Égypte*. There are also dailies in Greek (*Fws*) and Armenian (*Arev*).

Imported editions of all major British, French, German, and Italian daily and weekly newspapers – as well as *USA Today, The Wall Street Journal, The International Herald Tribune*, and *The European* – are generally available in hotels and at larger newsstands, usually a day or two late. Regional weekly publications in English include *The Middle East Times, The Arab Observer, Arab News*. Local English-language monthlies are *Business Monthly*, published by the American Chamber of Commerce, which carries business news, *Cairoscope*, which supplies a useful directory of current events, and *Cairo Today*, which offers features of special interest to both residents and visitors. *Places in Egypt* is a bi-monthly directory sold at newsstands and distributed free of charge by major hotels. The Ministry of Culture produces *Prism*, a quarterly covering the arts. Many European and American magazines are also available.

POSTAL SERVICES

Though improved since 1980, postal services remain erratic and there is no particular reason to suppose that a postcard sent to or from Cairo will ever arrive. The Central Post Office in Cairo, in Maydan al-Ataba, is open from 8 a.m. to 7 p.m. daily except Friday and smaller post offices are found in all areas of the city. Postage is cheap, but varies depending on whether the mail is going elsewhere in the Middle East or further afield. All parcels entering the country from abroad – even packages of books – are subject to customs regulations and taxation, usually at 100 percent of their perceived value, regardless of their use or worth. Most residents therefore instruct their friends and families abroad simply not to send anything to them in Egypt.

Couriers to and from Cairo are reliable and quick. They include:

DHL: 20 Gamal ad-Din Abu'l-Mohassin, Garden City. Tel: 355-7301, 356-0194

Federal Express: 1079 Corniche, Garden City. Tel: 355-1063, 355-2803; 31 Sh. Golf, Maadi. Tel: 350-7172; 24 Sh. Suria, Mohandisin. Tel: 349-0986, 360-1276; telex: 2355 YTS UN

IML Air Couriers: 2 Sh. Mustafa Kamil, Maadi. Tel: 350-1241, 350-1240; 16 Sh. Adli, Cairo. Tel: 390-8099, 390-7669, 392-1950; 25 Sh. Ibrahim, Heliopolis. Tel: 259-1945, 269-1311

Middle East Courier Service: 1 Sh. Mahmud Hafez at Sh. Safir, Heliopolis. Tel: 243-6328, 245-9281.

SOS Sky International: 45 Sh. Shehab, Mohandisin. Tel: 346-0028, 346-2503

TNT Skypak: 33 Sh. Duqqi, Cairo. Tel: 348-8204, 348-7228

World Courier Egypt: 17 Sh. Qasr an-Nil, Cairo. Tel: 777-678, 753-611

TELEPHONE, TELEX & FAX

Access to long-distance and international lines is limited and is subscribed to separately from normal service. Long-distance or trunk calls (i.e, to destinations outside Cairo) can therefore be made from few private phones, though they may be made from a post office or from any large hotel. Hotels, naturally, charge for the service. For holders of a Calling Card or similar credit device who wish to call the US, AT&T offers a service called USADirect, which gives direct access to an operator in the US and charges costs of calls at American internal rates. From Cairo the operator's number 356-0200; from outside Cairo prefix this number with "02".

Internal and overseas telegrams may be sent from hotels or main post offices, telexes and faxes from the business centres found in all major hotels and from many government offices. For telex information and complaints, call: 938-786, 930-709. For fax information and complaints, telephone: 767-644.

EMERGENCIES

SECURITY & CRIME

Except for the dangers of traffic, air pollution, and inadequately controlled construction, Cairo is one of the safest cities in the world at any time of the day or night. Mugging and aggravated assault, common in the West, are very rare. This fact – which should of course not be foolishly taken for granted – is due partly to effective policing, but mainly to the prevalence of an acute moral consciousness, especially among the city's poor, which is reinforced by both Islam and Christianity.

Petty crimes such as pickpocketing and purse-snatching, however, are unfortunately on the increase. Apart from sensation-seeking by the occasional middle-aged adventuress, imported films and television series have given rise to basic misconceptions about Western women: they are widely regarded as more highly sexed than Egyptian women and their relative freedom is interpreted as indicating that they are not only available, but ready and willing. Partially in consequence of these misconceptions, rape is by no means unknown, though Cairo is far less dangerous than, say, the west bank at Luxor. As in any other city, it is not advisable to venture into isolated areas alone at night; and the same care should be exercised with personal possessions as would be exercised anywhere.

LOSS OF BELONGINGS

Loss or theft should be immediately reported to the nearest police station, where a hand-written report will be filed. At the same time at least one copy of this report should be made, which will also have to be hand-written, since there are few photocopiers. This copy will certainly be needed later, when to secure it from scratch would mean going back to the police station, requesting that the appropriate file be produced, then hiring a scribe to make a hand-written copy, which would then have to be checked against the original, authorised as a true copy, and finally stamped with fiscal stamps.

Reporting to the police is vital and necessary. Loss or theft of passports must be additionally reported to the appropriate consul, who will require a copy of the police report before issuing a temporary replacement. Loss or theft of credit cards should be reported to the issuing agencies, who may also require copies of the police report or its number. In many cases stolen goods are recovered.

POLICE

In emergencies: dial 122

Police Headquarters, with connections to all stations: Tel: 930-022
Abdin. Sh. Gumhuriyyah at Sh. Abd al-Aziz. Tel: 916-604
Qasr an-Nil. Sh. Qasr an-Nil. Tel: 355-7351
Garden City. 11 Sh. Aysha at-Taymuriyya. Tel: 354-0686
Bulaq. Wakalat al-Karnub. Tel: 741-426, 770-539
Gazirah. 2 Sh. Hasan Sabri, Zamalek. Tel: 340-1719
Mohandisin Sh. al-Quds ash-Sherif. Tel: 347-9216
Aguza. Sh. an-Nil. Tel: 413-102
Duqqi. Maydan al-Galaa (facing the Sheraton Hotel). Tel: 348-5501
Gizah. Sh. Al-Bahr al-Azam. Tel: 723-428
Pyramids. Sh. al-Haram (Pyramids Road). Tel: 853-955
Heliopolis (Misr al-Gadidah). Sh. Dimashq. Maydan al-Gama. Tel: 432-305
Old Cairo (Misr al-Qadimah). Maydan al-Mamalik, Rawdah. Tel: 841-328
Maadi. 70 Road 13, Maadi. Tel: 250-3958, 250-2584

MEDICAL SERVICES

Medical services in Cairo are adequate in emergencies for basic care, but not for serious injury or illness. Several hospitals have emergency departments. A cash deposit is usually required for admission. Nursing standards are very low. If a lengthy stay is required, a friend or relative should therefore move in to take care of basic needs. Ambulance services exist (*see below*), but training and equipment leave something to be desired and it is often as fast and as comfortable to take a taxi.

Pharmacies are usually open from 10 a.m. to 10 p.m. Most pharmacists are highly trained and up-to-date in their knowledge; and all of them speak some English, which is the language of instruction in their field. Drugs are cheap in Egypt; and since many are sold without the additional expense of prescriptions purchased from physicians, pharmacists are expected to exercise more initiative and more judgement than is usual elsewhere. For information about pharmacies open in each district on a 24-hour basis, phone 140. For medical/pharmaceutical information, Tel: 755-439 (night), 749-012 (daytime).

AMBULANCE SERVICE & MAJOR HOSPITALS

In emergencies: dial 121

Ambulance service, with connections to all districts: Tel: 770-018/123/230
Ambulance service, Gizah. Tel: 720-385
Ambulance service, Heliopolis. Tel: 244-4327
Ambulance service, Maadi. Tel: 350-2873
As-Salam Hospital. 3 Sh. Suria, Mohandisin. Tel: 340-7561
Anglo-American Hospital. Zamalek. Tel: 341-8631
Arab Contractors Medical Centre. Al-Gebel al-Ahdar, Madinat Nasr. Tel: 832-534
Cairo Medical Centre. Maydan Roxy, Heliopolis. Tel: 680-237
Nile Badrawi Hospital. Corniche, Maadi. Tel: 363-8688, 363-8167/8
As-Salam International Hospital. Corniche, Maadi. Tel: 363-8050, 363-4194, 363-8424

LEFT LUGGAGE

There is no left luggage depot in Cairo. Most hotels are very obliging in this respect, however, and will often allow guests to leave their bags in a back room or cloakroom for a few hours or even for a few days.

GETTING AROUND

ORIENTATION

Cairo proper is east of the Nile and now centres on Maydan at-Tahrir. Nearby suburbs, which have become joined to the city by continuous urbanisation, are Maadi to the south on the river and Heliopolis (Misr al-Gadidah) in the desert to the northeast, not far from Cairo International Airport. Across the river is the separately administered governate of Gizah. Of the two islands in the river between Cairo and Gizah, the southern is called Rawdah and contains the districts of Rawdah and Manyal. On the northern island, Gazirat al-Bulaq, referred to simply as Gazirah, is the suburb of Zamalek.

Apart from the suburban districts of Imbaba, Mohandisin, Aguza, Duqqi, and Gizah itself, the governate of Gizah runs some 50 miles (85 km) south. It thus includes the site of ancient Memphis with its necropolis and the entirety of the Fayyum. The Memphite necropolis alone is some 40 miles (70 km) long. Near its northern end is the Gizah Plateau, where the most famous of Egypt's many pyramids stand above the village of Nazlat Saman, a 40-minute drive from Maydan at-Tahrir. Six miles (10 km) north of Gizah is the pyramid of Abu Rawash, marking the northernmost boundary of the Memphite necropolis. South of Gizah are the pyramids of Zawyat al-Aryan and Abu Sir and the great temple complex of Saqqarah, with the pyramids of Dahshur, al-Lisht, and Maydum lying beyond.

FROM THE AIRPORT

The airport is 15 miles (25 km) northeast of the centre of the city. A limousine service called Limo Misr maintains a fleet of blue Mercedes sedans that operate at reasonable fixed fares. Special buses to the city centre leave the airport every 20 minutes, stopping at the Nile Hilton, Ramses Hilton and Méridien hotels. Fare is LE 2.50. The red and white public bus number 400 will also take you into town.

The easiest way otherwise to get from the airport to Cairo is by taxi. It is usually necessary to bargain to fix a price in advance. At night add 30–50 percent to the following approximate daytime fares:

Heliopolis	LE 6.00
Maydan at-Tahrir	LE 6.00
Gizah	LE 15.00
Pyramids	LE 15.00
Maadi	LE 15.00

PUBLIC TRANSPORT

THE METRO

Cairo has a small but efficient rail transit system, called the Metro, which was created between 1983 and 1987 by French firms, who linked two lines running into the southern and northeastern suburbs with an underground stretch running beneath the centre of the city. East-west stretches running under the river are shown on some maps, but they exist only as plans that are many years from implementation. The Metro currently links the main railway station at Ramsis Square (Maydan Ramsis) with Heliopolis, Matariyyah and Marg to the northeast and with Maadi and Helwan to the south. Stops are at half-kilometre intervals.

The five underground stops beneath the centre of the city are named after nationalist leaders: the Ramsis Station stop is called Mubarak, and the stations southwards in order are Urabi (Shari Galaa), Nasir (Maydan Tawfiqqiyyah), Sadat (Maydan at-Tahrir), and Saad Zaghlul (the People's Assembly).

Other useful stops are: Sayyidah Zaynab (Munira), Malek as-Saleh (Shari Salah Salem), Mar Girgis (Misr al-Qadimah, "Old Cairo").

Metro stations are clean and a no-smoking rule is strictly enforced, but there are no sanitary conveniences. Entrances are marked by signs consisting of a red M on a black octagonal background. Fares are 25, 40, or 50 piastres depending on the destination.

TAXIS

No matter where one is or what the hour, a taxi can usually be found. Since taxi-drivers are on the prowl for customers, just holding out an arm will usually suffice; at busier times it helps to shout a destination.

Taxi-drivers do not see themselves as public servants, but as purveyors of accommodation – which may range in quality from decrepit to luxurious – and even as temporary hosts. They will not stop unless they fancy your company or your destination. It is considered odd and somewhat unmannerly for a lone male passenger to install himself in an empty back seat by himself rather than up front next to the driver.

Since drivers may or may not know exactly where a given destination is, it is best if the passenger knows the way. Taxi-drivers are not required by law, in fact, to know anything about the city at all. No Egyptians ever consult maps, moreover, and very few can even read them. What everyone likes is to stop someone and ask directions, even though the process is time-consuming and the directions supplied are often wrong.

Meters are almost never used and there is no tipping. Fares are what have been established by current custom. If the customary fare is unknown, a price should be established in advance, simply to avoid an argument at the final destination. Taxis to or from the major hotels are apt to try to charge a premium, though prices are reasonable in any case.

PRIVATE TRANSPORT

CAR RENTAL

To rent a self-drive car you must be at least 25 years old and possess an International Driving Licence. Agents can be found at all major hotels. Cars with drivers may also be hired by the day: rates are negotiable. Drivers are professional and are generally good at their jobs, but have no background that should lead anyone to expect them also to act as guides. The successful driver in Cairo must above all be alert, quick to take advantage of openings, defensive of the space around his vehicle.

Rules of the road have arisen out of actual practice. No one automatically has the right of way, for example: that privilege must be claimed, either by arriving on the spot first or by virtue of having the bigger and heavier vehicle. Lanes mean little, even if they are indicated on the road: though there may already be as many lanes as can fit on the road, someone will always try to make one more; and since everyone moves at his own choice of speed, overtaking from either side is therefore not only permitted, but usual. Traffic lights should be treated warily: a green light does not mean that one is actually recognised as having the right of way; and at important lights a traffic policeman is always stationed to do the actual directing. Petrol is cheap, sold by the litre and has a low octane rating, which means that tune-ups are required frequently.

Parking is fender-to-fender, bumper-to-bumper. At parking spots there is normally an attendant guardian (*munedi*), who will have bought the right to park and keep watch over cars at this location and will expect to be paid (LE 1 or 2). The hand brake should be left off so that he can push the car forward or backward as may be necessary to make room.

Checkpoints are occasionally set up on certain streets, especially at night. You may be asked to show identification, a driver's licence and a motor vehicle registration card. If you have a serious accident in Cairo, stop immediately and let someone summon the police. Outside Cairo, however, it is unsafe to linger even if your intention is to offer assistance: the rule is not to stop, but to drive to the nearest police station and report the accident.

WHERE TO STAY

In the years preceding World War I, European royalty and aristocracy were drawn to the city by its medieval streets and buildings and stayed in its recently constructed grand hotels. The old streets and buildings still exist, but the grand hotels have either disappeared or undergone transformation since into something quite different.

All seven of the most famous were opened before 1911. Shepheard's was burnt to the ground in 1952 and never rebuilt: the present Shepheards Hotel, which has no connection with the old one but the name, is state-owned and stands on a completely different site. The gracious old two-storeyed Semiramis, the favourite hotel of the grandfather of the present Aga Khan, has been supplanted with a concrete high-rise; and the fashionable Savoy, chief rival of Shepheard's, has also disappeared. The Mena House and the Gazirah Palace still exist, but have been remodelled, augmented, and expanded to the point where they are actually new hotels. The Continental, which likewise still exists, has sunk well below the luxury-class level; and the Heliopolis Palace, once said to be the largest hotel in the world, is currently being used as governmental office space.

Hotels in Egypt are officially classified as belonging to one of six categories. These categories have more to do with price, however, which is fixed by the government, than with quality of accommodation or service. Egyptian hotels thus range from "☆☆☆☆☆" (i.e. expensive) to "unclassified" (i.e. very cheap). Price also varies according to the nature of the booking: it is much higher for individuals than for groups. Charges to cover several taxes will appear as small percentages of the price on your final hotel bill.

Cairo's largest hotels are financed in part and managed by such well-known international chains as Hilton, Holiday Inn, Intercontinental, Marriott, Méridien, Mövenpick, Oberoi, Sheraton, or Sonesta. In 1988 the role of the government in hotel management was further reduced and the operation of many other hotels that had continued to be managed as public-sector enterprises was handed over to private firms. New training programmes, new employment practices, and new concepts of service were introduced in an effort to raise standards to the private-sector level and make the hotels comparable with other international hotels worldwide.

The list below, based on the official rating system, is not all-inclusive, but shows establishments recommended by seasoned travellers, including some that offer low-budget accommodation.

For backpackers the area around Maydan Talat Harb (Maydan Sulayman Pasha), just east of Maydan at-Tahrir, abounds in other cheap hotels and pensions, some of which are relatively clean and comfortable. The office of the Egyptian Youth Hostels Federation, which is affiliated with the International Youth Hostels Federation, is at 7 Shari Abd al-Hamid Said (near the Cinema Odéon, between Shari Champollion and Shari Talat Harb), tel: 758-099. The hostel itself is at 135 Sh. Abd al-Aziz as-Saud (Manyal Corniche) Manyal, on the island of Rawdah. Reservations are necessary and can be made by phone, tel: 840-729.

HOTELS

Price ranges for double rooms with bath are ☆☆☆☆☆, $60–100; ☆☆☆☆, $35–60; ☆☆☆, $20–40; ☆☆, $10–30; ☆, $6–20. In three, four, and five star hotels, payment must be made in foreign currency, by credit card, or in Egyptian currency with a bank exchange receipt.

There are no organised facilities for camping. Motels and bed and breakfast accommodation does not exist in Egypt.

☆☆☆☆☆
Cairo Concorde, Cairo International Airport. Tel: 664-242. Located on the fringes of the airport, the Concorde is handy for people who need airport facilities, but far from the centre of Cairo.

Cairo Marriott, Sh. Saray al Gazirah, Zamalek. Tel: 340-8888. The Marriott Hotel has built this facility around the former palace of the Khedive Ismail. Antique furniture graces the halls and public rooms. Restaurants include: Almaz Nightclub operating in the garden during the summer months; Empress Nightclub, open year round in one of the rooms of the palace; Eugénie's Lounge, an elegant cocktail bar in the former rooms of the Empress Eugénie; Garden Promenade, open air café in the Khedive Ismail's garden; Gezira Grill, French cuisine elegantly served in the former billiard room; Omar's Café, coffeeshop with good snacks and dining; Roy Rogers, a salad bar, with hamburgers and other fast foods; the View, an elegant lounge at the top of the hotel with a panorama of the city.

Cairo Sheraton, Midan el Galaa, Dokki. Tel: 348-8600/8700. One of the first international hotels in Cairo, near the city centre. Aladin, Middle-Eastern cuisine and entertainment; Alhambra, a nightclub with excellent oriental floor show; Arousa al Nil, continental and Middle-Eastern cuisine; La Mamma, one of the best Italian restaurants in Cairo.

Gezira Sheraton, Gazirah. Tel: 341-3442/1333/1555. South of the Cairo Opera House, the Gezira Sheraton has a superb view of the Nile. Gezira Andalus Café, 24-hr coffeeshop; Abu Kir, seafood out of doors on the Nile; outdoor summer nightclub with an oriental show; Le Gandool Bar; Paradise Island, a floating restaurant on the Nile offering barbecues and mezzes. The Grill has a Nile view and international cuisine. Kebabgy al Gezirah offers oriental food.

Heliopolis Mövenpick, Hurriyyah, Heliopolis. Tel: 664-242, 247-0077, 679-799. Near the airport. In Mövenpick tradition it offers good food: Al Sarraya, French restaurant; Il Giardino, an Italian *taverna* with snacks and live entertainment; Orangerie, buffet breakfast, lunch and dinner; Gourmet Shop, a pastry shop with Swiss sweets; Karawan, Middle-Eastern cuisine and barbecues in a garden atmosphere; Mövenpick, for Swiss and Middle-Eastern meals and snacks with a special ice cream menu. Papillon disco; St Germain bar.

Heliopolis Sheraton, Airport Road, Heliopolis. Tel: 667-700, 665-500. Near the airport. Now recovered from a devastating fire, the Heliopolis Sheraton has a bright airy lobby with plants and live birds. Dining facilities include: Alfredo's, an Italian restaurant; Vienna Café, a pastry shop; Bierstube, offering German cuisine and special food festivals; King Tut, formal dining with a continental menu; Oriental Tent, a village atmosphere, with an Egyptian buffet; and Al Zahraa Coffeeshop, a daily buffet with Lebanese, Italian, international and Chinese entrées. Bars include Al Sakia and the Swan Pub, with Victorian décor serving English-style meals. The disco is Le Baron.

Hyatt Al Salam, 61 Abdel Hamid Badawi, Heliopolis. Tel: 245-5155/2155. Although the Hyatt is far from the centre of town, it is housed in a former palace with lovely grounds. Restaurants include Café Jardin Coffeeshop, with a buffet; Marquis for light snacks; Ezbetna, for traditional Egyptian foods; Whispers, a bar offering a happy hour. Ya Salam is the Nightclub and Vito's is the disco.

Mena House Oberoi, end of Sh. al-Haram (Pyramid's Road), Gizah. Tel: 855-444, 857-999, 855-174. A historic landmark refurbished by the Oberoi chain, the Mena House is the only hotel in Egypt to have a golf course. Outlets include: the Greenery Coffeeshop, a buffet in the garden; Khan al Khalili, a coffeeshop featuring international and Middle-Eastern entrées; the Mogul Room offers Indian food and is one of the best restaurants in Egypt; the Rubayyat is the main dining room with continental and Middle-Eastern meals and live entertainment. Bars include the Mameluke Bar and El Sultan Lounge. Nightclubs are Oasis Summer Nightclub and Abu Nawas Nightclub. The disco is The Saddle.

Meridien, Rawdah Island, entered from the Corniche in Garden City. Tel: 362-1717. A riverfront hotel in the heart of the city. Fontana Coffeeshop offers international and Middle-Eastern meals and snacks. Kasr al Rashid provides a Middle-Eastern atmosphere, food and entertainment. La Belle Epoque is a nightclub and restaurant. La Palme d'Or offers French dining to live music. Nafoura is a summer restaurant with Middle-Eastern specialities.

Meridien Heliopolis, 51 Oruba, Heliopolis. Tel: 290-5055/1819. Located on the busy airport road. Outlets include Le Marco Polo Restaurant for Italian food and Café St Germain for snacks. Cakes and pastries at La Boulangerie.

Nile Hilton, Corniche, Midan Tahrir. Tel: 750-666, 740-777. One of the first international hotels in Cairo, the Hilton, located on the Nile in the city centre, has an authentic ancient Egyptian statue in the lobby. Abu Ali's Café serves *sheesha*, green tea, and light snacks on the terrace; Belvedere is the winter night club while the Tropicana is the summer night club around the pool; Ibis Cafe has continental cuisine; Jackie's is the popular disco. The main dining room is the Rotisserie, which offers international cuisine. La Pizzeria offers Italian pizzas and an open buffet; Le Gateau is a pastry shop. Bars include the Safari Bar, Lobby Bar, and the Taverne du Champ de Mars, an Art Nouveau pub offering drinks, snacks, and daily buffet.

Pullman Maadi Towers, Corniche, Maadi. Tel: 350-6092, 350-6093. On the Nile to the south of the city centre, the Pullman offers a wonderful panorama of the desert plateau on the west bank of the Nile including the pyramids of Gizah, Saqqarah, and Dahshur. Outlets include Le Clovis for international cuisine; Maadi Café, open 24 hours; and Darna for traditional Egyptian food.

Ramada Renaissance, Cairo/Alexandria Desert Road. Tel: 538-995/6. North of the Pyramids in a former citrus and palm grove, this hotel has excellent grounds. Outlets include: Garden Coffeeshop featuring continental meals and snacks; Les Fontaines offers continental food; and Sultan, with Middle Eastern food. Habiba is the nightclub. Golden Club is the disco.

Ramses Hilton, 1115 Corniche, Maspero. Tel: 777-444, 758-000, 744-400. Located on the Nile in one of the busiest sections of the city, the 36-storey Ramses Hilton has no grounds, but its upper floors offer an interesting panorama of Cairo. Citadel Grill offers elegant dining with seafood and grills; Falafel offers Middle Eastern foods and snacks; La Patisserie coffeeshop has excellent cakes and ice cream specialities. Terrace Café coffeeshop presents international and Middle-Eastern meals and snacks. Bars include Club 36 with piano entertainment and a panorama of the city.

Safir Etape Hotel, 4 Midan Misaha, Duqqi. Tel: 348-2424/2828/2626. In a residential square not far from the city centre, the Safir is a favourite hotel for visitors from the Gulf states. Diar El Andalos caters Lebanese and Middle-Eastern cuisine with *sheesha*; Filaka coffeeshop has an excellent daily buffet; Gazirat al Dahab offers French and Middle-Eastern food. Khan Morgan is the bar.

Semiramis Intercontinental, Corniche, Garden City. Tel: 355-3900/3800. Built on the site of the legendary Semiramis Hotel in the centre of the city, the current hotel offers good facilities but no grounds. Restaurants include: Feluka Brasserie featuring Middle-Eastern and continental open buffets; Far East offering oriental foods; Semiramis Grill with French cuisine; Sultana's Disco offering international live shows.

Shepheard's Hotel, Corniche, Garden City. Tel: 355-3804/3814. Shepheard's has the name, but not the site or the grandeur of the original and famous Shepheard's Hotel of the 19th century. Caravan offers international and Middle-Eastern meals and snacks; Asia House offers oriental foods; Régence offers French cuisine; and Italiano has pastas and pizzas.

Siag Pyramids, 59 Mariutia, Saqqarah Road. Tel: 856-022/623, 857-399. Near the desert with a view of the Giza pyramids, the Siag is host to the Pharaoh's Rally every October. Dining room only, but excellent food.

Sonesta, 4 Tayaran, Nasr City. Tel: 611-066, 609-444. Le Café for pastries and breads; the Garden Grill is an open-air summer restaurant featuring grills; Gondola offers Italian dining; Borobodur offers Indonesian food; Greenhouse coffeeshop has international meals and snacks; Rib Room is a steakhouse. Bars include Arabic Lounge and Speke's Bar. The disco is Sindbad.

☆☆☆☆
Atlas Zamalek, 20 Gam'at al Dowal al Arabiya, Mohandisin. Tel: 346-4175/5782/6569. Chez Zanouba is Middle-Eastern dining while Kahraman is French dining. Tamango is the hottest dance spot in Cairo.

Baron Hotel, Heliopolis off Oruba, Heliopolis. Tel: 291-2468/7/5757. Le Baron coffeeshop features international and Middle-Eastern meals and snacks; the Terrace, caters an international buffet each evening; Baron Patisserie; Le Jardin is the daily buffet. Pasha is the bar.

Bel Air Cairo Hotel, Muqattam. Tel: 922-685/816/884. The only hotel on the Muqattam hills, but you must leave the grounds to have a view of the city.

Jolie Ville Mövenpick, Cairo/Alexandria Desert Road. Tel: 855-118/539/612. Newly reopened after a fire. Mövenpick Restaurant offers daily buffets; Orangerie, breakfast, lunch, and dinner buffets; Pavillon des Pyramides, French dining. Terrace, snacks.

Novotel, Cairo Airport, Heliopolis. Tel: 671-715, 679-080, 661-330.

☆☆☆
Cairo Inn, 26 Syria, Mohandisin. Tel: 349-0661/2/3. Eagle Arms English pub; Taberna Espanola with Spanish entertainment in the evening. Excellent Spanish food.

Cleopatra, 2 Bustan, Midan Tahrir. Tel: 708-751.

Egyptel, 93 Merghani, Heliopolis. Tel: 661-716.

El Borg, Saray al Gazirah, Zamalek. Tel: 341-7655.

El Nil, 12 Ahmed Ragheb, Garden City. Tel: 354-2808.

Khan al Khalili, 7 Bosta, Attaba. Tel: 900-271.

President, 22 Dr. Taha Hussein, Zamalek. Tel: 341-6751/3195. Cairo Cellar, excellent food. Lebanese *Mezzeh* a speciality.

☆☆
El Hussein, Midan Hussein, al-Azhar. Tel: 918-664/089.

El Nil Garden, 131 Abdel Aziz al Saoud, Manial. Tel: 985-767, 983-931.

Viennoise, 11 Mahmoud Bassiouni. Tel: 751-949, 743-153.

Windsor, 19 Alfy Bey. Tel: 915-277, 915-810.

Unclassified
Anglo-Swiss Pensione, 14 Champollion. Tel: 751-479.

Bodmin House, 17 Hasan Sabri, Zamalek. Tel: 340-2842.

Duqqi House, 42 Madina al Munawara, Duqqi. Tel: 705-611/713.

Garden City House, 23 Kamal el Din, Garden City. Tel: 354-8126. Rub elbows with archaeologists and anthropologists.

Hotel of Youth & Sports, Masaken, Madinat Nasr. Tel: 260-6991/2.

Mayfair Pension, 9 Aziz Uthman, Zamalek. Tel: 340-7315.

Pensione Roma, 169 Muhammad Farid (Emad ad-Din). Tel: 342-0055, 341-8447, 341-8448.

FOOD DIGEST

WHAT TO EAT

Although *ful mudames* (fava bean stew) is supposed to be the Egyptian national dish – in somewhat the same sense that hotdogs, chop suey, spaghetti, and fish and chips are supposed to be the national dishes of the US, China, Italy, and Britain – the real basis of every meal in every ordinary Egyptian household is several loaves of flatbread. Egyptians consume more wheat per capita, by a very wide margin, than any other people in the world; and their word for "bread" is not the usual Arabic word, *khubz*, but the word *aysh*, which also means "life".

The language itself thus declares that bread is central to the act of eating, which is what most Egyptians believe that life is all about. Certainly most would admit that they rank the consumption of food, as frequently and copiously as possible, above all other possible pleasures. In Cairo even lovers thus typically associate their ecstasies with eating: dates and milk, for example, are guaranteed to sustain male vigour and rigour throughout trysts as long as 36 hours, while jellied calves' feet are said to make the perfect casserole for a couple on their second honeymoon. In a city where there is no lack of wit or verbal malice, the only thing ever spoken of without a trace of spite is food. And it is spoken of so ubiquitously and incessantly that the city as a whole often seems almost obsessed.

Unlike Aleppo, Bath, Bologna, Vienna, Kiev, or Boston, however, Cairo can claim no dishes as peculiarly or even characteristically its own; and in fact its culinary traditions are of relatively recent growth. Mamluk sultans and amirs undoubtedly ate well, for example, but medieval travellers from other Arab countries were shocked by the lack of sophistication in ordinary Cairene lunches and dinners, for which no one seemed to make any particular preparation; and before 1517, when the Ottoman conquerors brought a higher standard of cooking, even simple kitchens as such do not appear to have existed in any private dwellings.

ECLECTIC CUISINE

Cairene cookery has subsequently borrowed from every culture with which Egyptians have come into contact. A typical offering may derive from the classic and elegant cuisines of Turkey, Persia, Syria, and the Maghrib. Many of their basic ingredients are not grown or made in Egypt, however, and must be expensively imported. Cherries, dried apricots, raisins and sultanas, almonds, pistachios, pine nuts, walnuts, pomegranate juice, virgin olive oil, semolina, cracked wheat, and all but a very few common herbs and spices, for example, are either hard to find or simply unobtainable. They belong to a northern world of taste that stretches in space and time from the Caspian through the Caucasus, the Balkans, medieval Sicily and Andalusia to the Atlantic, a world that is only peripherally and incidentally Egyptian. In Cairo the Lebanese *mezzeh* of a hundred different hors d'oeuvres thus dwindles to four or five, while Persian and Turkish delicacies survive only in curtailed adaptations.

To the confusion of many foreigners, Syrian, Persian, Turkish and even Maghribine-style dishes are often indicated on Cairene menus as "Oriental". This quaint adjective functioned before 1914 to distinguish the possessions of the Ottoman Sultan from those of other European sovereigns. In European languages it is now a confusing misnomer, which becomes even more confusing when translated into Arabic, since Morocco, Algeria, and Tunisia belong to what in Arabic is referred to as "the Occident" and cannot by definition have national cuisines that are "Oriental".

"Oriental" dishes in any case have nothing at all in common with what is understood to be Oriental cooking elsewhere – the cuisines of India, China, Japan, Korea, or Southeast Asia, which are served in Cairo, but only in specialized restaurants and are either ignored or unknown in Egyptian private houses.

Far closer to authentic Egyptian taste than Syrian, Turkish or Persian food and thus in fact more likely to appear on Cairene tables are plain substantial dishes based on local meat, fish and – especially – vegetables, the most common of which are not native in origin, but were introduced from Asia, Europe, or America during the last century. Given the origins of their ingredients, it is not surprising that many such dishes are likely to have evolved from Italian, French, English, or even German household cookery of four or five generations ago. Robust and filling, they can be made exclusively of Egyptian-grown or Egyptian-made produce, and with the passage of time they have therefore become "traditionally" Egyptian. For example, in a recent edition the English-language daily newspaper, the *Egyptian Gazette*, published recipes for two dishes described in a headline as "Oriental": cream of tomato soup and a leek and potato soup that was obviously a simplified version of Vichyssoise.

Fresh tomatoes are apt to be added to whatever is served uncooked, while a national tendency to stew everything else in tomato sauce is not only recognised throughout the rest of the Arab World, but specifically celebrated in a famous Egyptian popular song. The addiction to tomatoes represents a heavy debt to Christopher Columbus and his discovery of the New World.

Old and deep-rooted native tradition, on the other hand, is represented in a multitude of pickles or in classic dishes like lentil soup or Egyptian-style *mulukhiyyah*, Jew's-mallow stewed with chicken or rabbit and served with rice, a green slime that one either loves or hates. The smell of *mulukhiyyah* is so seductive and its effect is so soporific that

one of the Fatimid caliphs tried – unsuccessfully, of course – to banish it from the city.

STREET FOOD

Like all cities from Athens eastward, Cairo offers a wide variety of street food, beginning a couple of hours after dawn, when vendors appear with loaves of bread and cart-loads of hot food at strategic points in every non-residential area. Many men eat breakfast on the street – bread, a bit of white cheese, pickles, and some *ful mudames,* ladled out of huge pots, which have a specialized shape that allows them to be buried overnight in smouldering rubbish, so that the beans can cook slowly. At lunchtime carts will appear to serve *makarona* (boiled pasta, with a choice of sauces) and *kusheri* (a mixture of pasta, rice and lentils, served with a hot sauce).

And as night begins to fall, another wheeled fleet arrives, lit by its own portable pressure lamps, to offer two or three kinds of roasted peanuts, *libb* (roasted melon seeds), *tirmis* (lupin seeds), baked sweet potatoes, and hard-kerneled maize that an old-fashioned American would identify instantly as "roasting ears".

Booths and small shops along major streets meanwhile operate all day long, selling *taamiya* (deep-fried beancakes, known elsewhere as *felafel*) *shawirma* (the Turkish *çevirme*, better know internationally as "doner kebab": slices of lamb stacked and broiled vertically, then slivered across the slices, to be served in a loaf of flatbread with *tahina*, a sauce made of sesame paste), or *fatir* (large thin pancakes folded around the buyer's choice of sweet or savoury stuffing).

In any market street there are mechanised roasters on which racks of skewered chicken are slowly doing to a golden turn, and a recent innovation is establishments selling fresh fish – of which Egypt offers splendid species from the Nile, the Mediterranean, or the Red Sea – broiled on the spot.

To accompany such food, specialised stands offer the juice of any fruit in season. They are most crowded during the months of mango harvest. At sugar-cane-cutting time green sheaves standing upright outside each establishment show that cane-juice, famous as a tonic, is on offer, freshly pressed. The season for the best citrus is short – from

November to May – but fresh strawberries and their juice are available in Egypt every day during at least nine months of the year. Picturesque street vendors still exist who carry enormous glass containers from which they dispense chilled decoctions of tamarind (*tamar hindi*), carob (*karub*), or licorice-root (*erq-sus*), which has given its name to the vendor himself, who is called an *erqsusi*.

Major hotels all provide upmarket imitations of these carts, booths, shops and stands, offering Cairene street food and drinks in versions that are more hygienic – and, of course, more expensive – but also quite authentic and tasty enough to have proven extremely popular with Cairenes themselves. Hardest to come by in hotels, strangely enough, is the fresh fruit juice that is so readily available elsewhere all over the city.

TRADITIONAL DRINKS

Among the drinks that hotels may offer are some of the "traditional" decoctions – meaning the ingredients are boiled – that can be bought in any good Cairo coffee house, in addition to coffee or tea. These drinks are far from mysterious, though some people are inclined to make them out to be. The clientèle of coffee-houses or chocolate houses in 18th-century London, for example, drank many of the same decoctions – made of cinnamon (*qirfa*, pronounced "erfa" in Cairo), ginger (*ganzabíl*), fenugreek (*helba*), aniseed (*yanssun*), or licorice-root (*erq-sus*) – that are still commonly ordered in any good coffee-house in 20th-century Cairo.

Popular in 18th-century Paris and Madrid as well as in London was *salep*, a hot drink made from the farinaceous root of *Orchis mascula*. The word *salep*, identical in French, Spanish and English, derives by way of Turkish from *sahlab*, the usual Arabic name for both the drink and the plant, but is in fact a polite euphemism for the plant's proper Arabic botanical name, which literally means "fox testicles".

The delicious red decoction made by boiling the dried blossoms of *Hibiscus sabdariffa* (*karkadih*), which originates in the Sudan, is drunk hot or cold and is available now as dehydrated powder in any Western health-food store under names like "hibiscus tea". Real Cairene coffee and tea are also decoctions (boiled drinks) and are therefore quite unlike the drinks made with the same ingredients in most of the West, where the usual preparation is by infusion.

Tea did not arrive until the late 19th century. Introduced by the British, it rapidly became the most popular drink among all classes of Cairenes, as it is throughout the Arab World, though no tea is grown in any Arab country. Typical Egyptian tea is not made from leaves – such niceties are known only in upper-class houses, where the Earl Grey or Lapsang Souchong that is served at five o'clock is always infused, Western-style – but from the cheapest tea-dust, which is boiled until, as one expert says, it remains just faintly translucent. Decanted into a glass, it is then cranked up with plenty of sugar, lacking which it would merely taste brackish and would probably fail to fortify. Generations of travellers have discovered its virtues as a restorative, miraculous when taken just before the breaking point on a hot, dusty, trying day.

BEER & WINE

The visitor is wise to ensure a supply of bottled drinks, especially water, and to confine drinking otherwise to what has been filtered, boiled, or treated chemically. The only brand of bottled water presently produced in Egypt, called *Báraka* (the name means "blessing") can be found nearly everywhere. Bottled soft drinks include good local versions of Coca Cola, Pepsi, Sport Cola, and 7-Up.

The local beer is a lager called Stella. It is generally available in two varieties, the commoner of which is made for the Egyptian market, and comes in large green or brown bottles. Connoisseurs rank it above the Export Stella, which comes in smaller bottles, is more expensive, sweeter, and somewhat insipid. A third variety, available in the late spring, is a good dark bock beer called Stella Marzen. A fourth variety, hard to find, is Stella Aswali, a dark beer from Aswan.

At the beginning of the 1990s, after several years during which production standards had sunk so far that most Egyptian wine was not only disgusting, but dangerous to drink, both reds and whites began to become more or less potable again. Quality still remains below the standard achieved by public- and private-sector producers in Lebanon, Syria, and Turkey, where utilitarian products are made that have one or two of the typical qualities of good wine. Egyptian wine, by contrast, even at its best, has no bouquet, aroma, or depth of taste, though it has at least shown signs of becoming consistent in quality.

Since all Egyptian wine is mass-produced by the same public sector firm from the same vineyards, differences among labels do not reflect soil or climate, but have been created for marketing purposes. The two best whites are Gianaclís Village (ask for *Qaryah Janaklís*), a dry wine named for the Greek cigarette-manufacturer who single-handedly revived the 5,000-year-old Egyptian wine-making industry a century ago; and Reine Cléopatre (ask for *Kliobatra*), a sweet and fairly consistent product throughout many years when all else had failed, drinkable even when somewhat heavy and sweet.

Other whites worth trying, perhaps, but not recommended include Cru des Ptolemées, Castel Nestor, and Nefertiti. Reds, more problematic than whites, are called Omar Khayyam (likely to be the least bad), Pharaons, Château Gianaclis. There is one rather acid rosé called Rubis d'Égypte. Headwaiters in Cairo's hotels and restaurants naturally try to sell imported wine, which tends to be mediocre – no restaurant in Cairo has a first-class wine-list – and over-priced, but is at least an alternative.

DINING OUT, DINING IN

Neither the cooking nor the service in typical old-fashioned Cairene public places could ever claim to equal the elegance ordinarily offered by establishments in Aleppo, Beirut or Marrakesh, though lack of finesse may be made up for by sheer efficiency or a quality that Egyptians prize far more – abundance. Since 1980, however, dozens of new restaurants have appeared where the cooking, the service, the prices, and – obviously – the clientèle are more ambitious.

Major hotels, which are all managed by international chains, tend to serve "international" cuisine. Their menus make lavish use of imported ingredients and vary according to current eating fashions in the business circles of such financial capitals as New York or Zürich. Each also operates one or two specialized restaurants, however, or sponsors occasional "festivals" when cooks are brought in from other hotels in the same chain, especially those in exotic locations – Bangkok, say, or Helsinki – to create a week of culinary ethnicity.

The best Cairene cooking, eating, and drinking, of course, is still in private houses. Families that pride themselves on their food are apt to keep a few recipes for Turkish dishes, many of them actually originated in the harem of the Ottoman sultan, as carefully guarded secrets, never shared with outsiders except in the form of finished products.

And all Cairenes of every class delight in the real glories of the Egyptian table, which are fresh vegetables in their proper seasons and fresh fish, prepared in the simplest way. To end a meal in a well-organised private house, several desserts will be presented, ranging from pastries – never made at home, since Cairo's patisseries now rival those of any Mediterranean city in quality and variety – to a *bombe* of ice cream and chocolate.

Also on offer are likely to be two classic puddings, *Aysh es-Saray* ("Bread of the Palace"), a sure cure for the most raging sweet tooth, and *Umm Ali* ("Mother of Ali"), a bread pudding eaten hot. The latter, they say in Cairo, was introduced into Egypt, through the Khedivial court, by one of Ismail the Magnificent's favourite foreign concubines, a Dublin girl called Molly O'Malley. Lively, red-headed, and endlessly inventive, Molly wrought improvements upon the Irish version until she had created this delightful dish, to which she gave her own last name.

WHERE TO EAT

Hotels offer restaurants ranging from small coffee shops to smart supper clubs. Outside hotels there is even more variety. The following is a list of some of the more popular establishments. (*See also Bars, under Nightlife, page 275.*)

Aberdeen Steak House
76 Sh. 9 at Sh. 83, Maadi. Tel: 350-8730

After Eight
6 Sh. Qasr an-Nil. Tel: 740-855

Al Dar
Saqqarah Road. Tel: 852-289

Andrea's (speciality: grilled chicken) 14 Maryutiyyah Canal (Kirdassah Road). Tel: 851-133; 47 Sh. 7, Maadi. Tel: 351-1369; Al-Hadaba al-Alia, Muqattam. Tel: 902-017.

Angus Chargrilled Specialities, 34 Sh. Yehya Ibrahim, Zamalek. Tel: 341-1321.

Arabesque, 6 Sh. Qasr an-Nil, Cairo. Tel: 759-896.

Asia House (Indian/Chinese), Shepheards Hotel, Corniche, Cairo. Tel: 355-3900.

Balmoral (Chinese, with take-away and delivery service), 157 Sh. 26 July, Zamalek. Tel: 340-6761, 340-5473.

Bon Appetit (French), 21 Sh. Wadi an-Nil, Mohandisin. Tel: 346-4937.

Caroll, 12 Sh. Qasr an-Nil. Tel: 746-739.

La Cloche d'Or, 3 Sh. Abu'l-Feda, Zamalek. Tel: 340-2314, 340-2268.

Cellar, 22 Sh. Taha Husay, (President Hotel), Zamalek Tel: 341-3195, 341-6751.

Chin Chin (Chinese), At Four Corners. 4 Sh. Hasan Sabri., Zamalek. Tel: 341-3961/ 340-1647.

Cho's (Chinese, Korean and Western), 7A Rd. 252 Digla. Tel: 352-6118.

Don Quichotte (French/International), 9A Sh. Ahmad Hishmat, Zamalek. Tel: 340-6415.

El Patio, 5 Sh. Sayyid al-Bakri, Zamalek. Tel: 340-2645.

Estoril, 114 Sh. Talat Harb (also entered from passage behind Air France between Sh. Talat Harb and Qasr an-Nil). Tel: 743-102. A Cairo institution.

Felfela (Egyptian, 15 Sh. Hoda Shaarawi, Cairo. Tel: 742-751.

Flying Fish, 166 Sh. an-Nil, Aguza. Tel: 349-3234.

Gazirat al Dahab, Safir Hotel, Maydan Missaha, Duqqi. Tel: 348-3828, 348-2424.

Ibis Café, Nile Hilton Hotel. Tel: 765-666, 767-444.

Justine (French), at Four Corners. 4 Sh. Hasan Sabri, Zamalek. Tel: 341-3961, 340-1647.

Khan al-Khalili, 5 al-Badestan, Khan al-Khalili. Tel: 903-788, 932-262. No alcohol.

Kowloon (Chinese), Cleopatra Hotel, 2 Sh. Abd as-Salam Araf (Sh. Bustan), Maydan at-Tahrir. Tel: 759-831.

La Charmerie (French), Sh. 26 July, Zamalek. Tel: 340-2645.

La Mamma (Italian), Cairo Sheraton Hotel, Gizah. Tel: 348-8600, 348-8700.

La Piazza (Italian), Four Corners, 4 Sh. Hasan Sabri, Zamalek. Tel: 341-2961, 340-4385.

La Terrine, 105 Sh. Higaz, Heliopolis. Tel: 257-8634.

Lolita Italian Restaurant and Take-Away, 15 Sh. 9B Maadi. Tel: 351-5465, 351-5587.

Matchpoint, at Four Corners, 4 Sh. Hasan Sabri, Zamalek. Tel: 341-3961, 340-1647.

Moghul Room (Indian), Mena House Oberoi Hotel, Pyramids Road (Shari al-Haram), Gizah. Tel: 85-5444, 85-7999, ext: 661.

Naniwa (Japanese), Ramses Hilton Hotel Annexe. Tel: 752-3999; 3 Sh. Lubnan, Mohandisin. Tel: 346-5943.

Nile Pharaoh (floating restaurant, luncheon and dinner cruises), 31 Sh. An-Nil, Gizah. Tel: 738-957, 738-914.

Okamoto (Japanese), 7 Sh. Ahmad Urabi, Aguza. Tel: 349-5774.

Omam Restaurants Four restaurants in one building: **Al Fanous** (Moroccan), **Chandani** (Indian), **Il Camino** (Italian) and **Sakura** (Japanese). Borg

Riyadh, 5 Sh. Wissa Wasif (off Gizah Corniche, Sh. Gamal Abd an-Nasir) 6th Floor, Gizah. Tel: 737-595/592. No alcohol.

Papillon (Lebanese). Sh. 26 July, Tersana Shopping Centre. Mohandisin. Tel: 3487-1672.

Paprika (Lebanese), 1129 Corniche, near the Radio and Television Building, Maspero. Tel: 749-447.

Petit Swiss Chalet, 9 Sh. 151 Maadi. Tel 350-4941.

Pizza Hut, 64 Sh. Musaddeq, Duqqi. Tel: 360-8048, 349-7609; 85 Sh. 9 Maadi. Tel: 375-9362; Maydan Messaha, Duqqi. Tel: 706-899, 361-1347; Sh. Ahram, Misr al-Gadidah (Heliopolis). Tel: 258-0518, 259-113.

Pub 28, 28 Sh. Sheger ad-Durr, Zamalek. Tel: 340-0927.

Prestige Pizzeria, 43 Sh. Gazirat al-Arab, Mohandisin. Tel: 347-0383.

Rôtisserie, Nile Hilton Hotel. Tel: 765-666, 767-444.

Scarabée (floating restaurant, luncheon and dinner cruises), docks in front of Shepheards. Tel: 984-967.

Seahorse, 5 Corniche. Tel: 363-8830.

Spaghetteria, Semiramis Intercontinental Hotel. Tel: 355-7171.

Silver Fish, 39 Mohiy ad-Din Abu' l-Izz St. Duqqi. Tel: 349-2272/73.

Swiss Chalet, 10 Sh. An-Nakhil, Mohandisin. Tel: 707-799.

Swiss Air Restaurants (Le Château and Le Chalet), Sh. An-Nil (Gizah Corniche, Sh. Gamal Abd an-Nasir), Gizah. Tel: 728-488.

Tandoori (Indian), 11 Sh. Shehab, Mohandisin. Tel: 340-6301.

Tikka Grill, 47 Al-Batal Ahmad Abd al-Aziz, Mohandisin. Tel: 340-0393.

Tirol (Austrian), 38 Sh. Gazirat al-Arab, Mohandisin.

Tokyo (Japanese), 2 Sayyid al-Bakri, Zamalek. Tel: 351-0502.

Vienna (Austrian), Sh. Al-Batal Ahmad Abd al-Aziz, Mohandisin. Tel: 346-6940.

Umda (Egyptian style fast food), Sh. Gamiat ad-Dawal al-Arabiyyah (next to the Atlas Zamalek Hotel), Mohandisin.

THINGS TO DO

MUSEUMS

The most famous of the city's museums is the Egyptian Antiquities Museum, but many others are well worth visiting. The usual hours are from 9 a.m. to 4 p.m. daily except Friday, when all museums are closed between approximately 11.30 a.m. and 1 p.m.

Agricultural Museum: Ministry of Agriculture, Duqqi. Tel: 702-366, 700-063, 702-879, 702-933. The oldest in the world (founded 1938), with 27 acres (11 hectares) of garden, contains a **Museum of Ancient Egyptian Agriculture**, a **Natural History Museum**, a **Museum of the Social Life of the Arab Nations**, and a **Cotton Museum**.

Amr Ibrahim Palace (Qasr Ali Ibrahim): Corner of Sh. Gazirah and Sh. Shaykh al-Marsafi (next to the Marriott Hotel), Zamalek. Tel: 987-495. An exquisite neo-Islamic house confiscated during the Revolution from Amr Ibrahim, a great-great-grandson of Ibrahim Pasha.

Bayt Gamal ad-Din: East of the Qasabah between the Fakahani Mosque and the Ghuriyyah. Residence of a 17th-century gold merchant.

Bayt al-Kiridliyyah: (*See Gayer-Anderson House, below.*)

Bayt Ibrahim Katkhuda as-Sinnari: 17

Harat Monge, off Shari an-Nasiriyya, Sayyidah Zaynab. Tel: 938-565. An 18th-century townhouse, one of three requisitioned for Bonaparte's *savants* in 1798

Bayt as-Sihaymi: Darb al-Asfar, Gamaliyyah. An Ottoman-period townhouse, largely intact, with Chinese porcelain made for the Arab market.

Coptic Museum: Mar Girgis, Old Cairo (Misr al-Qadimah). Tel: 841-766. Arts of Egypt's Christian era: textiles, metalwork, woodwork, ceramics, glass.

Egyptian Antiquities Museum: Maydan at-Tahrir. Tel: 754-319. The world's greatest collection of Pharaonic antiquities, including the Menkauré triads, the finds from the tomb of Hetepheres, and the treasures of Tutankhamun.

Entomological Society Museum: 14 Sh. Ramsis, near Main Railway Station. Tel: 354-5350.

Ethnological Museum: 100 Sh. Qasr al-Ayni (ground floor of the Geographical Society building). Tel: 354-5450.

Higher Institute of Folklore Museum: Sh. Borsa al-Khediwiyyah (Rue de la Bourse Khédiviale). Tel: 752-460.

Gayer-Anderson House: Adjoining Ibn Tulun Mosque. Tel: 354-6950. Two houses, 16th and 17th century, joined together and furnished with his collections by Major Robert Gayer-Anderson Pasha, who lived here between 1935 and 1942.

Gawharah Palace Museum (Qasr al-Gawharah): Citadel. Tel: 926-187. Muhammad Ali's Citadel *salamlik* (reception palace), restored since 1971 and fitted with furniture formerly owned by the Muhammad Ali family. The name of the palace means *bijou* or jewel, but there has never been a "jewel collection" in it.

Gazirah Museum: Planetarium building, Gazirah Exhibition Grounds, next to the National Cultural Centre. Tel: 806-982. Paintings, bibelots, and objets d'art confiscated from the Muhammad Ali family.

Geological Museum: Corniche, Old Cairo (Misr al-Qadimah), entrance from Sh. Asar an-Nabi. Tel: 354-6950, 982-608, 982-580

Helwan Palace Museum: Helwan. Tel: 340-5198. Closed to the public.

Islamic Art Museum: Corner of Sh. Port Said, Sh. Qal'a (Sh. Muhammad Ali), and Sh. Sami al-Barudi, Abdiin. Tel: 341-8672. Important collections of arms and armour, ceramics, coins, carpets and textiles, manuscripts and printed papers, metalwork, stonework and woodwork from the period of the city's greatest glory.

Manastirli Palace and the Nilometer: Southern end of Rawdah. Restored in 1990, this early 19th-century *salamlik* is the public portion of a palace complex that belonged to a distinguished Cairene Turkish family. The Nilometer is the oldest intact Islamic monument in Cairo.

Manyal Palace Museum: Rawdah Island. Tel: 936-124. A complex of gardens and buildings constructed between 1901 and 1929 and bequeathed to the nation in 1955 by Prince Muhammad Ali, younger brother of Khedive Abbas II Hilmi and first cousin of King Faruq. Apart from the prince's residence with all its furnishings, there are buildings housing splendid collections of family memorabilia, costumes, calligraphy, glass, porcelain, silver, and trophies of the hunt.

Military Museum: Citadel. Tel: 920-955. Housed in the Harim Palace, chief residence of rulers belonging to Muhammad Ali's family from 1827 to 1874, itself worth seeing. Collections include uniforms, weapons and models.

Muhammad Ali Museum: Qasr ash-Shubra, Shubra. Closed to the public at time of press.

Muhammad Mahmud and Emilienne Luce Khalil Collection: Installed between 1971 and 1991 in the Amr Ibrahim Palace (*see above*), but now returned to the **Muhammad Mahmud and Emilienne Luce Khalil Museum** on the Gizah Corniche (Sh. Gamal Abd an-Nasir) in Gizah. Paintings, chiefly 19th and 20th-century French, including works by Ingres (2), Delacroix (8), Corot (12), Daumier (4), Courbet (4), Millet (6), Renoir (6), Degas (2), Fantin-Latour (2), Manet, Monet (5), Pissarro (6), sisley (5), Toulouse-Lautrec, Gauguin (3), Van Gogh and others, sculpture (Houdon, Barye, Carpeaux, and Rodin), chinoiserie, japonaiserie, and turquoiserie. Bequeathed with their house to the nation by Muhammad Mahmud Khalil (died 1955), landowner, industrialist, and politician, and his French wife, Emilienne Luce Khalil (died 1962).

Mukhtar Museum: Gazirah near Galaa Bridge. Tel: 805-198. Designed by Ramses Wissa Wasif, founder of the Harraniyyah weaving project, and dedicated to Mahmud Mukhtar, sculptor of *Awakening Egypt*, the monument at the Gizah end of the Kubri Gaamah (University Bridge), as well as the monumental statues of Saad Zaghlul in Cairo and Alexandria.

Musafir-khana: Darb at-Tablawi, Gamaliyyah, behind the mosque of Sayyidna Husayn. Tel: 920-472. Townhouse built in 1779, birthplace of Khedive Ismail.

Museum of Hygiene and Medicine: Maydan Sakakini, Abbasiyyah. Housed in the extraordinary Sakakini Palace, built in 1898 by the Syrian financier Henri Sakakini Pasha, head of the firm of Sakakini Frères, Cairo agent for the Dervieux (Paris) and Oppenheim (London) banks.

Museum of Modern Art: (Museum of Twentieth-Century Egyptian Art). Gazirah Exhibition Grounds.

Museum of the People's Assemby: In the People's Assembly (Meglis ash-Shaab) Building, Shari Meglis ash-Shaab. Photographs, documents, including Khedive Ismail's charter for the first parliamentary assembly and copies of the 1923 Constitution and its republican successors; and the State Coach used for the opening of sessions by Ismail, Fu'ad, and Faruq.

Mustafa Kamil Museum. May Salah ad-Din, below the Citadel. Tel: 919-943. Houses the tomb and memorabilia of the founder (1874–1908) of the Nationalist Party.

Nagi Museum: Below the Gizah Pyramids. Dedicated to the life and work of Muhammad Nagi (1888–1956), Alexandrian neo-Impressionist painter.

National Museum for Civilisation (Museum of Egyptian Civilisation): Planetarium building, Gazirah Exhibition Grounds, next to the National Cultural Centre. Tel: 340-5198

National Police Museum: The Citadel. Uniforms, weapons and various criminological exhibits.

Ornithological Museum: Gizah Zoo, Sh. Gizah (Sh. Murad). Tel: 726-313, 726-233

Post Office Museum: Maydan al-Atabah. P.O. Bldg, 2nd floor. Tel: 917-575

Royal Carriage Museum: 82 Sh. 6 July, Bulaq. Tel: 774-437. Entry from behind the Ministry of Foreign Affairs on the Corniche or from next to the Abu'l-Ila mosque on Sh. 26 July. A world-class collection of 78 viceregal, khedivial, and royal horse-drawn vehicles representing 22 types, with displays of harness, livery and trappings.

Saad Zaghlul Museum: Bayt al-Umma, 2 Sh. Saad Zaghlul, Munira. Tel: 534-5399. Residence of the nationalist leader (1854–1927) who inspired the 1919 Revolution, founder of the Wafd (opposition party), Prime Minister 1924–25.

Shawqi Museum: 6 Sh. Ahmad Shawqi, between Sh. Gizah (Sh. Murad) and the Gizah Corniche (Sh. Gamal Abd an-Nasir). Tel: 729-947. Elegant residence of Ahmad Shawqi (1868–1932), court poet to Khedive Abbas II Hilmi, exiled by the British between 1915 and 1919.

Solar Boat Museum: Beside Cheops Pyramid, Gizah. Tel: 857-928. Houses the Old Kingdom solar boat found on the site and painstakingly reassembled.

State Railway Museum: Sh. Bab al-Hadid (Main Railway Station). Tel: 977-393. Splendid collection of viceregal rolling stock and British-made models.

ANCIENT SITES

Memphis and its Necropolis: Of Memphis, the capital of Egypt throughout much of its history, there is little to see but ruins. A small museum compound contains a sphinx and a colossus of Ramses II. Much more is visible in the ancient city's enormous necropolis, which stretches along the plateau above the the river and is entered at Saqqarah, just west of the site of the city itself.

At Saqqarah is a complex of temples and tombs dating from the Old Kingdom onward. Among outstanding attractions are the reliefs in a group of 6th-Dynasty tombs, all possibly designed by the same hand. South of Saqqarah are the pyramids of Dahshur, which require special permission to visit; a few miles north and visible from the Saqqarah plateau are the 5th-Dynasty pyramids of Abu Sir, while still further north are the three great 4th-Dynasty pyramids of Gizah, the Sphinx and the Solar Boat Museum. A Sound and Light show (*Son et Lumière*) takes place every evening at 6.30 p.m. and 7.30 p.m., in English, French German or Arabic. (Check the programme first.)

CHRISTIAN SITES

Misr al-Qadimah: The quarter of the city that contains the major Christian monuments is Misr al-Qadimah ("Old Cairo"), where the remains of Roman Babylon still stand. Legend has it that the Holy Family took refuge from the wicked King Herod here. There are several interesting churches, as well as an important synagogue and a historic mosque marking the site of the first Muslim house of worship built in Africa.

MEDIEVAL CAIRO

The Historic Zone: An imperial capital for most of the period between AD 870 and 1517, Cairo has a resplendent past of which an extraordinary amount has been preserved. Until the onset of mass tourism in the 1960s, in fact, when tastes changed, its medieval streets and buildings were a major attraction for foreign visitors. Earliest intact monuments are the 8th9th-century Nilometre and the 9th-century mosque of Ibn Tulun, a masterpiece that is one of the glories of the Muslim architecture. More than 500 other buildings dating from the 10th–16th centuries are clustered within a historic zone in which nearly all the streets are at least seven centuries old. Other medieval buildings are scattered throughout the city.

The historic zone includes the districts of Sayyidah Zaynab, Darb al-Ahmar, Al-Qahirah, the Citadel, and the so-called Cities of the Dead. It is defined roughly by the northern walls of the Fatimid enclosure on the north, Sh. Salah Salem on the east, the site of Fustat on the south, and Sh. Port Said on the west.

CULTURE PLUS

MUSIC

The **New Cairo Opera House** (The National Cultural Centre), a state-of-the-art facility built and equipped by the Japanese, was opened at the Gazirah Exhibition Grounds in 1988, a belated replacement for the much-loved old Khedivial Opera House at Azbakiyyah, burned in 1971. At the old Opera House there were recitals and symphonic concerts, as well as an annual season during which European (and, during its last decade, local) operatic companies performed. The New Opera House likewise affords a venue for artists and troupes from abroad, which perform either on the large stage of its main auditorium or in the Small Hall.

DANCE

The Cairene public adores ballet and modern dance, a taste that is readily catered to by several foreign governments. The New Opera House consequently offers more dance performances of higher quality than are likely to be seen in any other world capital except Moscow. Among performers have been the Royal Festival Ballet, the Paris Opera Ballet, the Moscow City Ballet, the Leningrad Classical Ballet, the Alvin Ailey troupe, the Harlem Dance Theatre, and the Ballet Béjart.

The **Cairo Ballet** is the product of the National Ballet Institute, which was founded with Soviet help in 1960 and, until 1972, when all Soviet advisers were expelled by order of President Sadat, students at the Institute were Russian-trained. Graduates entered the corps de ballet, which performed at the old Opera House – the repertoire included *Don Quichotte* and *The Fountain of Bakhchiserai* – and the best of them went on for further training and performing experience with the Bolshoi in Moscow. Standards have declined, however, in recent years, despite popular enthusiasm; and public performances in Egypt are rarer than private ones in Saudi Arabia, where it has become fashionable to hire the Cairo Ballet to add class to wedding receptions.

THEATRE

Several public- and private-sector theatres offer regular dramatic performances, but only in Arabic. All productions are subject to censorship. Comedy is popular, but is regarded as particularly dangerous: after references to politics, sex or religion have been removed, little is usually left but slapstick. Performances begin late and run well into the small hours. For Arabic-speakers the experience may be worthwhile. From time to time foreign productions, usually British, are presented at one of the larger public-sector theatres, always under the sponsorship of a foreign government. Performances are well advertised.

CINEMA

Egyptians are keen moviegoers and Egypt is the centre of film-making in the Arab World. Normally, however, there are several foreign films being screened in Cairo (with Arabic subtitles). Recommended: the Tahrir Cinema in Duqqi and Cosmos I and II.

ARTS

There are several very good public and private-sector art galleries in and around Cairo. Most hold regular exhibitions of both local and foreign artists. Public sector galleries include:

Akhenaten Gallery: The Centre for Art (Bayt al-Fann, Bayt Aysha Fahmi), 1 Maahad as-Swissri, Zamalek. Tel: 340-8211.
Al-Mustadira (Fine Arts Syndicate Gallery): National Cultural Centre, Gazirah Exhibition Grounds. Tel: 341-8005.
As-Salam Gallery: Mahmud Khalil Museum (Qasr Amr Ibrahim), 1 Sh. Gazirah, Zamalek. Tel: 341-8672.
Cairo Opera House Exhibition Hall: National Cultural Centre, Gazirah Exhibition Grounds Tel: 342-0592/8.
Egyptian Centre for International Cultural Cooperation: 11 Sh. Sheger ad-Durr, Zamalek. Tel: 341-5419.
Faculty of Fine Arts, Helwan University: 4 Sh. Muhammad Thaqib, Zamalek.
Nile Hall (An-Nil). National Cultural Centre, Gazirah Exhibition Grounds. Tel: 341-8796.
Saray an-Nasr: National Cultural Centre, Gazirah Exhibition Grounds. Tel: 340-5198
The Atelier: 2 Sh. Karim ad-Dawla, off Sh. Antikhana near Maydan Talat Harb (Sulayman Pasha).

Private-sector galleries frequently display ceramics and other handicrafts, as well as sculpture and painting. (For more information: *see Applied Arts and Handicrafts and Antiques under Shopping, page 277.*) Important private-sector galleries are:

Aida Gallery (Restaurant Kanit Tiyam): Kilometre 6, Saqqarah Road, Gizah. By appointment. Tel: 736-538, 538-141.
Arabesque: 6 Sh. Qasr an-Nil, Cairo. Tel: 759-896.
Dr. Ragab Gallery: 3 Corniche (Sh. Gamal Abd an-Nasir), Gizah. Tel: 348-8676.
El Patio: 6 Road 77C, parallel to Sh. Golf, Maadi. Tel: 351-6654.
Gallery Mervat Massoud: 6 Sh. Gazirah, Zamalek. By appointment. Tel: 341-2493
Four Seasons: 11 Sh. Hasan Sabri, Zamalek. Tel: 341-3601.
Imhotep: 118 Sh. Merghani, Heliopolis. Tel: 663-372.
Kahramana Gallery: 32 Sh. Ishaq Ya'qub, As-Sabaa Emarat, Heliopolis. Tel: 290-4644
Le Touch: Maydan Ittihad, connecting with Road 106, Maadi.
Mashrabeya: 8 Sh. Champollion (off Maydan at-Tahrir). Tel: 778-623.
Nile Gallery: 3 Sh. Abu al-Wafa, Pyramid Road 2 km from Maydan Gizah, Gizah.
Nostalgia: 6 Sh. Zakariya Rizk, Zamalek. Tel: 342-0880.
Riash: 6 Sh. Gazirat al-Wasta, Zamalek. Tel: 340-9994.
Safar Khan: 6 Sh. Brazil, Zamalek. Tel: 340-3314.
Sinouhi: 54 Sh. Abd al-Khaliq Tharwat, Cairo. Tel: 910-955.

CULTURAL & RESEARCH CENTRES

American Centre: 4 Sh. Ahmad Rageb, Garden City. Tel: 354-9601.
American Research Centre (ARCE): 2 Maydan Qasr ad-Dubbarah (Simòn Bolívar), Garden City. Tel: 355-3052, 354-8239.
Austrian Archaeological Centre: 8A Sh. Ismail Muhammad, Apt. 62, Zamalek. Tel: 340-6781.
Austrian Cultural Centre: 1103 Corniche, Garden City. Tel: 354-4063.
British Council: 192 Sh. an-Nil. Aguza. Tel: 345-3281.
Canadian Cultural Centre: Canadian Embassy, 6 Sh. Muhammad Fahmi as-Sayyid, Garden City. Tel: 354-3119, 354-3159.
Canadian Institute: 32 Sh. 103, Maadi. Tel: 350-7214.
Chinese Cultural Centre: 4 Sh. Ibn Batutah, Gizah. Tel: 852-261.

Egyptian Centre for International Cultural Cooperation: 11 Sh. Sheger ad-Durr, Zamalek. Tel: 341-5419.

French Cultural Centre: 1 Sh. Madrasat al-Huquq al-Faransiyya, Munira. Tel: 355-3725.

German Archaeological Institute (Deutsches Archäologisches Institut): 22 Gazirat al-Wasta, Zamalek, entrance on Sh. Abu'l Feda. Tel: 340-1460, 340-2321.

Goethe Institute (German Cultural Centre): 5 Sh. Bustan (Abd as-Salam Aref), Zamalek. Tel: 759-877.

Greek Cultural Centre: 14 Sh. Emad ad-Din (Muhammad Farid). Tel: 753-962, 753-833.

Indian Information Service: 37 Sh. Talat Harb (Sulayman Pasha). Tel: 745-162, 745-243.

Institut Dominicain d'Études Orientales: Sh. Masna at-Tarabish, Abbasiyyah. Tel: 925-509.

Institut Français de l'Archéologie Orientale (IFAO, French Institute): 3 Shaykh Ali Yusuf, Munira. Tel: 354-8245.

Israeli Academic Centre in Cairo: 92 Sh. An-Nil (Gamal Abd an-Nasir), Duqqi. Tel: 348-8995, 349-62342.

Italian Cultural Institute: 3 Shaykh al-Marsafi, Zamalek. Tel: 340-8791.

Japanese Cultural Centre: 2 Sh. Abd al-Qader Hamza, Garden City. Tel: 355-3962, 355-3963, 355-3964.

Netherlands Institute of Archaeology and Arabic Studies: 1 Sh. Mahmud Azmi, Zamalek. Tel: 340-0076.

Polish Centre for Mediterranean Archaeology: 14 Sh. Baron Empain, Heliopolis.

Soviet Cultural Centre: 127 Sh. Tahrir, Duqqi. Tel: 348-7079, 340-2915.

Spanish Cultural Centre: 20 Sh. Adli. Tel: 393-6476.

Swiss Cultural Centre. 10 Sh. Abd al-Khaliq Tharwat. Tel: 758-133, 758-284.

Swiss Institute of Archaeology and Architectural Studies (Schweizerisches Institut für Archäologie-und Baukunstgeschichte): 11–13 Sh. Maahad as-Swissri, Zamalek. Tel: 340-9359.

NIGHTLIFE

BARS

Old Cairo hands wax wistful over memories of the vanished Cecil Bar, Aladin, the Strand, the Turf Club, and the bars at the National Hotel and Groppi's Corner House. Most surviving bars are in the larger hotels.

American Corner: 8 Maydan Amman, near the Shooting Club, Duqqi. Tel: 349-7326.

Carmen (Flamenco Hotel): Tel: 340-0815.

Cosmopolitan Hotel: Sh. Ibn Thalab, off Sh. Qasr an-Nil. Tel: 392-7877, 392-7522.

El Gondool (El Gezirah Sheraton Hotel): Tel: 341-1555, 341-1333.

Estoril: 114 Talat Harb (also entered from passage behind Air France at Maydan Talat Harb). Tel: 743-102.

Five Bells Bar: 13 Sh. Ismail Muhammad, Zamalek. Tel: 340-8980.

Mashrabia Bar (Cairo Sheraton Hotel): Tel: 348-9600, 348-8700.

Oasis Bar (Cairo Sheraton Hotel): Tel: 348-9600, 348-8700.

Pub 13 (Sweet Hotel): 39 Road 13, Maadi. Tel: 350-1708, 350-4544.

Pub 28: 28 Sh. Sheger ad-Durr, Zamalek. Tel: 340-0972.

Saint Germain Bar (Cairo Heliopolis Mövenpick Hotel): Tel: 247-0077, 697-799

Sevilla (Flamenco Hotel): Tel: 340-0815, 340-0816.

Speke's Bar (Cairo Sonesta Hotel): Tel: 611-066, 609-444.

Surprise: 5 Said El Bakri, Zamalek. Tel: 340-2645.

Taverne du Champ de Mars (Nile Hilton Hotel): Tel: 765-666, 767-444.

The Cave: 381 Pyramids Road (Sh. al-Haram). (No Telephone).

Vienna Lounge: 37 Sh. Al-Batal Ahmad Abd al-Aziz. Mohandisin. Tel: 346-6940.

Windsor Hotel: 19 Sh. Alfi Bey, Cairo. Tel: 915-277, 915-810.

NIGHTCLUBS

Nightclubs open after 9 p.m. Generally on offer are "Oriental" food and a cabaret with at least one belly dancer. Apart from up-market nightclubs in each major hotel, there are a great many cheaper ones all over town, especially around Azbakiyyah, on Sh. Abu'l Feda in Zamalek, and along the Pyramids Road (Sh. al-Haram). For better nightclubs, reservations are recommended.

Abu el Feda: Sh. Abu'l-Feda, Zamalek. Tel: 340-0736

Abu Nawas (Mena House Oberoi Hotel): Tel: 3877-444

Al Hambra (Cairo Sheraton Hotel, Duqqi): Tel: 348-8600

Al Karawan (Cairo-Heliopolis Mövenpick Hotel): Tel: 247-0077

Alaa ad-Din (Cairo Sheraton Hotel, Duqqi): Tel: 348-8600

Ali Baba (Shepheards Hotel, Corniche): Tel: 355-3800

Almaz (Cairo Marriott Hotel): Zamalek. Tel: 341-1856

Arizona: Pyramids Road (Sh. al-Haram). Tel: 850-204

Auberge des Pyramides: Pyramids Road (Sh. al-Haram). Tel: 852-548

Belvedere (Nile Hilton Hotel): Tel: 740-777

El Samar (El Gezira Sheraton Hotel): Gazirah. Tel: 341-1333, 3411-1555

Empress (Cairo Marriott Hotel): Zamalek. Tel: 340-8888, ext: 8266

Habiba (Ramada Renaissance Hotel): Tel: 387-700, 387-0311

Haroun El Rashid (Semiramis Intercontinental Hotel): Tel: 355-7171

La Belle Époque (Méridien Hotel): Tel: 845-444

Layalina (El Gezira Sheraton Hotel): Gazirah. Tel: 341-1333, 3411-1555

Merryland: Sh. al-Higaz, Heliopolis. Tel: 244-8090

Salt and Pepper: Sh. Abu'l-Feda, Zamalek. Tel: 341-6656

Summer Night Club (Ramsis Hilton Hotel): Tel: 777-4444

Tropicana (Nile Hilton Hotel): Tel: 767-444, 765-666

Two Seasons (Ramsis Hilton Hotel): Tel: 744-400

Versailles Palace: 10 Sh. Muhammad Thaqib, Zamalek. Tel: 341-3199

Ya Salam (El Salam Hotel): Tel: 245-5155, ext: 7003

DISCOS

An established institution, discothèques appeared in Cairo and Beirut in the late 1950s, several years before they had spread from France to the rest of Europe and America. Discos in some hotels are operated as private clubs and are theoretically open only to hotel guests or to members. Minimum charges range from LE 6 to LE 15 per person.

Cairo Airport Stereo: Cairo International Airport. Tel: 665-255

Club Med Disco (Club Méditerranée, Manyal Palace): Manyal. Tel: 844-524, 846-014

Club 36 (Ramsis Hilton Roof): Tel: 744-400

Churchill (Baron Hotel): Heliopolis. Tel: 291-2468

Emanuelle: 49 Sh. al-Thawra, Ard al-Golf, Heliopolis. Tel: 291-3246

Golden Club (Ramada Renaissance Hotel): Cairo-Alexandria Desert Road. 2.5 km from the Pyramids. Tel: 538-111

Granada City: Sh. Granada, Heliopolis. Tel: 439-804

Jackie's (Nile Hilton Hotel): Tel: 767-444, 765-666

Le Barracuda (Méridien Hotel Heliopolis): Heliopolis. Tel: 290-5055

Le Caméléon (Safir Hotel): Maydan Missaha, Duqqi. Tel: 348-2828

Le Papillon (Heliopolis Mövenpick): Airport Road. Tel: 664-977, 679-799

Maxi's Disco: 41 Sh. Hasan Sabri, Zamalek. Tel: 341-2961

Pub 13 Disco (Sweet Hotel): 39 Road 13, Maadi. Tel: 350-1708, 350-4544

Rasputin (Green Pyramids Hotel): Off Pyramids Road. Tel: 856-778

Régine's (El Gezira Sheraton Hotel): Gazirah. Tel: 341-1555

Saddle (Mena House Oberoi): Pyramids. Tel: 387-7444, 387-3424

Sinbad (Sonesta Hotel): Madinat Nasr. Tel: 611-606, 609-444

Sultana's (Semiramis Hotel): Garden City. Tel: 355-7171

Tamerina (Siag Pyramids Hotel): Saqqarah Road. Tel: 850-874

Tamango (Atlas Zamalek Hotel):

Mohandisin. Tel: 346-4175, 346-6569
Vito's (El Salam Hotel): Heliopolis. Tel: 245-2155
Why Not (Belair Hotel): Muqattam. Tel: 910-000, 922-685, 916-177

GAMBLING

It is illegal for Egyptians to gamble anywhere except at the race-track, where pari-mutuel betting is allowed. There is a gambling casino in each of the city's larger hotels, offering the usual *vingt-et-un* (black-jack), baccarat, and craps tables, roulette wheels and slot machines. Gambling is legal for foreigners only and is conducted solely in hard currency, with dollars preferred. A gambler must be over 18 and should carry a passport to identify himself or herself as such. Except within the walls of these hotels the word *casino* in Cairo otherwise normally signifies a tea-house.

SHOPPING

WHAT TO BUY

The Pharaonic, Romano-Byzantine and medieval eras produced artisans and craftsmen of amazing virtuosity, as is demonstrated by the examples of their work in Cairo's three major museums. After the Turkish Conquest in 1517, however, a gap in craft traditions was created when thousands of the best artisans were carried off to Istanbul to embellish the court of the Ottomans. The first half of the 19th century brought additional shocks: the destruction of guilds was followed by an influx of cheap Western factory-made goods after Muhammad Ali was forced to sign the Treaty of London in 1841. Traditional craftsmanship had been dealt a mortal blow.

Efforts made to revive crafts towards the end of the century met with considerable success, however, and by 1930 many crafts-men held permanent positions attached to important households, in which Islamic art had come to be recognised at its true worth. But the Revolution put an end to such patronage – the government's efforts to act as a collectivist substitute for moneyed connoisseurs has never been more than half-hearted – and craftwork fell in esteem, to be delegated either to the otherwise unemployable or to children whose job was simply to turn out shoddy non-functional goods for the tourist market.

WHERE TO LOOK

Simple, beautiful, and useful things can nevertheless still be found in the modern *suqs* and elsewhere. Excellent machine-made fabrics, for example, are available on and around Shari al-Azhar where it is crossed by Shari Muizz li-Din. North of Shari al-Azhar are cotton goods. South of Shari al-Azhar, in the Tunisian rug market, one street to the west of the old Silkmercers' Bazaar – where the shoppers are apt to be *beduw*, Sudanese drovers or other working people who really know about such things – simple flatwoven rugs and pure handwoven woollen shawls, the kind peasants wrap around their heads and shoulders in winter, are sold. Handweaving is done in innumerable back alleys, where rag rugs are on sale for almost nothing.

Leather slippers and sandals, handbags, briefcases, and ottomans are not only of good quality, but seem to improve in design and construction: they can be found in boutiques, major hotels and in the Khan al-Khalili bazaar, though everyone claims there are better buys in Alexandria. In the Khiyamiyyah or Tentmakers' Bazaar craftsmen still make appliqué, sitting crosslegged in their tiny shops: hundreds of metres of the tenting they make are erected in the streets with amazing alacrity as temporary shelters for festivals or funerals; and smaller pieces of appliqué, in the form of bedspreads or cushion covers, make wonderful presents – to oneself, if to no-one else – and are easy to pack. The striped canvas bags on sale in the same area are useful and attractive and as a consequence may now be seen all over the world. Copper and brass pots line the Coppersmiths' Bazaar; and gold- and silverwork are executed in a maze of nearby alleys.

Dozens of different sorts of clay pots, storage jars, incense burners, and casseroles are still made in the potteries near Fustat, while brooms, mats, and other simple household objects made of rattan and palm fibre are sold in many streets.

These things are all made for ordinary people in the poorer quarters of the city. Thanks to the almost unvarying good weather in Egypt, much of life is lived outdoors and in public. Whether they like it or not, Cairenes in these quarters are thus seen continually all day long. One result is that they typically find privacy odd and suspect. Another is that they are very conscious of appearances, of manners and dress.

PERSONAL PRIORITIES

A cook or camel merchant may be unable to read, but when he is ordering a new *gallabiyya* he will be meticulously careful about the quality and colour of the material he buys, about the style and measurements, the bindings and trimmings, down to the last crocheted button. He has his own personal flair – his way of shaping and wearing his cap or turban, though it varies from season to season, will be unique to him – and never wants to cut less than a respectable and even elegant figure in front of his cronies at the coffeehouse.

Clothes are important and everyone wears them with some sense of style. Though the prescription for older women is to wear black in the street, younger women and women coming to town from the country wear brilliant colours with joyous abandon, adding touches that are as expensive as they can afford, a pearl pin here, a flounce or a ribbon there. Even the poorest have earrings and necklaces. Girl babies have tiny gold earrings in their pierced ears almost before they can smile. In the crowds at Cairo markets or along the banks of the Nile on holidays or feast-days, the kaleidoscopic parade of flowered cotton in flaming oranges, shocking pinks, purples, acid greens, electric and peacock blues, of cut velvet insets and eye-catching frills, tucks, and pleats, is dazzling.

Household furnishings, by contrast, are basic. The poor may sleep in a bed under a cover, but probably sit either on an upholstered bench or the floor, gathering for meals round a low table to eat from plastic bowls.

Brides are given a set of copper cooking pots and basins tough enough to last a lifetime, and all the other moveables necessary to a household can usually be piled in the back of a single small Toyota.

The new middle classes have more trouble – and only in part because they have m choice – determining what clothes a nishings are appropriate to their sta along by a tide of consumerism a lated by advertising, they are in want too much and too fast. Wome dren, and furniture are overdressed household fixtures are too fussy. Even years ago there were almost no ready-made clothes, no packaged products, and choices were easy because there was much less to choose from. Today the tiny new flats are swept with nylon brooms, the clothes are washed with imported soap in a washing machine assembled in Egypt, and hung on a plastic washing line by plastic pegs. The one traditional element is likely to be a roomful of gilt chairs and settees in the perennially popular Franco-Italian style referred to locally as *Luigi Khamastasher*.

FRIENDS OF ART

Luckily there is a fairly strong countercurrent to the tide of declining craftsmanship and shoddy goods. It emanates from a number of educated artist-craftsmen, who have set up their own ateliers to produce beautiful and useful things. Many of them have been motivated by ideas traceable to Hamid Said, a London-trained artist who believed that simple and attractive architecture and furnishings could be made as they were during the great eras of Egyptian art, when they were made, he believes, in a spirit of love: love of the Creator, love of natural materials, and love of nature itself. Said and his wife, Ehsan Khalil, a painter and designer, gathered about themselves a notable group of men and women who shared his philosophy. This group called themselves the Friends of Art and Life.

Prominent among the Friends were two architects whose different influences, after 50 years, are now indelible in Egypt. One of them was Hasan Bey Fathy, who designed houses that could be constructed using local materials and modular techniques derived from the practice of village masons. Often thwarted in Egypt, he nevertheless taught two generations of students and was lionised abroad, where the significance of his work was recognised. His influence on succeeding generations has thus been enormous. Based upon the domes, vaults and *mastabahs* (built-in benches of stone, baked brick, or mud-brick) that used to characterise the best Upper Egyptian and Nubian vernacular architecture, his designs are imitated throughout the Arab world and as far away as the American Southwest, while the philosophy behind them has become the governing way of thinking for every serious architect working in the region.

With their calculatedly human scale, his houses seem monumental, but are never pompous. The domes and vaults are functional as well as beautiful – Hasan Bey did extensive research on temperature and convection control – and their size is kept modest by fidelity to the building materials and the laws of parabolic stress. They create spaces, intimate rather than grand, in which the use of *mastabahs* practically dictates the style of furnishing: simple, elegant, and handmade along traditional lines.

It was Hasan Fathy's dream to create an architecture for the poor. Ironically, however, it was the rich who understood and appreciated his ideas and who developed a taste for private houses designed by Fathy and his pupils. Many of them are to be seen in the orchards and palm groves that line the road to Saqqarah. Their requirement for appropriate furnishings and fabrics for their lifestyles eventually created a whole new market for fine craftsmanship.

The other architect among the Friends of Art and Life was Ramses Wissa Wassef. His domed and vaulted mud-brick school at the village of Harraniyyah just off the Saqqarah road is world famous. Drawing on the old Coptic tradition of tapestry-weaving, he and his wife Sophie taught village children to use their imaginations and their perceptions of the world around them. The children learned to create pictures with wool, which was coloured by vegetable dyes made from plants they grew themselves. The children of 40 years ago are now middle-aged virtuosi, while succeeding generations continue to learn the art of making beautiful tapestries. The school also teaches pottery and batik. The best of the work is displayed in a vaulted museum designed by Sophie Wissa Wassef.

In other domed and vaulted houses nearby are an art gallery, the atelier of an artist in glass-making, Zakaria Konani, and his jeweller wife, both of them Friends of Art and Life, and the studios of several potters, painters, and writers, either Friends themselves or former pupils and devotees.

WORKSHOP INDUSTRIES

Like-minded artists, craftsmen and jewellers are finding a growing demand for their work. A large new atelier in the Harraniyyah area employs over 70 workers making jewellery and decorative mirrors, lanterns and other handcrafted items, sold in boutiques all over Cairo. The success of Wissa Wassef's innovative venture is confirmed by the dozens of tapestry and carpet workshops that have sprung up all along the Saqqarah road, at Kirdassah, and even in the tourist bazaar of Khan al-Khalili, selling imitations of the Harraniyyah creations. The scenes they depict are very similar, but the materials and the workmanship are cruder, and consequently they are much cheaper than the genuine article. They are nevertheless handmade and can have considerable charm.

Several boutiques now specialise in silver and "Bedouin" jewellery, using up-to-date versions of traditional designs, such as tiny Qur'an cases, the eye of Horus or the hand of Fatma. It is possible to buy turquoise, coral, lapis lazuli, or ceramic beads – which the patient amateur may find himself picking out from among thousands heaped together in a tin box – then buy the connecting pieces of silver and appropriate clasps. One can then combine them oneself or have them strung together by a favourite jeweller.

A devoted student of Hasan Fathy with a degree in Islamic art and architecture runs a boutique in Duqqi. Specializing in Bedouin dresses and embroidery, she also sells jewellery, pottery, glass, brass, and fabrics and offers a good choice of Bedouin rugs. She knows many artisans still working in the old quarters of Cairo and can have fabrics and furniture custom-made or adapted to modern use. Other boutique owners have followed suit.

Today there is considerable demand for finely turned wooden screens made of tiny bits of mahogany, rosewood, beech and pine called *mashrabiyyah* and workshops producing it have become quite profitable. This fine old craft dates back to the Middle Ages, when the screens were used solely for shading windows, and purists nowadays claim its use in furniture is inappropriate. A more popular school of thought, however, sees *mashrabiyyah* as an art in itself and finds no reason why it should not be used for the backs of sofas, chairs, for the tops of coffee-tables, tea trolleys and bars. Its use is a question of taste and meanwhile the brisk demand is keeping the craft alive and well. There is a workshop on the road to Kirdassah, a large factory in Duqqi, and many of the village carpenters in Maadi and elsewhere have turned over their traditional carpentry shops to the manufacture of *mashrabiyyah* furniture.

WHERE TO SHOP

APPLIED ART & HANDICRAFTS

Distinctly up-market from the old-fashioned tourist goods are a wealth of high-quality hand-made articles that are either produced by Egyptian artisans or imported from elsewhere in the region (*see also Carpets, Ceramics, and Tapestries, below*).

Alrowaq (Ar-Riwaq): 3 Sh. 269 off Sh. Nasr, Maadi al-Gadidah (New Maadi).
Anas Al-Wogoud Gallery: 23B Sh. Ismail Muhammad Zamalek, Apt 40, 6th floor. Tel: 341-8189.
Association Chrétienne de la Haute-Égypte: 85A Sh. Ramsis. Tel: 752-381, 754-723. Weaving and embroidery.
Bashayer: 58 Sh. Musaddeq, Duqqi. Tel: 713-233. Owner: Hasan Salem. Rugs, jewellery, pottery, paintings, textiles, wood furniture and brass.
El Ain Gallery: 73 Sh. Al-Husayn, Duqqi. Owners: Azza and Randa Fahmy. Jewellery and brass, wooden furniture, folk painting on glass and silk, pottery, blown glass, basketry, *gallabiyyas*, shawls and upholstery fabrics.
El Patio Gallery: 4 Sh. 77C, golf area, Maadi. Owner: Lamia Hassanein. Rugs, pottery, paintings, blown glass, copper-framed mirrors, *mashrabiyyah* and textiles.
Emeraude: 54 Sh. Abu Bakr as-Siddiq. Maydan Safir, Heliopolis. Tel: 243-1542.

Jenny: Semiramis Intercontinental Hotel.
National Art Development Institute of Mashrabeya (NADIM): Sh. Al-Mesana, south of the Coca Cola production centre, Duqqi. Tel: 715-927, 714-219. Owner: Asaad Nadim. *Mashrabiyyah*, inlaid wood, appliqué work and brass.
Nomad: Cairo Marriott Hotel. Tel: 341-2132. Also at: 14 Sh. Saray al-Gazirah, first floor. Tel: 341-1917. Thursday, Friday and Saturday from 10 a.m. to 3 p.m. Owner: Carol Sidki. Brasswork, basketry, rugs, appliqué work, shawls, camel saddles and jewellery.
Om El Saad: Sh. Musaddeq, Duqqi. Tel: 349-8685.
Shahira Mehrez and Companions: 12 Sh. Abu Emama. Duqqi, left side, third floor. Closed Friday. Summer hours: 10 a.m. to 3 p.m. and 5 p.m. to 8 p.m; winter hours: 10 a.m. to 7 p.m. Tel: 348-7814. Owner: Shahira Mehrez. *Gallabiyyas*, rugs, shawls, embroidery, fabrics, jewellery, brass, folklore-inspired paintings on glass.
Tiffany Egypt: Nasr Building, Maydan Gazaa'ir off Sh. Nasr, Maadi al-Gadidah (New Maadi). Tel: 352-6620, 352-1590; Fax: 352-5796. Owner: Samir Mahmud. Makers of art-class lamps, including reproductions of Tiffany models; suppliers for the European market, where their work is old at six times the Cairo price.

ANTIQUES

It is illegal to sell Egyptian-made objects – or non-Egyptian-made objects officially deemed to have "historical" importance – if they are more than 100 years old. This restriction means that all objects for sale as antiques are apt to be of 20th-century European manufacture.

Avenue 30: Gazirat al-Wasta, Zamalek. Tel: 340-6058. Owners: Farida Greiss and Eloui Farid.
Gallerie Classique: 32 Sh. Bahgat Ali, Zamalek. Tel: 341-1719. Owner: Nihad Bahgat.
Husayn Ahmad: 16 Sh. Hoda Shaarawi.
Mahrus Muhammad Al-Assal: 21 Sh. Hoda Shaarawi. Tel: 393-8852.
Noubi Antiquaire: 157 Sh. 26 July, Zamalek. Tel: 340-1385. Owner: Nubi Muhammad Ahmad.

Sami Shehata: 5 Sh. Muhammad Sidqi, off Sh. Hoda Shaarawi. Tel: 393-3047.

Sinouhi: 54 Sh. Abd al-Khaliq Tharwat, Cairo. Tel: 910-955. Owners: Omar and Leila Rashad. The first and still probably the best of these boutiques. Antiques, paintings and graphics by Margo Veillon and Hasan Sulayman.

Zann's Too: 3 Sh. 152, Sh. an-Nahda at the Nile end of the Metro overpass, Maadi. Owners: Anni Zein El-Din and Samir Sananiri. Books, silver, bibelots, old prints, paintings of Amy Nimr.

CARPETS

Export of high-quality handmade Persian or Turkish carpets is forbidden and few come onto the market. Export of lower-quality locally-made carpets is extremely difficult for everyone except tourists, who may carry them out in their luggage, but should be provided with two documents: a bank receipt, marked "For the Purchase of a Handmade Carpet", showing exchange of foreign currency for the purchase of the carpet and a receipt for the purchase itself.

Woollen carpets have been made from the Ptolemaic period onward in Egypt and production reached a high point under the Mamluks. Most carpets manufactured in Egypt today are machine-made, but there are centres producing both flat-woven (*kelim*) and knotted carpets. Though not very inspired in their designs – usually adaptations of Persian patterns that have simply been assigned to a weaver for production – the hand-knotted carpets are serviceable, reasonably priced and Woolmarked.

Handmade flat-woven carpets in styles identified with Helwan, Asyut and Aswan come from those towns in Upper Egypt and are cheap, even with Cairo dealers' mark-ups added. Bedouin carpets are obtained mainly at Hammam, 38 miles (60 km) west of Alexandria, where they are brought for sale and are quite cheap there. In Cairo they are often marked up several hundred percent. Selections are visible in the Suq al-Attarin (Herbalists'/Perfumers' Market), behind and south of the *madrasah* of al-Ghuri, at the village of Kirdassah, near the Gizah pyramids on Maryutiyyah Canal Road, and in many of the shops listed *above under Applied Arts and Handicrafts*.

CLOTHES

Egypt has wonderful fabrics and boasts many excellent couturier-designers. Some work chiefly on commission for particular clients: their artistry is apt to result in unique and expensive garments that are displayed only by special arrangement. Others have created lines of ready-made clothes that compete successfully with such international labels as Benetton or Stefanel (also made in Egypt and sold at local prices). Between these two extremes are many other kinds of clothing, all found in private-sector boutiques like the following:

Benetton: 11 Sh. Hasan Sabri, Zamalek; 23 Sh. Shehab, Mohandisin; 114 Sh. Muhammad Farid (Emad ad-Din); 2 Sh. Ibrahim Laqani, Heliopolis; 51 Sh. 9, Maadi.

Chiavistelli: 4-A Sh. Ibn al-Nabih, Zamalek.

Concrete: 12 Sh. 216/306 Digla. Tel: 352-8980.

De Luca: 4-D Sh. al-Gazirah, Zamalek.

Ed-Dukkan: Ramses Hilton Hotel Annex.

Eve: 2 Sh. Taha Husayn (Sh. Willcocks), Zamalek.

George Dib: Semiramis Intercontinental Hotel. Tel: 355-7171.

Marie-Louise: 1 Sh. al-Batal Ahmad Abd al-Aziz, Mohandisin. Tel: 342-2973.

Miss Egypt: Nile Hilton Hotel. Tel: 765-666, 767-444.

Mix and Match: 21 Maydan Mazhar, off Sh. Brazil, Zamalek. Tel: 340-9602.

MM: 110 Sh. 26 of July, Zamalek. Tel: 341-4482; 8 Sh. Qasr an-Nil. Tel: 743-346; 20 Sh. Talat Harb. Tel: 778-204.

Mobaco: 242 Sh. Sudan, Mohandisin. Tel: 347-3791; 19 Talat Harb. Tel: 393-4630; 31 Sh. Mukhtar, New Maadi. Tel: 350-6738; 47 Sh. Beirut, Heliopolis. Tel: 290-7835; Nile Hilton Hotel. Tel: 765-666, 767-444; Semiramis Intercontinental Hotel. Tel: 355-7171.

NafNaf: 23 Sh. Suria, Mohandisin.

Nes: 6 Sh. Ibn Nabih, Zamalek. Tel: 340-8410.

Octopus: 8 Maydan Shaykh Marsafi, Zamalek. Tel: 340-4683; 6 Sh. Arhab (off Sh. an-Nil.), Gizah; 25 Misr-Helwan Agricultural Road, Maadi; 15 Sh. Baghdad, Heliopolis. Tel: 664-338; 92 Sh. al-Higaz, Heliopolis. Tel: 243-7769.

On Safari: 10 Sh. Michel Lutfallah, Zamalek. Tel: 340-1909. High-quality travel clothing.

The Shirt Shop: Cairo Marriott Hotel, Zamalek. Tel: 340-8888.
Stefanel: 6 Sh. Ismail Muhammad, Zamalek; 64 Sh. 9, Maadi; 18 Sh. Baghdad, Qubbah, Heliopolis; 39 Sh. Sherif, Central Cairo.
Top Shop: Cairo Marriott Hotel, Zamalek. Tel: 340-8888.
Valentina: 56 Sh. Dimashq, Mohandisin. Tel: 349-0221.
Zann's: 20 Sh. Ismail Muhammad, Zamalek. Tel: 340-0169.

Public-sector ready-to-wear clothes, especially those for men, are often well made of high-quality cotton, are very durable, and are a superb buy.

GLASS

So-called "Muski" glass – crude glass made and blown in the Husayniyyah and in the Northern Cemetery – is available at the glassblowers' establishments, in the Khan al-Khalili, and in many shops. It comes in turquoise, brown, blue, pink and green in the form of a variety of objects, including Christmas decorations. Cracks and bubbles make each piece unique, but very fragile.

JEWELLERY

The best jewellery in Cairo is made by craftsmen working on commission for a handful of designers, who sell their work either privately or through shops specializing in art and handicrafts. Bedouin silver (i.e, pieces made for the *badawi* market) sometimes appears for sale. The best pieces are found in shops specialising in art and handicrafts or in Khan al-Khalili (*see below*), where they are cheap, but not nearly as cheap as in the Yemen or in Siwah. Gold is sold by weight according to the latest London "fix" regardless of workmanship and can be a bargain. Gold cartouches, with a name spelled out in hieroglyphic characters, have become standard everywhere.

PAPYRUS

Cyperus papyrus is the sedge from which papyrus was made in ancient Egypt. Until it was re-introduced a few decades ago by Dr Hasan Ragab, former Egyptian ambassador to the People's Republic of China, the plant had been virtually extinct in Egypt for over a millennium. The technique of papyrus-making, never written down, had long been forgotten. Dr Ragab is the founder of the Papyrus Institute, which occupies two houseboats moored to the Gizah bank of the Nile, where manufacturing techniques were originally re-evolved. Papyrus is now available everywhere in various sizes and qualities, with or without pharaonic motifs.

The Papyrus Institute also includes an art gallery (*see Arts, above*). At Dr Ragab's Pharaonic Village the ex-diplomat has recreated vignettes of life in pharaonic times, using actors. The visitor tours an island by boat, watches scenes involving activities such as the making of papyrus, and visits reconstructions of the houses of a peasant and a nobleman.

TAPESTRIES

Trained as children, the artist-weavers of the hamlet of Harraniyyah, near the Gizah pyramids on the Saqqarah Road, are world-famous. The superb tapestries produces at the centre created for them by Ramsis Wissa Wassef, a distinguished architect, and his wife Sophie Habib Ghorgy, the daughter of a well-known sculptor, have been the subject of major exhibitions in Paris (at the Centre Pompidou) and London (at the Barbican). They are created from pure vegetable-dyed wool and the museum on the premises that displays them is well worth seeing. A few finished pieces are offered for sale. For visitors who find real Harraniyyah work expensive, many cheaper imitations are produced elsewhere, which are inferior in both craftsmanship and inspriation, but still worth having.

Embroidered tapestries are made at Akhmim, a village in Upper Egypt, under the sponsorship of the Association Chrétienne de la Haute-Égypte, 85A Sh. Ramsis (Tel: 752-381, 754-723) and sold in Cairo at Coptic Orthodox Christmastide, in early January, every other year (i.e. January 1993, 1995, etc). Much prized and consequently widely imitated, they can occasionally be found at other outlets, as can the attractive counterpanes and napery that are woven at Akhmim.

The village of Kirdassah, on the Maryutiyyah Canal Road. offers a wide selection of handmade imitations of Wissa

Wassef weaving and Akhmim embroidery, as well as carpets and fabrics.

TOURIST GOODS

For anything other than food, Cairenes do most of their shopping in well-known public-sector department stores and in private-sector galleries and boutiques. Tourists, however, are almost certain to do major shopping in the **Khan al-Khalili bazaar**, a market area loosely installed in the ruins of the Khan al-Khalili, a 14th-century caravanserai, of which little remains. The ruins now merge with the ramshackle streets and buildings that form one corner of the Gamaliyyah quarter, near the mosque of Sayyidna Husayn. The bazaar was formerly a Turkish enclave specializing in imported glassware and fine carpets, neither of which has been a significant part of its stock in trade since the 1950s.

The tradition of selling goods of the same type in the same area keeps trading competitive and means that in the neighbourhood of the ruins of Khan al-Khalili there are whole streets of spice merchants, perfumers, coppersmiths, goldsmiths, and jewellers. The Khan al-Khalili bazaar itself is not quite a traditional market, however, but one that has grown up in response to the tourist trade; and the common denominator now among the goods on offer is that they are the sort of wares that tourists are supposed to be interested in. Trade in anything more than 100 years old is forbidden. As measured by the standards of Damascus or Istanbul, the craftsmanship displayed in most new items is indifferent; and handmade goods of more interesting design and higher quality will be found, in fact, in many boutiques elsewhere in the city specializing in art and handicrafts. Bargaining is expected: do not be outraged at the trader's opening price, which he rarely hopes to get.

The Khan al-Khalili bazaar provides at least a kind of introduction to monuments of the city's historic zone, some of the finest of which are literally just around the corner and are missed by many tourists altogether. Also just around the corner, stretched along 100 metres or so of the the Qasabah, are three real centuries-old bazaars: the Suq an-Nahhasin (the Coppersmiths' Market) and the Suq as-Sagha (the Goldsmiths' Market), where ordinary Egyptians shop for household cooking vessels and gold, and the Suq al-Attarin (Herbalists'/Perfumers' Market), where people from all over Cairo come to buy incense, herbs, and spices.

Many of the best dealers in the neighbourhood of Khan al-Khalili also maintain retail premises elsewhere, offering selections of cloth, jewellery, herbs, spices, incense, floral essences, and copper and brassware that are at least equal to those displayed in the Khan al-Khalili bazaar in quality and are easier and perhaps even cheaper to buy. Examples:

Atlas: Semiramis Intercontinental Hotel. Tel: 355-7171. Cloth, cushion covers, *gallabiyyas*.
Hamdi and Galal: 72 Sh. 9, Maadi. Tel: 351-6707. Copper and brassware.
Ar-Rihani (Rifai M. Rifai and Co): 93 Sh. 9, Maadi. Tel: 350-5080. A well-stocked traditional-style *attar* (druggist, spice-dealer, perfume-seller). Spices, herbs, essences and aromatic oils, perfumes.
Onix: 72 Sh. 9, Maadi. Tel: 351-3860. Silver, old and new, in all forms.
Sirgany: Cairo Sonesta Hotel. 4 Sh. at-Tayaran, Nasr City. Tel: 80-9444. A firm established in the Suq as-Sagha since 1776. Gold and jewellery.

BOOKSHOPS

Academic Bookshop: 121 Sh. Tahrir, Duqqi.
Al Ahram: 165 Muhammad Farid (Emad ad-Din). Tel: 390-4499.
Alexandria Bookshop.134 Sh. Umar ibn al-Khattab, Heliopolis.
American University in Cairo (AUC) Bookstore: 113 Sh. Qasr al-Ayni. (Maydan at-Tahrir). Entrances on Sh. Muhammad Mahmud and on Sh. Shaykh Rihan. Tel: 357-5377.
Anglo-Egyptian: 165 Muhammad Farid (Emad ad-Din). Tel: 914-337.
Everyman Bookshop: Sh.12 Baghdad St. Heliopolis.
L'Orientaliste: 15 Sh. Qasr an-Nil. Tel: 753-418.
Lehnert and Landrock: 44 Sh. Sherif. Tel: 392-7606.
Livres de France: Sh. Qasr an-Nil at Sh. Sherif. Tel: 393-5512.
Ra Bookshop: Cairo Marriott Hotel, Zamalek.

Reader's Corner: 33 Sh. Abd al-Khaliq Tharwat. Tel: 748-801.
Zamalek Bookstore: 19 Sh. Sheger ad-Durr, Zamalek. Tel: 341-9197.

SPORTS

SPECTATOR

Cairenes love football and the fortunes of the two first-division Cairo teams, Zamalek and Ahli, are followed with zeal.

Horse-races take place on Saturday and Sunday from mid-November through May alternatively at the Gazirah Sporting Club track (Tel: 341-5709) and at the Heliopolis Hippodrome.

PARTICIPANT

There are a several sports clubs in Cairo. Best known is the Gazirah Sporting Club in Zamalek, though the Shooting Club in Duqqi has become the most exclusive. Many clubs offer temporary memberships or will allow day-visitors to use facilities for a fee. The Shooting Club, in which membership even for long-established residents is extremely difficult to obtain, is an exception. Major hotels also operate clubs and maintain health facilities with saunas, swimming pools and tennis courts.

Popular and accessible are golf and riding. The only two golf courses now extant are at the Mena House and the Gazirah Sporting Club, where equipment may be rented and green fees are very reasonable. Fridays at the Mena House are reserved for members only. There are several stables near the Gizah pyramids, where horses can be purchased or rented by the hour, day or month and where lessons are given.

SPORTS CLUBS

Automobile Club of Egypt: 10 Sh Qasr an-Nil. Tel: 743-355.
British Golfing Society: Meets the last Saturday of each month at the Mena House for competitions. A statutory restriction to British passport holders is not strictly enforced and newcomers may play as guests.
British Sub-Aqua Club: 21 Sh. Lubnan, Mohandisin. Tel: 346-1105/09/10/23.
Cairo Divers Club: Open to divers and non divers. First Monday of each month at Semiramis Intercontinental Hotel. Diving instruction and certificates, diving trips.
Cairo Hash House Harriers: Runs Friday afternoons followed by picnics and social hours.
Cairo Rugby Club: 2 Sh. 161, Maadi. Weekly training Wednesday 5 p.m. at Victory College, Maadi. Social evenings Monday and Wednesday.
Cairo Yacht Club: 3 Shari an-Nil (Gizah Corniche, Shari Gamal Abd an-Nasir), Gizah. Tel: 348-9415.
Egyptian Rowing Club: 11 Shari an-Nil (Gizah Corniche, Shari Gamal Abd an-Nasir), Gizah. Tel: 731-639.
Gazirah Sporting Club: Sh. Saray al-Gazirah, Zamalek. Tel: 340-6000.
Gizah Yacht Club: 101 Shari an-Nil (Gizah Corniche, Shari Gamal Abd an-Nasir), Gizah. Tel: 348-2420.
Heliolido Sporting Club: Sh. Galaa, Heliopolis. Tel: 243-6002.
Heliopolis Sporting Club: 17 Sh. Mirghani, Heliopolis. Tel: 604-585.
Heliopolis Racing Club: Near Hyatt El Salam Hotel, Heliopolis. Tel: 245-4090.
Maadi Sporting Club: Sh. Dimashq, Maadi. Tel: 350-5504.
Maadi Yacht Club: Corniche, Maadi. Tel: 350-5169.
Mena House Golf Club: Mena House, Gizah. Tel: 875-999.
National Sporting Club: Near Cairo Tower, Gazirah. Tel: 340-2112.
Sakkara Country Club: Saqqarah Road. Tel: 348-4871.
Shooting Club: Sh. Nadi as-Seid, Duqqi. Tel: 704-333.
Tewfiqiyyah Club: Madinat al-Awadaf, Cairo. Tel: 346-1930.
Zamalek Sporting Club: Mohandisin. Tel: 346-6685, 347-6677.

PHOTOGRAPHY

"Egyptians enjoy being photographed," says one expert, "but only if they're ready for you." Studio portraits are extremely popular, street photographers taking posed portraits with home-made box cameras are still common, and Cairenes love looking at pictures of themselves and their friends. Indeed, some are so eager to be photographed that their persistence can be troublesome.

Others, however, may resent it as an intrusion upon their privacy. Small gatherings should be asked for their permission before a shot is taken. In larger gatherings the sheer density of the crowd is likely to be too inhibiting for most work. Egyptian photographers say that unposed pictures of people have to be taken quickly and unobtrusively or – if there are objections – not at all.

Because few of its inhabitants have ever conceived of their city in visual terms, Cairo is less photogenic than its history and monuments might suggest: it offers only a handful of the "photo opportunities" that characterise Western cities, which are often organised around vistas. Ordinary Western and Asian ideas of what a picture is, moreover, or of what makes it good or bad are not generally understood. They derive from a shared visual culture that somehow seems to have missed the Middle East. Even Egyptian photographers thus have trouble with the officiousness of self-appointed street corner censors, who are apt to announce that to take pictures of anything in view is *mamnua* – forbidden.

Such declarations may be either attempts at extortion, instances of spy-fever, or throwbacks to the period between 1960 and 1980, when pictures of any objects that might suggest that Egypt was "backward" were prohibited. Among such despised objects, of course, are most of the things – the people, streets, and buildings of the historic zone, for example – that are worth shooting. An appropriate response to the would-be censor is a polite request to see his identity-card. It is useless to argue.

In certain areas regarded as of military importance, however, photography is officially and strictly forbidden. In such restricted areas, which include not only the zones around air-bases and army camps, but also the approaches to all bridges, as well as the bridges themselves, post-offices and many other quite ordinary governmental buildings, signs announcing the prohibition are usually posted, but not always.

The Egyptian Antiquities Organisation allows photography in most of the mosques, tombs and museums under its jurisdiction, but fees levied at many places have reached preposterous levels: LE 1,000 for the use of a tripod, LE 60 per photograph in the study collection of the Islamic Museum, plus an additional charge for general permission to photography, etc.

Contrary to what one might suppose, the best time of year for most photography in Cairo is the winter, when dust and glare are reduced and a more interesting and useful light is available than in the summer. Thanks to dust and pollution, Cairo's skies are rarely clear at season, however, and ASA100 is often too slow for ordinary photography, especially with telephoto lenses. Colour negative film (Kodak Gold, Kodacolor, Ektar, Agfacolor, Fujicolor) is plentiful and cheap, but black and white film (Ilford, Pan F) and slide film (Kodachrome, Ektachrome, Fujichrome, Agfachrome) are more difficult to come by. Processing of colour negative film is fast, but generally uninspired. Slides or transparencies, however, can only be handled by two or three establishments and Kodachrome must be sent to Europe for processing.

LANGUAGE

The system used to transliterate Arabic words and proper names in this book is designed to help the reader use them and be understood even if he or she does not know a word of the language. Though reasonably accurate, it is also very simplified and leaves at least eight Arabic letters and sounds unrepresented.

Most Cairenes know a few words of English, though real ability to use languages other than Arabic is confined to the educated. A few words of colloquial Egyptian Arabic are therefore useful. The words and phrases listed below are not transliterated, but spelled more or less phonetically, according to the following rules:

Vowels
’ = glottal stop
a = a as in *father*
aa = a as in Standard English *bad, mad, glad*
e = e as in *very*
ee = ee as in *between*
i = i as in *if, stiff*
o = o as in *boss*
oo = o as in *fool*
u = u as in *put*

Consonants
All consonants are pronounced individually and as in English with the following exceptions:

kh = ch as in Scottish *loch*
sh = sh as in *shut*
gh = Arabic *ghayn*, usually described as resembling a (gutteral) Parisian *r*.
q = Arabic *qaf*, frequently pronounced in Cairo as a k or a glottal stop.

WORDS & PHRASES

airport	*matár*
boat	*mérkeb*
bridge	*kubri*
car	*arabiyya, sayára*
embassy	*sefára*
hospital	*mustáshfa*
hotel	*fúnduq*
post office	*bosta*
restaurant	*matáam*
square, maydan	*midáan*
street	*shaari*
right	*yeméen*
left	*shemáal*
and/or	*wa/walla*
yes/no	*aywa/laa’*
please/thank you	*minfadlak/shukran*
big/little	*kibeer/sughayyar*
good/bad	*kwáyyis/mish kwáyyis*
possible	*mumkin*
impossible	*mish mumkin*
here/there	*hena/henáak*
hot/cold	*sukn/baarid*
many/few	*kiteer/olayyel*
up/down	*fo’ (foq)/taht*
more/enough	*kamáan/kefáya*
breakfast	*íftar*
dinner	*asha*
today	*innahárda*
tomorrow	*bokra*
yesterday	*embáareh*
morning	*is-sobh*
noon	*id-dohr*
afternoon	*bad id-dohr*
at night	*belayl*
next week	*il esbool-iggáy*
next time	*il mara-iggáya*
last time	*il-mara illi fáatit*
after a while	*bad shwayya*
I/you	*ana/enta*
he/she	*huwwa/hiyya*
they/we	*humma/ehna*

NUMBERS

1	*wáhid*
2	*itnéyn*
3	*taláatah*
4	*arbá*
5	*khamsa*
6	*sitta*
7	*séba*
8	*tamánya*
9	*tíssah*
10	*áshara*
11	*hedásher*
12	*itnásher*
13	*talatásher*
14	*arbatasher*

15	*khamastásher*
16	*sitásher*
17	*sabatásher*
18	*tamantásher*
19	*tissatásher*
20	*ashréen*
30	*talatéen*
40	*arbaéen*
50	*khamséen*
60	*sittéen*
70	*sabaéen*
80	*tamanéen*
90	*tissaéen*
100	*meeya, meet*

MONEY

50 piastres
khamseen 'ersh (qersh)

75 piastres
khamsa wa sebaeen 'ersh (qersh)

money	*filóos*
change/no change	*fakka/mafeesh fakka*
the bill	*il hesáb*
this/ that	*di/da*
how much	*bekáam?*
how much do you want (to a male)	*ayiz kaam?*
how much do you want? (to a female)	*ayza kaam?*
all/half	*kull/nus*

DAYS OF THE WEEK

Sunday/Monday
yowm el had/yowm il-itnéyn

Tuesday/Wednesday
yowm it-taláat/yowm il-árba

Thursday/Friday
yowm il-khamées/yowm ig-góma

Saturday
yowm is-sabt

MONTHS

January/ February/ March
yanáyer/febráyer/máris

April/ May/ June
abreel/mayoo/yoonyoo

July/ August/ September
yoolyoo/aghustus/sibtímbir

October/November/December
októbir/nofímbir/disímbir

COMMON EXPRESSIONS

Hello, welcome	*ahlan wa sahlan*
Good morning	*sabáh-il-kheir*
Good evening	*masáal-kheir*
goodbye	*mas-saláama*
what is your name?	*íssmak ey?* (to a male)
	íssmik ey? (to a female)
How are you?	*izzáyak* (to a male)
	izzáyik (to a female)
I am fine,	*kwayiss* (male)
	kwayíssa (female)
thank God	*il-hamdo li-lah* (standard reply)

Often heard is "insha'Allah," which means "God willing" and is a reminder that all things are ultimately in the hands of Providence. The standard reply to a casual "See you tomorrow," for instance, is "Insha'Allah".

FURTHER READING

Abu-Lughod, Janet. *Cairo: 1001 Years of the City Victorious*. Princeton: Princeton University Press, 1971.

Aldridge, James. *Cairo*. London: Macmillan, 1970.

Antoniou, Jim, et al. *The Conservation of the Old City of Cairo*. London: UNESCO, 1980.

Atiya, Nayra. *Khul-Khaal: Five Egyptian Women Tell Their Stories*. Syracuse: Syracuse University Press, 1982; Cairo: The American University in Cairo Press, 1984.

Baedeker, Karl. *Egypt and the Sudan: Handbook for Travellers*. Seventh Edition. Leipzig: Karl Baedeker, 1914.

Baedeker, Karl. *Egypt and the Suda*

book for Travellers. Eighth Edition. Leipzig: Karl Baedeker, 1929. (Contains new chapters by Monneret de Villard and K.A.C. Creswell.) Reprinted London and Newton Abbot: David and Charles; New York: Hippocrene Books, Inc, 1985.

Baines, John and Malek, Jaromir. *Atlas of Ancient Egypt.* Oxford: Phaidon, 1980.

Baud, Marcel. *Égypte.* Paris: Librairie Hachette, 1950.

Behrens-Abouseif, Doris. *Azbakiyya and Its Environs: From Azbak to Ismail, 1476–1879.* Cairo: Institut Français de l'Archéologie Orientale, 1985.

Behrens-Abouseif, Doris. *Islamic Architecture in Cairo: An Introduction.* Leiden: E.J. Brill; Cairo: The American University in Cairo Press, 1989.

Behrens-Abouseif, Doris. *The Minarets of Cairo.* Cairo: The American University in Cairo Press, 1985.

Berque, Jacques. *Egypt: Imperialism and Revolution.* London: Faber and Faber, 1972.

Budge, Wallace. *The Nile: Notes for Travellers in Egypt.* Ninth Edition. London and Cairo: Thomas Cook and Sons, 1905.

Burckhardt, John Lewis. *Arabic Proverbs; or the Manners and Customs of the Modern Egyptians Illustrated from Their Proverbial Sayings Current at Cairo, Translated and Explained.* With an introduction by Sir William Ousely. London: The Association for Promoting the Discovery of the Interior of Africa, 1830. Reprint London: Curzon Press, 1984.

Butler, Alfred J. *Babylon of Egypt: A Study in the History of Old Cairo.* Oxford: Clarendon Press, 1914.

Le Caire. Autrement, hors série no. 12 (février 1985). Paris: *Autrement,* 1985.

Carman, Barry and McPherson, John, eds. *Bimbashi McPherson: A Life in Egypt.* London: British Broadcasting Corporation, 1983.

Cecil, Lord Edward. *The Leisure of an Egyptian Official.* London: Hodder and Stoughton, 1921.

Clerget, Marcel. *Le Caire: Étude de géographie urbaine et d'histoire économique.* Cairo: Imprimerie E. & R. Schindler, 1934. Two volumes.

Cooper, Artemis. *Cairo in the War, 1939–1945.* London: Hamish Hamilton, 1989.

. . . . istina. *Das islamische Kairo: Ein Reisebuch.* Göttingen: Lamuv, 1990.

Evin, Ahmet, ed. *The Expanding Metropolis: Coping with the Urban Growth of Cairo.* Proceedings of Seminar Nine in the Series "Architectural Transformations in the Islamic World". Held at Cairo, Egypt, November 11–15, 1984. Singapore: Concept Media Pte for the Aga Khan Award for Architecture, 1985.

Fargeon, Maurice. *Les Juifs en Égypte depuis les Origines jusqu'à ce jour: histoire générale suivie d'un aperçu documentaire.* Cairo: Imprimerie Paul Barbey, 1938.

Hautecœur, Louis and Wiet, Gaston. *Les Mosquées du Caire.* Paris: Librairie Ernest Leroux, 1932.

Hopwood, Derek. *Tales of Empire: The British in the Middle East 1880–1952.* London: I.B. Tauris, 1989.

Ilbert, Robert. *Heliopolis: Le Caire 1905–1922: Genèse d'une ville.* Paris: Centre National de la Recherche Scientifique, 1981.

Kessler, Christel. *The Carved Stone Domes of Cairo.* London and Cairo: AARP and the American University in Cairo Press, 1976.

Kubiak, Wladyslaw B. *Al-Fustat: Its Foundation and Early Development.* Cairo: The American University in Cairo Press, 1987.

Lane, Edward William. *Cairo Fifty Years Ago.* Edited by Stanley Lane-Poole. London: John Murray, 1896.

Lane, Edward William. *An Account of the Manners and Customs of the Modern Egyptians.* London: Charles Knight, 1836. Two volumes. Second Edition. London: The Society for the Diffusion of Useful Knowledge, 1837. Everyman Edition, based on the fifth edition (1860) as edited by Edward Stanley Poole. London and Toronto: J.M. Dent; New York E.P. Dutton, 1908, reprinted many times. Reprint of eighth (1895) edition: London and Cairo: East-West Publications and Livres de France, 1978, 1981.

Lane, Edward William. *The Thousand and One Nights, commonly called in England, The Arabian Nights' Entertainments: A New Translation from the Arabic with Copious Notes.* Reprint of the edition of 1838. London and Cairo: East-West Publications and Livres de France, 1979–1981. Three volumes.

Lane-Poole, Stanley. *The Story of Cairo.*

London: J.M. Dent and Sons, 1902.

Lézine, Alexandre. *Trois palais d'époque ottomane au Caire.* Cairo: Institut Français de l'Archéologie Orientale, 1972.

Murnane, William. *The Penguin Guide to Ancient Egyptian Monuments.* Hammersmith: Penguin, 1983.

Napier, Priscilla. *A Late Beginner.* London: Michael Joseph, 1966.

Palmer, Monte, Ali, Leila, and Yassin, El Sayed. *The Egyptian Bureaucracy.* Syracuse: Syracuse Universiyt Apress, 1988.

Parker, Richard B., and Sabin, Robin. *Islamic Monuments in Cairo: A Practical Guide.* Third edition, revised and enlarged by Caroline Williams. Cairo: The American University in Cairo Press, 1985.

Petrie, Flinders, Bevan, Edwyn, Milne, J.E., and Lane-Poole, Stanley. *A History of Egypt.* London: Methuen, 1894–1901. Six volumes.

Raymond, André and Wiet, Gaston. *Les marchés du Caire: Traduction annotée du texte de Maqrizi.* Cairo: Institut Français de l'Archéologie Orientale, 1985.

Revault, Jacques and Maury, Bernard. *Palais et Maisons du Caire du XIVe au XVIIIe siècle.* Cairo: Institut Français de l'Archéologie Orientale. Four volumes.

Richards, Alan and Waterbury, John. *A Political Economy of the Middle East: State, Class, and Economic Development.* Boulder and Cairo: Westview and the American University in Cairo Press, 1990.

Rodenbeck, John and Youssef, Hisham, eds. *Egypt.* Second Edition. Hong Kong and Singapore: APA Publications, 1989. Second Edition, 1989.

Rugh, Andrea. *Family in Contemporary Egypt.* Cairo: The American University in Cairo Press, 1985.

Russell, Dorothea (Lady Russell Pasha). *Medieval Cairo and the Monasteries of Wadi Natrun: A Historical Guide.* London: Weidenfeld and Nicolson, 1962.

Ruthven, Malise and the Editors of Time-Life Books. *Cairo.* Amsterdam: Life Books, 1980.

Sabry, M. *L'Empire Égyptien sous Mohamed-Ali et la question d'"Orient (1811–1849).* Paris: Librairie Orientaliste Paul Geuthner, 1930.

Scharab, Muhammad. *Kairo: Stadt und Architektur im Zeitalter des Europäischen Kolonialismus.* Tübingen: Verlag Ernest Wasmuth, 1989.

Schölch, Alexander. *Egypt for the Egyptians! The Socio-Political Crisis in Egypt 1878–1882.* St. Antony's Middle East Monographs, no. 14. London: Ithaca Press, 1981.

Searight, Sarah. *The British in the Middle East.* New York: Atheneum, 1970.

Seton-Williams, Veronica and Stocks, Peter. *Egypt.* London: Ernest Benn, 1983. Second Edition, 1986.

Stewart, Desmond. *Great Cairo, Mother of the World.* Second Edition. Cairo: The American University in Cairo Press, 1981.

Storrs, Ronald. *Orientations.* London: Ivor Nicholson and Watson, 1937.

Vatikiotis, P.J. *The History of Egypt from Muhammad Ali to Sadat.* Second Edition. London: Weidenfeld and Nicholson, 1980.

Wahba, Magdi, et al., eds. *Colloque International sur l'Histoire du Caire.* Cairo: Ministry of Culture, 1972.

Waterbury, John. *The Egypt of Nasser and Sadat: The Political Economy of Two Regimes.* Princeton: Princeton University Press, 1983.

Wiet, Gaston. *Cairo: City of Art and Commerce.* Trans. Seymour Feiler. Norman: University of Oklahoma Press, 1964.

Wikan, Unni. *Life Among the Poor in Cairo.* Translated by Ann Henning. London: Tavistock, 1980.

Woolfson, Marion. *Prophets in Babylon: Jews in the Arab World.* London and Boston: Faber and Faber, 1980.

DIRECTORIES

Amin, Naguib. *Cairo A-Z.* Cairo: The Palm Press, 1988. Available at larger bookshops and most hotel newsstands. A complete atlas of the city, with maps, a streetfinder, index, and a small yellow-page telephone directory. (*NB*: No complete official telephone directory has been published since 1961, though all numbers then extant have been changed several times, while the city's population has quintupled and the telephone system itself has been totally replaced. This book, the *Cairo Telephone List* and the *Yellow Pages* listed below, and private lists are therefore only published sources even for ordinary telephone numbers.)

Cairo Telephone List. Cairo: published annually in December by Coca Cola and the Maadi Women's Guild. Available from the Maadi Community Church Centre, Sh. Port Said and Sh. 17, Maadi (Tel: 361-2755); the American Chamber of Commerce, Marriott Hotel, Zamalek (Tel: 340-888 Ext. 1541); Community Services Association, 4 Sh. 21, Maadi (Tel: 350-5284); the Women's Association, 3 Sh. Salah ad-Din, Mohandisin (Tel: 346-3521); Heliopolis Community Church, 17 Sh. Seti, Heliopolis (Misr al-Gadidah) (Tel: 660-339, 668-476). This phone book represents a tiny fraction of the telephones in Cairo, but lists most foreign firms or organisations, as well as most of the foreigners and many of the Egyptians associated with such firms or organizations.

Cairo Yellow Pages, July 1989. Cairo: Yellow Pages Egypt, 1989.

USEFUL ADDRESSES

EMBASSIES & CONSULATES

Argentina
8 Sh. as-Saleh Ayyub, Apt 2, Zamalek
Tel: 430-1501, 340-5234, 341-7765

Australia
Cairo Plaza, 5th floor, Corniche, Bulaq
Tel: 777-900, 777-273, 777-994

Austria
Corner of Sh. an-Nil and Sh. Wissa Wasif
5th Floor, Gizah
Tel: 737-640, 737-658, 737-602

Belgium
20 Sh. Kemal ash-Shinnawi, Garden City
Tel: 354-7494/95/96

ammad Fahmi as-Sayyid, Garden
54-3110

Consulate:
5 Sh. Al-Fadi, off Talat Harb
Tel: 393-4316

Cyprus
23 Sh. Ismail Muhammad, Zamalek
Tel: 341-1288, 341-0327

Czechoslovakia
4 Sh. Duqqi, Gizah
Tel: 348-5531

Denmark
12 Sh. Hasan Sabri, Zamalek
Tel: 340-2502, 340-7411, 340-8673

European Community
6 Sh. Ibn Zanki, Zamalek
Tel: 340-8388

Finland
10 Al-Kamil Muhammad, Zamalek
Tel: 341-3722, 341-1487, 340-2801

France
29 an-Nil (Gizah Corniche
Gamal Abd an-Nasir), Gizah
Tel: 728-275, 728-649, 728-497

Germany
8A Sh. Hasan Sabri, Zamalek
Tel: 341-0015, 340-6017, 340-3687

Greece
18 Sh. Aysha at-Taymuriyya
Garden City
Tel: 355-0443, 355-1074, 355-5915

Hungary
29 Sh. Muhammad Mazhar, Zamalek
Tel: 340-0659, 340-8634

India
5 Sh. Aziz Abaza, Zamalek
Tel: 340-6053, 341-3051, 341-0052

Iraq
9 Muhammad Mazhar, Zamalek
Tel: 340-9815, 340-2633, 340-2794

Ireland
3 Sh. Abu'l-Feda, Zamalek
Tel: 340-8264, 340-8547, 340-4653

Israel
6 Ibn Malek, Gizah
Tel: 726-000, 726-264, 729-329

Italy
15 Abd ar-Rahman Fahmi, Garden City
Tel: 354-3195, 354-0658, 354-0657

Japan
Cairo Centre Building
14 Sh. Ibrahim Nagib, 3rd Floor
Garden City
Tel: 354-4518, 355-3962/63/64, 354-9283,
3551-477, 355-7573

Jordan
6 al-Gohayni, Duqqi
Tel: 348-5566, 348-6169, 348-7543

Kenya
20 Bulus Hanna, Duqqi
Tel: 704-455, 704-546

Lebanon
5 Ahmad Nessim, Gizah
Tel: 728-315, 728-266, 728-454

Libya
7 as-Saleh Ayyub, Zamalek
Tel: 805-863/64

Morocco
10 as-Saleh Ayyub, Zamalek
Tel: 340-9677, 340-9849, 341-4718

Netherlands
18 Sh. Hasan Sabri, Zamalek
Tel: 340-8744, 340-6434, 340-6872

Norway
8 Sh. al-Gazirah, Zamalek
Tel: 340-8046, 341-3955, 340-3340

Poland
5 Sh. Aziz Uthman
Tel: 340-5416, 340-9583, 341-7456

Saudi Arabia
2 Ahmad Nessim, Gizah
Tel: 728-012, 726-037

Singapore
40 Sh. Babel, Duqqi
Tel: 704-645, 704-744, 701-472

Spain
9 Sh. Hod al-Laban, Garden City
Tel: 354-7069

Sudan
3 al-Ibrahimi, Garden City
Tel: 354-5043, 354-5044, 354-9661

Sweden
13 Muhammad Mazhar, Zamalek
Tel: 340-5377

Switzerland.
10 Sh. Abd al-Khaliq Tharwat
Tel: 758-133

Tunisia
26 Sh. al-Gazirah, Zamalek
Tel: 341-8962, 340-4940

Turkey
Corner of Sh. Ibn Sina and Sh. an-Nil
(Gizah Corniche, Gamal Abd an-Nasir),
Gizah
Tel: 726-115, 726-044, 730-249

Consulate:
25 Sh. al-Falaki, Bab El Luq
Tel: 354-8364, 354-3736

United Arab Emirates
4 Ibn Sina, Gizah
Tel: 729-107, 729-226, 729-955

United Kingdom
7 Sh. at-Tambak (Ahmad Ragab)
Garden City
Tel: 354-0850, 354-0852

USA
Sh. Amrika Latiniyyah, Garden City
Tel: 355-7371, 354-8211

USSR
95 Sh. al-Gizah, Gizah
Tel: 348-9353/54/55

Vatican (Saint Siège)
5 Muhammad Mazhar, Zamalek.
Tel: 340-2250, 340-6152

Yemen
28 Amin ar-Rafi, Duqqi
Tel: 983-796, 983-035

Yugoslavia
33 Sh. as-Saleh Ayyub, Zamalek
Tel: 340-4473

BUSINESS ORGANISATIONS

American Chamber of Commerce in Egypt. Suite 1541, Marriott Hotel. Tel: 340-8888, Ext: 514.

Cairo Chamber of Commerce. Tel: 354-8491.

Egypt-US Business Council. El Nil Tower, 21 Sh. Gizah , Gizah.

Egyptian Businessmen's Association. Tel: 737-285.

European Economic Community Delegation. 4 Sh. Gazirah, Zamalek. Tel: 340-8388.

Federation of Egyptian Chambers of Commerce. Tel: 987-103.

Federation of Egyptian Industries. Tel: 748-945.
French Chamber of Commerce. 4 Maydan Falaki, Bab al Luq. Tel: 354-2897, 354-2898, 354-8491.

German Agency for Technical Cooperation. German Embassy, 8A Sh. Hasan Sabri, Zamalek. Tel: 341-2445.

German-Arab Chamber of Commerce. 3 Sh. Sherif Pasha. Tel: 769-327, 741-754.

Greek-Arab Chamber of Commerce. 10 Sh. Sulayman al-Halabi. Tel: 741-190.

International Executive Service Corps. Nile Hilton Centre. Tel: 776-771, ext: 22-23.

Italian-Arab Chamber of Commerce. 33 Sh. Abd al-Khaliq Tharwat. Tel: 760-275.

Japanese Chamber of Commerce. 31 Sh. 26 July. Tel: 740-942, 740-659.

Netherlands Development Corporation. 13 Sh. Gizah, Gizah. Tel: 723-054.

Rotary International. Cairo Central: Tuesday 2 p.m., Nile Hilton Hotel; **Cairo North:** Wednesday 2 p.m., Nile Hilton Hotel; **Cairo South:** Sunday 8 p.m., Maadi Yacht Club; **Cairo West:** Mondays 2 p.m., Meridien Hotel; **Zamalek:** Monday 8.30 p.m., Nile Hilton Hotel; **Heliopolis:** Monday 2.30 p.m., Heliopolis Sheraton; **Gizah:** Wednesday 2.15 p.m., Cairo Sheraton, Gizah; **Gizah, Pyramids Area:** Monday 2.30 p.m., Cairo Sheraton, Gizah.

ART/PHOTO CREDITS

Photography by

Page 87, 90, 220, 223	**Jean-Claude Aunos**
14/15, 135, 153, 178, 233, 235R	**Marcus Brooke**
69, 98, 169, 195, 234	**Andrew Eames**
22/23, 60L, 89, 94, 97, 212/213, 226, 238, 239	**Tor Eigeland**
130, 131R, 179, 209	**Patrick Godeau**
49	**Robert Harding**
54, 58	**Illustrated London News**
Cover, 12/13, 30, 76/77, 99, 185, 204	**Lyle Lawson**
7, 16/17, 20, 24, 32, 33, 45, 78, 80, 108, 109, 112, 114/115, 120/121, 127, 136/137, 139, 146, 150/151, 152, 155, 156, 161, 162/163, 164, 170L, 170R, 171, 176/177, 188/189, 190, 207L, 207R, 208, 211, 224, 228/229, 230, 236, 237, 244, 246, 248	**Richard Nowitz**
37, 73, 93, 101, 107, 126, 132, 133, 166, 215, 221, 235L	**Christine Osborne**
72, 75, 79, 91, 113, 131L, 158, 174, 242, 245, 247	**Eddy Posthuma de Boer**
186	**John Rodenbeck**
51, 53, 124/125	**Thomas Cook**
26, 27, 28/29, 35L, 47, 55, 56/57, 59, 60R, 62, 63, 65, 92, 232	**Topham Picture Source**
40/41, 42, 201	**Wallace Collection**
1, 18/19, 38L, 38R, 50, 64, 66, 67, 68, 70/71, 81, 83, 85, 96, 104, 106, 110, 111, 116/117, 118/119, 129, 134, 138, 140L, 140R, 142, 143, 144, 145, 147, 148, 149, 154L, 157, 159, 160, 165, 167, 168, 172, 173, 175, 181, 182, 183, 184, 187, 192, 193, 194, 196, 199, 200, 202/203, 205, 210, 214, 218, 219, 225, 231, 240/241, 243	**Marcus Wilson-Smith**

Maps	**Berndtson & Berndtson**
Illustrations	**Klaus Geisler**
Visual Consultant	**V. Barl**

INDEX